The HeliD0143167

PF 3999 .A32 H45 1992
Heliand. English.
 The Heliand : the Saxon Gospel : a
translation and commentary

endi oc thinoro uuordo so self alloro barno bezt · that thu us bedon
leres uugoronthine · so iohannes duot diurlic dopori dago gehuui
licas · is uuerod mid uuordun · huuo sie uualdand sculun godan gro
tan · do thinun iungorun so self geriht us that gerum ·

Thohabda eft the rikeo garu san aftar thiu sunudrohtines god
uuodd angegin · Than gi god uuilleas uueros mid iuuuon uuordun
uualdand grotean · allaro cuningo craftigostan · than quedad gi
so ic iu leriu · Fadar is usa firiho barno · the is an them hohon himi
larikea · Geuuihid si thin namo uuordo gehuuilico · Cuma
thin craftag riki · Uuerda thin uuilleo obar thesa uuerold al so
sama an erdo · so thar uppa ist an them hohon himil rikea · Gef
us dago gehuuilikes raddrohtin thegodo · thina helaga helpa ·
Endi alat us hebenes uuard managoro mensculdio · al so uue
odrum mannum doan · Nelat us far ledean letha uuihti so ford
an iro uuilleon so uui uuirdige sind · Ac help us uuidar allun ubi
· lon dadiun · So sculun biddean than gi te bede hnigad · uueros
mid iuuuom uuordun · that iu uualdand god lederalate an leut
cunnea · ef gi than uuilliad alatan liudeo gehuuilicun thero
sacono endi thero sundeono the sie uuid iu selbon hir uureda ge
uuirkeat · than alatid iu uualdand god · fadar alamahtig firin
uuerk mikil managoro men sculdeo · Ef iu than uuirdid
iuuua mod te starc that gi ne uuilleat odrun erlun alatan uue
ron uuamdadi · than ne uuil iu oc uualdand god · grim uuero
fargeban · ac gi sculun is geld niman suido ledlicon · telanguru

The Heliand

The Saxon Gospel

A translation and commentary by
G. RONALD MURPHY, S. J.

New York   Oxford
OXFORD UNIVERSITY PRESS
1992

PF
3999
.A32
H45
1992

Oxford University Press

Oxford   New York   Toronto
Delhi   Bombay   Calcutta   Madras   Karachi
Kuala Lumpur   Singapore   Hong Kong   Tokyo
Nairobi   Dar es Salaam   Cape Town
Melbourne   Auckland

and associated companies in
Berlin   Ibadan

Copyright © 1992 by Oxford University Press, Inc.

Published by Oxford University Press, Inc.
200 Madison Avenue, New York, New York 10016

Oxford is a registered trademark of Oxford University Press

All rights reserved. No part of this publication may be reproduced,
stored in a retrieval system, or transmitted, in any form or by any means,
electronic, mechanical, photocopying, recording or otherwise,
without the prior permission of the publisher.

Library of Congress Cataloging-in-Publication Data
Heliand. English
The Heliand : the Saxon Gospel :
a translation and commentary /
by G. Ronald Murphy.
p.   cm.   Includes bibliographical references (p. 231).
ISBN 0-19-507375-4 (cloth). — ISBN 0-19-507376-2 (pbk.)
I. Murphy, G. Ronald. 1938—   . II. Title.
PF3999.A32H4   1992   839'.1—dc20   92-3774

2   4   6   8   9   7   5   3   1

Printed in the United States of America
on acid-free paper

To my students

Acknowledgments

I begin my list of thank-you's with a renewed special bow to Cynthia Read, senior editor at Oxford University Press, for a helpful spirit that extended far beyond the realm of required professional interest and concern. Her constant enthusiasm, confidence, and can-do attitude, helped enormously to make this project a pleasure.

Georgetown University graciously gave me the sabbatical time so that this project could be completed at the Research and Study Center at Centreville, Maryland, with the kind support of the Raskob Foundation. My department at Georgetown helped as well with encouragement and assistance in reading and correcting text. In this regard I am especially indebted to Professor Heidi Byrnes and her unfailing eagle-eye. Colleagues at other academic institutions who deserve great thanks for their careful reading and critical suggestions (and to be cherished for their real and selfless interest) are Professors Irmengard Rauch and Winfred Lehmann. Dr. Hermann Hauke of the manuscript department of the Bayerische Staats-bibliothek went out of his way to make the Munich manuscript *M* of the *Heliand* available to me during my stay in Munich and initiated many a delightful conversation on religious infighting during the more recent history of Bavaria. Back home, the librarians of the Lauinger Library's inter-library loan section deserve a medal for their knightly faithfulness to service, for constantly seeking and unfailingly finding.

When it comes to faithfulness I do not have the words to thank Richard J. O'Brien, S.J., for his hours at the computer bringing my poor "small-disk" efforts at producing computer text into the big-disk world of camera-ready copy. His hard work enabled me to concentrate my attention and energy where I most wanted, on the poetry and meaning of the *Heliand* itself.

Personal encouragement came to me from many quarters, from my family, from Cynthia McMullen, from Sr. Virginia, from Dr. Gene d'Aquili, from Jim McKee, S.J., from my students, and from the many Jesuits who have shared this form of happy labor. Thank you all.

Acknowledgment is also due to those translators who in the past have made works from other times and cultures come home to me and who have been an inspiration. Their number is great, but let me single out Rieu's famous translation of the *Iliad* as the one that first opened my eyes to the touching humanity and poetry of that great epic. In connection with previous translations of the *Heliand*, I have diligently consulted the Modern German version of Felix Genzmer and the English version of Mariana Scott. While I have not followed the style of either, I found them helpful companions with whom I could often disagree and who would still, equally often, keep me from stumbling or from throwing up my hands over some frustratingly difficult passage.

I extend my thanks also to Professor Reinhold Grimm, editor of *The German Quarterly*, and Professor Valters Nollendorfs, editor of *Monatshefte*, for their kindness in permitting me to include Appendices 3 and 4, which originally appeared as articles from my pen in their respective journals.

The last shall be first. Let me therefore lastly thank the unknown poet himself. Because of his effort and insight, every day of work on the translation brought home to me some new appreciation of the gospel story. In the midst of the Dark Ages, the author of the *Heliand* was the first person to look at the whole gospel narrative through Northern European eyes and the first to bring what he saw, for the sake of Northern Christianity, to full and lasting expression, to "write it down in a bright-shining book."

Contents

Introduction to the Translation

The *Heliand* has a unique aura in the history of world literature. Its contemplative integration of Northern-European magic, sooth-saying, wizardry, fatalistic warrior virtues, personal mysticism, and the Christian gospel story give it a compelling power and charm. The *Heliand* was written in Old Saxon over a thousand years ago in the first half of the ninth century by an author whose mysterious identity has remained unknown. Whoever he was, he was an enormously gifted religious poet capable of profound intercultural communication. He rewrote and reimagined the events and words of the gospel as if they had taken place and been spoken in his own country and time, in the chieftain society of a defeated people, forcibly Christianized by Charlemagne: the Saxons. By the power of his imagination the unknown poet-monk (perhaps ex-warrior) created a unique cultural synthesis beween Christianity and Germanic warrior-society—a synthesis that would ultimately lead to the culture of knighthood and become the foundation of medieval Europe.

Why translate such a work? If the *Heliand* is a translation of the gospel, will not a translation of the *Heliand* into English simply read like the King James Version? If the *Heliand* were only a translation, the question would be perfectly justified, but the *Heliand* is not a translation in a literal sense, it is a reimagining of the gospel, as the reader will see immediately, and the task of the translator of the *Heliand* is to bring the reimagined gospel story into English. In doing so, I have set as a goal a "visual principle" for translation. For example, the poet often uses *burg* to Saxonize biblical place names such as *Nazarethburg, Bethlehemaburg,* and so forth. If one follows a principle of philological similarity in translation, these places become, in English, *'Nazarethburg, Bethlehemburg,'* or *'Nazarethborough, Bethlehemborough.'* I think that such a translation does not tell the modern reader what the poet was doing. One must ask the question what a Saxon *burg* looked like. Was it a stone castle? *'Castle'* is also often given as the (High Medieval) translation of *burg,* in view of the meaning of *Burg* in modern German. Stone fortifications, however, were not to be found in Saxony until the very late ninth century, when Viking invasions forced a change. Charlemagne had his stone palace and chapel at Aix-la-Chapelle, but the only stone walls in Saxony appear to have been the new monastic chapels at Fulda, Corvey, and Verden. A Saxon *burg* was a hill-fort (and its accompanying community), a central hill-fort with high earthen walls topped by a wooden palisade, surrounded by the smaller thatch-roofed houses beneath the hill of those who were not of the warrior (upper) class. The warrior-nobility prided themselves, it seems from the *Heliand,* on being born within the walls. Following the visual rather than philological principle, I have thus translated *Nazarethburg,* for example, as 'hill-fort Nazareth,' or 'Fort Nazareth.'

A second principle I have tried to follow is a historical one. *Degen* can be rendered 'knight.' The *Heliand,* however, was written at the time and in the culture of the unmounted warrior. Indeed a Saxon fear of cavalry seems to be expressed in the *Heliand;* and one remembers that their cousins, the Anglo-Saxons, fought the mounted Normans on foot in 1066. Since the word *knight,* in our times, however, conjures up much later images of the mounted knight of the High Middle Ages and the crusades, I have generally avoided the word and have made the decision to remain with the older English word *thane* or to use *warrior* for the ubiquitous *degen.*

In general I have not attempted to include alliteration in the translation, but where it was possible and natural it will be found in the text. The *Heliand,* as we now have it, consists of some 5984 lines (twice the length of *Beowulf*) of alliterative verse, and while I stand in admiration of those who have attempted with great success to translate the entire epic into the alliterative verse of modern languages, I have also seen occasions in such translations where the need for similarity of sound in a line has successfully tempted the translator to use far-fetched vocabulary and occasionally to lose the poetic point for the sake of the sound.

The poetic power of the *Heliand* lies in its imagery and in the charm created by hearing Northern equivalents for the familiar Mediterranean concepts of the Bible. This poetry I have done everything to preserve and convey to the reader. The translator is assisted in this task by the very form which the author frequently used. The poetic 'alliteration' which carries the burden of meaning so often in the *Heliand* is what we might call 'concept alliteration,' or 'concept rhyme.' As in the ancient Hebrew poetry of the psalms, *mountain*, to give an example, can be rhymed with *hill*, the *side of a mountain* with the *slope of a hill, fishes* with *whales, snow* with *hail*, and so forth, on the basis of some familiar similarity in the semantic meaning of the words rather than on a similarity of their sound. This technique fits in perfectly with the author's central purpose of finding Northern-European equivalents to 'rhyme' with Biblical concepts. *They put Him on a cross* is rhymed in the following line with *they hanged Him from a tree*.

I have tried to follow the author's lead in the choice of technical religious vocabulary. Where the author has refused to make use of a loan word from Latin, even though other authors of his day did so, and insists on the Saxon religious word, even when it must have held deeply pagan connotations, I have followed his lead. When he uses a Latin loan word, even though his contemporaries were using a Germanic word, I have followed. For example, he never uses *tempal*, the common Saxon loan word from Latin *templum* for the temple in Jerusalem, but daringly uses the Germanic *uuiha* (and several other Saxon words) which clearly indicated a Germanic place of (pagan) worship to his hearers. To create a parallel feeling in English I have avoided the common English word *temple* and used *shrine* instead. On the other hand, the Jewish feast of Passover is translated as the Germanic feast of *ostar* 'Easter' by his contemporaries, but the *Heliand* poet retains the liturgical Latin *Pascha*. Though I am not sure of the reason for the author's doing this, I have not translated

Pascha as *Easter* but have kept the loan word *Pascha* as did the author. My reason for doing this is an attempt to reproduce as much as possible in the translation the varying surprise effects that the use of nonfamiliar and familiar words would have had on the *Heliand's* audience.

The audience of the *Heliand* was probably to be found in mead-hall and monastery. The epic poem seems not to have been designed for use in the church as a part of official worship, but is intended to bring the gospel home to the Saxons in a poetic environment in order to help the Saxons cease their vacillation between their warrior-loyalty to the old gods and to the "mighty Christ." Internal evidence, as well as liturgical tradition, would indicate that the epic was designed for after-dinner singing in the mead-hall and the cloister. It is clearly addressed to the Saxon warrior-nobility, and the mead-hall scenes in the *Heliand* (the wedding-feast at Cana) show a familiar touch, one that might deliberately reproduce the very situation in which a singer of the *Heliand* might find himself. One occasionally hears as well an exhortation that sounds much more like an oblique address to the monks who are in charge of the conversion of the Saxons, rather than to the Saxon nobility themselves.

Two important preoccupations of the author that serve to tie the whole of the *Heliand* together are the beauty of light and the power of God's words. The world is light, for the author, a creation caused by God's first spoken words, "Let there be light." The world is most frequently referred to as "this light," heaven is called "the other light." When a new human being is born, it is described as an addition of brilliance to the light. John the Baptist, for example, comes "shining to the light of mankind."

Spoken words possess internal power; the Creator himself used them to call the light-world from non-existence into being. God's words, then, in the Celto-Germanic world, are seen as magic, and give their magic power to the few who know them. For this reason, it is very important at the wedding-feast of Cana in the *Heliand* that no one learn the magic words by which Christ turns water to wine. The four evangelists alone were taught what to write and sing—God's spells—by the greatest of masters, the Creator.

In so describing the four gospels, the *Heliand* poet has both managed to speak in the language of Germanic mythology, in which the god Woden is described as having taught the runes and magic to men, and has also gone beyond that mythology. It is not a mortal god who taught Christians their magic words, but the immortal Creator-God, who himself used them.

The work was no doubt written to be sung or chanted in an epic style. Neums, musical notations for the singer, can still be found in the manuscripts, though their interpretation today remains unclear. The division of the epic into untitled (the titles in this edition are the translator's) songs or *fitts* 'episodes' goes back to the author himself, in the opinion of most scholars. While I agree with this position, there are some places in the epic where one can wonder whether the exact placement of the end of a given song and the beginning of the next is the author's own or the (possibly mistaken) decision of a subsequent copyist.

Some awareness of the ninth-century cultural and social environment of the Saxons is extremely helpful in reading and interpreting the poem. I would urge the interested reader to consult the companion volume, *The Saxon Savior: the Germanic Transformation of the Gospel in the Ninth-Century Heliand* (New York: Oxford University Press, 1989) for a more complete treatment of the religious and cultural setting of this great work.

For the curious (and the brave), the following lines are the beginning of the first song of the *Heliand*.

> *Manega uuaron, the sia iro mod gespon,*
> *. . . , that sia bigunnun uuord godes,*
> *reckean that giruni, that thie riceo Crist*
> *undar mancunnea marida gifrumida*
> *mid uuordun endi mid uuercun. That uuolda tho uuisara filo*
> *liudo barno loбon, lera Cristes,*
> *helag uuord godas, endi mid iro handon scriбan*
> *berehtlico an buok, huo sia is gibodscip scoldin*
> *frummian, firiho barn. Than uuarun thoh sia fiori te thiu*
> *under thera menigo, thia habdon maht godes,*
> *helpa fan himila, helagna gest,*

craft fan Criste,— sia uurdun gicorana te thio,
that sie than euangelium enan scoldun
an buok scriƀan endi so manag gibod godes,
helag himilisc uuord: sia ne muosta helido than mer,
firiho barno frummian, neuan that sia fiori te thio
thuru craft godas gecorana uurdun,
Matheus endi Marcus,— so uuarun thia man hetana—
Lucas endi Iohannes; sia uuarun gode lieƀa,
uuirdiga ti them giuuirkie. Habda im uualdand god,
them helidon an iro hertan helagna gest
fasto bifohlan endi ferahtan hugi,
so manag uuislik uuord endi giuuit mikil,
that sea scoldin ahebbean helagaro stemnun
godspell that guoda, that ni haƀit enigan gigadon huergin,
thiu uuord an thesaro uueroldi, that io uualdand mer,
drohtin diurie eftho derƀi thing,
firinuuerc fellie eftho fiundo nid,
strid uuiderstande—, huand hie habda starkan hugi,
mildean endi guodan, thie thes mester uuas,
adalordfrumo alomahtig.[1]

---

[1] *Heliand und Genesis.* Herausgegeben von Otto Behaghel. 9. Auflage, bearbeitet von Burkhard Taeger (Tübingen: Niemeyer, 1984), p. 7-8.

The Heliand

The Heliand

Song 1

The Creator's spell, by which the whole world is held together is taught to four heroes.[1]

There were many whose hearts told them that they should begin to tell the secret runes,[2] the word of God, the famous feats that the powerful Christ accomplished in words and in deeds among human beings. There were many of the wise who wanted to praise the teaching of Christ, the holy Word of God, and wanted to write a bright-shining[3] book with their own hands, telling how the sons of men should carry out His commands. Among all these, however, there were only four who had the power of God, help from heaven, the Holy Spirit, the strength from Christ to do it. They were chosen. They alone were to write down the evangelium in a book, and to write down the commands of God, the holy heavenly word. No one else among the heroic sons of men was to attempt it, since these four

---

[1] Song titles do not appear in the original text but have been supplied by the translator.

[2] *giruni*. The word not only implies that the gospel is a secret mystery, but that it is of the power of the magic spells and charms written in the runes of the Northern world. This same rich expression, *giruni*, will be used by the author to introduce the 'secret runes' of the Lord's Prayer.

[3] *berehtlico* 'brightly'. Possibly the poet is thinking of the brilliantly illuminated gospel manuscripts of the eighth and ninth centuries.

had been picked by the power of God: Matthew and Mark, Luke and John were their names. They were dear to God, worthy of the work. The ruling God had placed the Holy Spirit firmly in those heroes' hearts, together with many a wise word, as well as a devout attitude and a powerful mind, so that they could lift up their holy voices to chant God's spell.[4] There is nothing like it in words anywhere in this world! Nothing can ever glorify the Ruler, our dear Chieftain, more! Nor is there anything that can better fell[5] every evil creature or work of wickedness, nor better withstand the hatred and aggression of enemies. This is so, because the one who taught them God's Spell, though generous and good, had a powerful mind: the noble, the almighty Creator Himself.

These four were to write it down with their own fingers; they were to compose, sing, and proclaim what they had seen and heard of Christ's powerful strength—all the many wonderful things, in word and deed, that the mighty Chieftain Himself said, taught, and accomplished among human beings—and also all the things which the Ruler spoke from the beginning, when He, by His own power, first made the world and formed the whole universe with one word. The heavens and the earth and all that is contained within them, both inorganic and organic, everything, was firmly held in place by the Divine words.[6] He then determined which of the peoples was to rule

---

[4] *godspell* 'God's speech, gospel'. Originally, in Anglo-Saxon, it was 'the good speech', but in the *Heliand* the 'good' is understood as 'God's.' It is not possible to distinguish easily between the two words by spelling, thus the change must have come easily. In addition, the author desires very much to explain the gospel as not just good speech, but God's speech.

[5] *fellie*. The hidden image is that of the tree, the place of Woden worship in Germanic religion. That worship included human sacrifice, usually by hanging the victims, often prisoners of war, from the tree. While admitting that the tree of such religion must be felled, the author praises 'God's spell' as the proper weapon to do the task, thereby rendering small support, and implicitly criticizing the violent conversion method of Charlemagne and Boniface in Saxony. See *The Saxon Savior*, Ch. 2.

[6] The author, who was obviously enamored of the power of words, seems to have been very much impressed by the first chapter of the book of *Genesis*, where the entire universe is described as being created by a series of spoken words. Each of the seven days of creation begins with God speaking and saying, *Fiat* . . . 'Let there be .

the greatest territory, and at what times the ages of the world were to come to an end. One age still stood before the sons of men; five were past.[7] The blessed sixth age was to come by the power of God the Holy Spirit and the birth of Christ. He is the Best of Healers, come here to the middle world to be a help to many, to give human beings an advantage against the hatred of the enemy and the hidden snare.

At that time the Christian God granted to the Roman people the greatest kingdom. He strengthened the heart of their army so that they had conquered every nation. Those helmet-lovers from hill-fort Rome[8] had won an empire. Their military governors were in every land and they had authority over the people of every noble race.

In Jerusalem, Herod was chosen to be king over the Jewish people. Caesar, ruling the empire from the hill-fort Rome, placed him there—among the warrior-companions[9]—even though Herod did not belong by clan to the noble and well-born descendants of Israel. He did not come from their kinsmen. It was only thanks to Caesar in hill-fort Rome, who ruled the empire, that the descendants of Israel, those fighting men renowned for their toughness, had to obey

---

. . ' The author makes an essential connection between the creating power of those primal words 'which hold everything firmly in place,' the Word, the gospel's words, and the powerful magic words of Germanic religion.

[7] The author may have taken the division of the time between the creation and the coming of the Messiah into five ages from St. Augustine's division as given at the end of *The City of God*.

[8] *Rumuburg*. The image of Rome created by the use of the Saxon *burg* is that of a hill-fort, a fortification built at the top of a hill surrounded by wooden palisades, a structure familiar in the North for thousands of years.

[9] *gisidi*. This is the group of bodyguards and warrior-companions personally chosen by a ruling chieftain. By explaining the difficulty of Herod's appointment as being caused by the fact that it took place in the reverse fashion (he is imposed upon the warrior-companions) the impropriety of his appointment is made clear in Saxon terms. So also, at the same time, is the impropriety of the appointment of Charlemagne's Frankish legates (also unrelated by kinship to the Saxons) to rule the Saxons, subtly placed in a gospel context.

him. They were Herod's very unwavering friends—as long as he held power, for as long as he had authority over the Jewish people.[10]

At that time there was in that place an old man, a man of experience and wisdom. He was from the people, from Levi's clan, Jacob's son, of good family. His name was Zachary. He was a blessedly happy man, since he loved to serve God and acted according to God's will. His wife did the same. She was an elderly woman. An heir had not been granted to them when they were young. They lived far from any vice and were highly respected. Their obedience was to the King of Heaven, they honored our Chieftain; they never desired to be the cause of anything bad or treacherous, illegal or sinful, among mankind. But they did live in a worried state of mind because they did not have an heir of their own; they had no children.

There, in Jerusalem, Zachary fulfilled the divine command whenever his turn came. Whenever the times informed him in their bright and clear way that he was to perform the holy worship of the Ruler at the shrine,[11] the divine service of God, the King of Heaven, he was very happy and carried it out with a devout mind.

---

[10] No doubt a description of a Saxon attitude of mind toward the Holy Roman Empire of Charlemagne as much as the Hebrew one toward the old Roman Empire of the Caesars.

[11] The word used here for the temple is *uuiha*. The word means 'holy place' and is the pagan word for *temple*. The author also uses the word *geld* for *worship*, which means 'worth' and is thus quite similar to our Anglo-Saxon 'worthship' or 'worship'. The word he uses parallel to *geld* is *iungarskepi*, which means 'discipleship' and sounds much more like a more literally Christianized word for worship and which I have thus translated as 'divine service'. This instance is almost paradigmatic for the author's technique when dealing with a difficult and unfamiliar image. He first renders the concept in a Northern, Germanic form, and immediately thereafter gives the more standard Southern and more literal Mediterranean form.

Song 2

Zachary sees the Chieftain's angel in the shrine.

Then the time came which had been foretold in words by wise men that Zachary was to attend to the shrine. Many of the Jewish people were gathered there in Jerusalem at the shrine to ask the Lord in His graciousness, to pray to the ruling God, the King of Heaven, most humbly, to remove evil from them. The people stood around the holy house as the exalted man went inside. The rest of the Hebrew people remained outside around the altar until the elder had finished doing the will of God.

Inside, the old man was carrying his incense to the altar and going around the altar with his censer, worshipping the Powerful One. He was performing his duty, the divine service, enthusiastically and with a clear mind (the way one should gladly follow one's lord), when feelings of fear came over him, and he became frightened at the altar. He saw, behind the altar, an angel of God inside the shrine. The angel spoke to him in words and told the old man not to be afraid or frightened of him. "Your deeds are precious to the Ruler," he said, "as well as your word. He is grateful for your service to Him and grateful that you think so much of His power alone. I am His angel. My name is Gabriel, I always stand before God, I am always in the presence of the All-Ruler, except when He wishes to send me off on His affairs. Now He has sent me on this journey and told me to let you know that a child will be born to you—from your elderly wife a child will be granted to you in this world—and he will be wise in words. Never in his lifetime will he drink hard cider or wine in this world: this is the way the workings of fate made him, time formed him, and the power of God as well.[12] God said that I should say to you that your child will be a warrior-companion of the

---

[12] Fate and time are the highest entities in Germanic religion (along with the cosmic tree). Their existence as potent forces in the natural world is not denied by the *Heliand*, and they are accorded a legitimate place in the author's scheme of things in tandem with (as here), or in subordination to, the power of God. See *The Saxon Savior*, Ch. 3.

King of Heaven. He said that you and your wife should care for him well and bring him up on loyalty, and that He would grant him many honors in God's kingdom.[13]   God said that this good man was to have the name John and He commanded that you call the child by that name when he comes. He said moreover that the child would become a warrior-companion of Christ, His own Son, in this world, and that both of them would be coming here very soon on His mission." Zachary then spoke in conversation with the Chieftain's very angel as he began to wonder about these events and these words. "How can this happen," he said, "at our age? It is all too late for us to bring about what you are saying with your words. It was a long time ago, back when we were twenty winters in this world, that this woman came to me. We have now been together, sharing bed and board, for seventy years since the day I took her to be my wife. If we were not able to accomplish this in our youth, if we were not able to produce our own heir, raised under our own roof, back then, how are we to do it now that we are old? Old age has taken away our physical strength. Our faces have gone slack, our loins are slow, our flesh is loose, our skin is not beautiful, our sexual desire is gone, our bodies are dried out, our appearances have changed—and so have our emotions and vitality—so many days have we been in this world.

---

[13] In this truly remarkable passage we have the earliest known blending of Germanic warrior virtue with Christian religion. God the All-Ruler is made to request that John be raised by Zachary to practice the warrior virtue of *treuwa* 'unflinching loyalty to one's chieftain, especially in battle'. God's reason is the astonishing Saxon concept that He wishes to make John *gisid heɓancuninges* 'a warrior-companion of the King of Heaven'. God then adds that John will also be a warrior-companion of His own Son, John will be *Kristes gisid*. The *Heliand* uses the image of warrior-companionship for discipleship throughout the poem to explain the role of Peter and the apostles, very movingly so in the scenes of the Passion and Death of Christ.

In this ninth-century synthesis lies the first full written expression and perhaps the origin itself of the Germanic-Christian knighthood of the Middle Ages.

This is why I wonder how what you are saying with your words could happen."[14]

Song 3

John comes to the light of mankind.

Then the King of Heaven's messenger became very angry that Zachary doubted his message and did not want to believe that God could restore to him the youth he once had at the beginning, if He so willed. The angel gave him as punishment that he would not be able to say a single word, not even move his mouth, "until a son is born to you, until your old woman bears you an earl, a newborn baby of good family, and he comes shining into this world. At that moment you will speak, you will regain the power of speech, and you will not be dumb any longer." It happened then and there. What the

---

[14] Fundamental to Saxon (Christian and pagan) doubt about the Christian God must have been doubt as to whether He was more powerful than the neutral, cosmic forces of fate and time. Neither Woden nor Thor, both powerful but mortal in Germanic mythology, were ever imagined as being capable of standing up to fate or time, much less of being capable of reversing a process of fate or time. In Mediterranean mythology, both Greco-Roman and Jewish, the person-god[s] are immortal, either defeating these neutral forces in battle or creating them by words 'in the Beginning.'

In Germanic mythology the personal gods have only a neutrally alloted time before the irrational forces of time and matter bring them their doom, their famous 'twilight of the gods'. The author tries to do justice to Germanic religious feeling by having a Saint Zachary present the case for the uncontrollable power of time in human life in very realistic terms. Zachary himself is depicted unmistakably: he enters a Germanic *wiha* 'shrine' to worship, and yet walks around the altar with the incense of Catholic ritual. He is the embodiment of the complex psychological situation of the converted Saxons.

The author then just as forcefully presents the Christian case by describing the birth of John in glowing terms, both human and military. The invented reaction of the two elderly men later in the story shows the possible responses of good earls to the demonstration of the All-Ruling God's control of fate and time in the birth of John.

angel of the All-Ruler said in the shrine came true: the old man lost his speech—though he kept a clear mind in his head.

Outside the shrine the people had been waiting all day long and everyone was wondering why the revered and good man was taking so long to perform his service. No other thane ever took so long at the shrine to perform the worship service with his hands. Then the good man came out of the sanctuary. The earls crowded in closer, they were extremely curious to hear what he would say to them and what truth he would let them know. He was not able to say a single spoken word to the warrior-companions of his retinue, he was only able to let the people know with his right hand that they should follow the teachings of our Ruler. The people understood that he had seen something directly from God, but that he could not say anything nor let them know about it.

So it was. He had performed the worship of our Ruler when it was his turn as determined by human beings.[15]

Soon thereafter the power of God, His mighty strength, was felt: the wife [Elisabeth], a woman in her old age, became pregnant—soon the husband, that godly man, would have an heir, an infant boy born in the hill-fort.

The woman awaited the workings of fate. The winter skidded by and the year measured its way past. John came to the light of mankind. His body was beautiful and his skin was fair, as were his hair and fingernails, and his cheeks shone! Many of their friends and many of the learned gathered there, amazed at what had happened and wondering how two such old people could bear a child—unless it was something ordained by God Himself. They recognized immediately that there was no other way for such a happy event to occur. Then, a man of many years both very intelligent and gifted with wise words, spoke and asked with great interest what the boy's name would be in this world: "I think that both in the manner of his birth and in the way he is, he is superior to us. For this reason I believe that God Himself has sent him directly to us from heaven."

---

[15] The idea seems to be: the sequence of the feasts of the year is determined by the cosmic movements of the sun and moon in time; the determination of which priest will serve at the altar for a given feast is made by more humble procedures!

Soon thereafter the mother of the child spoke, the one who had borne the child as a baby in her womb: "A solemn command came here last year from God," she said, "a solemn command that by God's instruction he was to be called John. Even if I had the power, I would not dare even to think about changing that in the slightest." Then an arrogant relative who was from her clan territory spoke up. "No nobleman ever born of our clan or kin has had that name before," he said. "Go and choose a more appealing name for him, one he might be able to like."

Then the older man spoke, the one who gave a great deal of good counsel. "I never advise any nobleman to start altering the Word of God. Just go and ask the father, a man of long experience, who in his wisdom has seated himself over there in his mead-hall.[16] Even though he cannot speak a single word, he can give us a message by writing the name in letters." At that, he approached Zachary and put a beech-wood stave[17] on his lap, asking him very earnestly to carve in wisely determined words what this holy child was to be called. Zachary took the book into his hands and the thoughts of his mind turned gladly to God. He wisely carved the name John, and immediately thereafter began speaking in his own words. He regained his power of speech and spoke with intelligence and wisdom. The affliction had left him, the hard punishment which holy God had powerfully inflicted upon him so that Zachary's memory would not forget Him, should He ever again send him one of His followers.[18]

---

[16] *uuinseli* lit. 'wine-hall' or 'drinking room'.

[17] *boc* lit. 'beech[-wood]; book'. Zachary is depicted as carving runic letters on beechwood, in the Germanic manner. The verb used, *uuritan*, signifies writing by incising letters in wood or stone; *scriban* (from Lat. *scribere*) is most commonly used for writing with ink on parchment.

[18] *iungron*. The word adds a delightful and important undertone. Throughout the Zachary story the author has carefully identified him with the Saxons: a nobleman-priest with his band of armed companions before a Saxon temple. The angel is referred to throughout with the two words one would expect: *bodo* 'messenger' and *engil* 'angel'. The ending of the story, where the author gives his own reason for God's inflicting the punishment on Zachary (so that his memory will not forget God, should He ever again send one of His 'angels'), turns the warning toward the audience by using a word that doesn't so much mean 'angel' at all but rather 'follower', 'servant', or 'disciple'.

Song 4

The All-Ruler's angel comes to Mary in Galileeland.

It was not long thereafter that it was all accomplished just as the all-mighty God had so often promised mankind—that He would send His heavenly Child, His own Son, to this world to free all the clans of people here from evil. His messenger Gabriel, the angel of the All-Ruler, then came to Galileeland. There he knew a lovely young woman, a girl who had reached her maidenhood. Her name was Mary. Joseph, a nobleman, was engaged to her, David's daughter. What a precious bride and virtuous woman she was! There in hill-fort Nazareth the angel of God addressed her face to face, calling her by her name and saying to her from God: "Health be with you, Mary. Your Lord is very fond of you.[19] You are precious to the Ruler for your wisdom, woman full of grace. You are to be sanctified more than any other woman. Do not waver in your mind and do not let yourself fear for your life. I have not come here to put you in any danger and I am not bringing you any kind of trick or deception. You are to become the mother of our Chieftain here among human beings. You will bear a child, the Son of the high King of Heaven. His name among the peoples will be Healer. The broad kingdom over which He will rule as a great leader will never come to an end."

Then the maiden, the most beautiful and radiant of women, replied to the angel of God: "How can that happen," she said, "that I would bear a child? I have never known man in my life." The angel of the All-Ruler had his answer ready for the woman: "By the power of God, the Holy Spirit will come to you from the meadows

---

[19] *thu bist thinun herron liof.* It is interesting that this lovely way of rendering the difficult Latin phrase *gratia plena* (which the poet repeats in the following line in a literal translation) is almost identical with that forcefully suggested by Martin Luther seven hundred years later. In his *Sendbrief vom Dolmetschen* he ridicules the idea of rendering *gratia plena* by 'full of grace' on the grounds that it makes grace or favor seem like a liquid (beer) being poured into a vat (Mary). He suggests instead *du bist deinem Herrn lieb* expresses the Lord's fondness far more movingly and how favored and 'dear' (*lieb*) Mary is to her Lord. The suggestion is identical with the Saxon phrase in the *Heliand*. Was Luther acquainted with the *Heliand*?

of heaven. From Him a child will be given to you in this world.
Divine power from the most high King of Heaven will shade you in
its shadow. Never among human beings was there ever as beautiful
or so great a birth as this one, when it comes, by the power of God,
to this wide world!" After this explanation the woman's mind
changed and was completely in accord with God's will. "I stand here
ready," she said, "to perform any service He may wish to give me. I
am the maid-servant of mankind's God. I now trust this thing. Let
it be done unto me according to your words, whatever my Lord
wills—nor is my mind in doubt, neither in word nor in deed."

And so I have heard it told that the woman very gladly received
the message of God with an easy mind, with good faith and with
transparent loyalty. The Holy Spirit became the baby in her
womb.[20] In her heart and feelings she realized what had happened
and she told whomever she wished, that the power of the All-Ruler
coming in holiness from heaven had gotten her pregnant.

Joseph's mind and emotions, however, were in turmoil, since he
had already bought the maiden—this virtuous woman, this lady of the
nobility—to be his bride. He could see that she had a child in her
body and ignored the fact that the woman had actually guarded
herself well. He did not yet know about the Ruler's merry

---

[20] *Uuard the helago gest that barn an ira bosma.* This is a very unusual passage.
In orthodox Christian theology from the earliest councils of the church it has always
been understood that it is the Second Person of the Trinity (the Son) who becomes
man in Jesus Christ. The First Person (the Father) does not, and the Third Person
(the Holy Spirit) is seen as entering the generality of the persons of the church at
Pentecost, but never as repeating the incarnation of the Son in one specific human
being alone. The author may have misunderstood the Creed of Nicea's relevant
phrase *et incarnatus est de Spiritu Sancto* 'He was made flesh by the Holy Spirit', or
possibly the Annunciation scene in Luke's gospel. The author may also have been
misled by his own purposes. If Christ, including His hair and fingernails (contrast
with John the Baptist), is entirely the product of the Holy Spirit and not at all
beholden to the workings of time and fate, then He is shown to be above the highest
Germanic divinities. This is a very docetist position. Cf. *The Saxon Savior*, Ch. 3.
(An alternate suggestion that the passage might mean 'The Holy Spirit came; the baby
was in her womb' is too difficult to reconcile with the text.)

message.[21] He no longer wanted her to be his bride, his wife within his hall, and he began to think in his mind how he could let her go in such a way that she would not at all get hurt or feel hardship. He also did not want all this made known afterwards to people—he was afraid that the sons of men might take her life. That was the custom of those people, the Hebrews, back then, according to the old law. If ever a woman lived or slept with anyone unlawfully, she always had to pay the price for it: her life for the love. There was no woman so good that she could remain alive long thereafter among those people or last long among the crowd.

Joseph, that wise and very good man, began to think in his heart of ways to let the girl go secretly. It was not long then before the messenger of the King of Heaven, the Chieftain's angel, came to him there and in a dream and told him to keep her and to love her in his heart: "Do not be angry with Mary, your young lady, she is a proper wife. Do not think too harshly of her. You are to keep her safe, you are to protect her well in this world. Continue with the betrothal which you made, and foster loving friendship between you. Do not let her be loathsome to you because there is a baby in her body. That child in her womb comes from the meadows of heaven by the command of God, the Holy Spirit. It is Jesus Christ, God's own boy, the Ruler's Son. Keep her well, in a holy way. Do not let your mind doubt or your emotions be disturbed." Joseph's mind was changed after these words. He took the maiden to be his wife and gave her his love. He acknowledged the power of God and the command of the Ruler. He had a great desire to be able to keep her in a holy way and he took care of her among his warrior-companions.

And she carried, all for the glory of God, the Holy Spirit, that Divine Man, until the workings of fate informed her powerfully that she should bring forth to the light of men the Best of all who have ever been born.

---

[21] *blidi gibodskepi* 'the happy [blithe] message'. A delightful allusion to the gospel itself as well as to Christmas! This is a happy rendition of the Latin *evangelium* (from the Greek *eu-* 'good' + *angelion* 'message'). In modern English one often hears 'the good news' as its translation, and in modern German *die frohe Botschaft* 'the happy message'.

Song 5

The Chieftain of mankind is born in David's hill-fort.

Then there came a decree from Fort Rome, from the great Octavian who had power over the whole world, an order from Caesar to his wide realm, sent to every king enthroned in his homeland and to all Caesar's army commanders governing the people of any territory.[22] It said that everyone living outside their own country should return to their homeland upon receipt of the message. It stated that all the warrior heroes were to return to their assembly place, each one was to go back to the clan of which he was a family member by birth in a hill-fort.

That command was sent out over the whole world. People came together at all the hill-forts. The messengers who had come from Caesar were men who could read and write, and they wrote everyone's name down very carefully in a report—both name and nationality—so that no human being could escape from paying the tax which each warrior had on his head.

The good Joseph went also with his household, just as God, ruling mightily, willed it. He made his way to his shining home, the hill-fort at Bethlehem. This was the assembly place for both of them, for Joseph the hero and for Mary the good, the holy girl. This was the place where in olden days the throne of the great and noble good King David stood for as long as he reigned, enthroned on high, an earl of the Hebrews. Joseph and Mary both belonged by birth to his household, they were of good family lineage, of David's own clan.

I have heard it told[23] that the shining workings [of fate] and the power of God told Mary that on this journey a son would be granted

---

[22] By eliminating the name of the specific governor given in Luke's gospel (Lk 2:2-3: *when Quirinius was governor of Syria*) and by making the statement on governor-ships a general statement in the plural, the author has created the possibility of his audience identifying closely with his story, since the occupied country of the Saxons was ruled by military legates (*missi*) sent from "Caesar" in Aix-la-Chapelle.

[23] *Thar gifragn ic* 'Then, I have learned' or 'I found out'. This appears to be an oral formula from heroic poetry indicating the beginning of an important passage. I translate it *I have heard it told. . .* whenever it occurs.

her, born in Bethlehem, the strongest child, the most powerful of all kings, the Great One come powerfully to the light of mankind—just as foretold by many visions and signs in this world many days before.

At that time it all came to pass, just as wise men had said long ago: that the Protector of People would come in a humble way, by His own power, to visit this kingdom of earth. His mother, that most beautiful woman, took Him, wrapped Him in clothes and precious jewels, and then with her two hands laid Him gently, the little man, that child, in a fodder-crib, even though He had the power of God, and was the Chieftain of mankind. There the mother sat in front of Him and remained awake, watching over the holy Child and holding it. And there was no doubt in the mind or in the heart of the holy maid.[24]

What had happened became known to many over this wide world. The guards heard it. As horse-servants they were outside, they were men on sentry duty, watching over the horses,[25] the beasts of the field: they saw the darkness split in two in the sky, and the light of God came shining through the clouds and surrounded the guards out in the fields. Those men began to feel fear in their

---

[24] This observation inserted by the author is no doubt a side remark aimed at his Saxons, urging them quietly, as he did in the Zachary story, not to doubt their new faith.

[25] The famous sheep and shepherds of Christmas Eve are transformed by the author into horses and horse-guards. This cannot be because sheep, wool, and shepherds were unknown in the North. Quite the opposite should have been the case in a climate where woolen clothing was preferred. The reason must lie in the social unacceptability of shepherds. The *Heliand* is at great pains to show that Joseph and Mary are upper class, *of good family. . . born inside the hill-fort,* and sheep herders cannot have been acceptable recipients for angelic messages in the eyes of the Saxon warrior nobility.

Saxon and Carolingian law accepted a rigid stratification of society into three classes. The serfs, servants, slaves were at the bottom of society; freemen: farmers, fishermen, artisans were the middle class; and the warrior nobility of the hill-forts and mead-halls were the upper class. Since horses were a prized item of the upper class, and the horse-guards (the marshalls and equerries of the High Middle Ages) who were responsible for the horses even at night, must have been their picked and trusted servants, the Christmas Eve scene is made familiar to the warrior class, and the alienation that might have been caused by retaining serfs' sheep and shepherds is avoided.

hearts. They saw the mighty angel of God coming toward them. He spoke to the guards face to face and told them that they should not fear any harm from the light. "I am going to tell you," he said, "something very wonderful, something very deeply desired. I want to let you know something very powerful: Christ is now born, on this very night, God's holy Child, the good Chieftain, at David's hill-fort. What happiness for the human race, a boon for all men! You can find Him, the most powerful Child, at Fort Bethlehem. Take what I now tell you in truthful words as a sign: He is there, wrapped up, lying in a fodder-crib—even though He is king over all the earth and the heavens and over the sons of all the peoples, the Ruler of the world." Just as he said that word, an enormous number of the holy army, the shining people of God, came down to the one angel from the meadows of heaven, saying many words of praise for the Lord of Peoples. They then began to sing a holy song as they wended their way through the clouds towards the meadows of heaven.

The guards heard how the angels in their power praised the all-mighty God most worshipfully in words: "Glory now be," they said, "to the Lord-Chieftain Himself, in the highest reaches of heaven, and peace on earth to the sons of men, men of good will, those who because of their clear minds recognize God!"

The herdsmen understood that something great had been told to them—a merry message! They decided to go to Bethlehem that night, they wanted very much to be able to see Christ Himself.[26]

---

[26] The reader may have noticed the complete omission in the *Heliand* of the *no room for them at the inn* part of the Nativity story. Apparently such inhospitable treatment of a 'well-born, noble' couple would have been unthinkable in a Saxon hill-fort, especially if it were the home fort of their own clan (and thus the author had transposed the story). The author would have been obliged to omit it for consistency's sake.

Song 6

The Baby is brought to the Ruler's shrine.

The angel of God had shown the horse-guards with a shining sign that they themselves could go to God's Baby Son. They soon found Him, the Chieftain of Clans, the Lord of Peoples. They praised God the Ruler with their words and made known widely all over the shining hill-fort what a brilliant, holy vision, from the meadows of heaven, they had been shown out there in the fields. The lady, the holy girl, the maid, kept in her mind and in her heart whatever she heard the men saying.

The mother, the loveliest of ladies, then fittingly brought up the Chieftain of many men, the holy heavenly Child, on love.[27]

Many of the heroes, the earls, very intelligent men, spoke on the eighth day with God's girl, saying that the Child should have the name 'Healer' just as the angel of God, Gabriel, said in truthful words when he, as God's messenger, gave this command to the woman. That had been at the moment she first conceived the Child as He came shining into this world. She very much wanted to keep the Child in this holy way, she was very glad to take care of Him.

The year slipped further by, until God's Son of Peace was forty days and forty nights of age. There was a duty which parents were obliged to perform, they had to bring Him to Jerusalem to the Ruler at His shrine. That was the way it was then, that was the country's custom, one that no woman among the Hebrews could omit. The first time a woman gave birth to a son, she always brought him to God's shrine. And so Joseph and Mary, those two good people, decided to leave Bethlehem. They had the baby with them, the holy Christ, and went to visit the house of God in Jerusalem. There they

---

[27] This forms a perfect companion piece to John the Baptist's upbringing. Zachary was informed that his son John was to be a warrior-companion (*gisid*) of the King of Heaven and Christ, and thus to be raised in the virtue of loyalty (*treuua*). Christ is to be the Chieftain of many such warriors and thus is brought up fittingly on the appropriate reciprocal virtue: love (*minnea*).

were to worship the Ruler at the shrine according to the ways of the Jewish people.

At the shrine they found a good, old man of noble birth at the altar. He had lived many of the winters and summers of his life at the shrine where he performed the divine praises with a clear mind. He had the Holy Spirit, a happy heart. Simeon was his name. The Ruler's power had shown him a long time ago that he would not leave this light, he would not make the journey from this world, before his wish was granted that he should see holy Christ Himself, the holy King of Heaven. At that moment his heart became extremely happy within him—he saw the Child coming into the shrine. He gave thanks to the Ruler, the all-mighty God, that he saw Him with his own eyes.

Simeon went toward Him, and gladly the old man took Him in his arms. He recognized all of it: the sign, the vision, and the Son of God as well, the holy King of Heaven. "Now, Lord," he said, "will I gladly ask you, since I am now very old, that you let your devoted servant go away from here, to travel under your peaceful protection to where my forefathers, brave warriors, went when they left this world. My wish is fulfilled on this most precious day, now that I have seen my Chieftain, my gracious Lord, just as it was promised to me long ago. You are a powerful light to all foreign peoples who have not yet recognized the All-Ruler's might, and Your coming, my Lord Chieftain, brings glory and honor to the sons of Israel, Your own clan, Your own dear people."

The old man spoke secretly with the good woman at the altar and in soothsaying told her how her Son would be the downfall of many of the sons of men and the help of many others here in the middle world—pleasure to those who follow His teaching, pain to those who do not want to hear the teachings of Christ. "You will have sorrow in the future," he said, "you will suffer pain in your heart when heroes' sons overwhelm Him with weapons. Then your great work will begin: to bear sorrow." The young girl understood the wise man's words completely.

Then an old woman also came walking into the sanctuary, Anna was her name, Phanuel's daughter. She had served her Chieftain well in gratitude, she was a mature woman. After her maidenhood, she, the noble girl, was married to an earl on his property. For seven winters she and her bridegroom ruled his lands together.

Then I have heard it told that sorrow came to her, that the mighty power of the Measurer[28] separated them, the cruel workings of fate.[29] After that she was a widow at the shrine of peace for eighty-four winters of her lifetime. And so she never went away from the shrine, but served God her Chieftain well there by day and by night.

She too came walking toward them at the same moment. She immediately recognized God's Child and let the heroes know, the warriors at the shrine, the great and welcome news, saying that the Rescuer's salvation had come to them, help from the King of Heaven: "Now the holy Christ, the Ruler Himself, has come to this shrine, to deliver the people, the poor people who, for so long now, have been waiting in this middle world, for such a long time. Now, let mankind rejoice over this!" Many of the people at the shrine were over-joyed—they heard the great and welcome news being said about God.

The woman had performed the sacred task there, the worship at the altar, just as it was commanded in their law and in the book in the bright shining hill-fort.[30] The holy family, Joseph and Mary, set off for home then and left Jerusalem. They always had the King of Heaven, the Son of the Chieftain, the Protector of Multitudes as their

---

[28] *metodes* 'of the Measurer'. *Metod* is one of the words for God or Fate as the ultimate determiner of the length of existence for any person or thing. In the *Heliand* it is clear that the author does not wish to use this word as the translation for the God of the Christians, even though this had been done in England.

[29] *uurdigiscapu* 'the workings of fate'. Whenever a death is involved the author prefers to have *giscapu* 'workings' bear the immediate responsibility for determining the event and, above all, its timing. If it is a case of the beginning of a life, then occasionally one sees, in some of the manuscripts, *godes* 'God's', inserted ahead of what some copyists must have seen as the too dangerously pagan concept of *giscapu* 'workings'.

[30] While it is clear that the presentation in the temple was commanded in the old law, it seems unclear (to me, at least) what the author is referring to as the book in the fort, unless he again means the Old Testament.

companion,[31] thus it was that the news did not spread any further in this world—than He wished, that was the King of Heaven's intention.

Song 7

Three thanes from the East, led by the workings of fate, follow a star.

Even though holy men there recognized Christ, still it had not yet become known at the king's court to the men who in their attitude were not very inclined to Him—and it remained hidden from them in word and in deed until men of the East, very wise men, three strong thanes, came to this people, walking the long road over the land to get there. They were following a bright-shining beacon, and with clear mind[32] were looking for God's Child. They wanted to kneel to Him, to go and become His followers—God's [fate-]workings were leading them on.

They found Herod there, the powerful man sitting in his hall, the slithery-mouthed king, angrily talking with his men—he always enjoyed murder. The wise men addressed him in his house properly and fittingly in the royal manner, and he soon asked what business brought these warriors out on a journey far from home. "Are you bringing wound gold to give to someone? Why[33] are you traveling

---

[31] A truly remarkable concept in Saxon terms. One could not even think of having a king as a warrior-companion, it should be the opposite, one might dream of being the companion of a king! In the *Heliand* the wonder of the Incarnation is expressed movingly by saying that Mary and Joseph had not an earthly warrior but the King of Heaven as one of their warrior-companions!

[32] This concept is not clarified until later in the work where clear-minded behavior is identified with single-minded devotion and unswerving loyalty to one's chief. Its opposite, therefore, would not be muddled or illogical thinking, but rather double-mindedness, vacillation in one's attitude and intentions.

[33] Or, possibly, 'To whom?'

like this, walking on foot?[34] I do not even know where you come from, earls of other peoples! I can see that you are of noble birth, clansmen of good family. Never before have such messengers come here from other peoples since I have ruled this noble and wide kingdom. You are to tell me truthfully in front of these people of our country why you have come to this land."

Then the men of the East answered him, those word-wise warriors. "We can easily tell you the truth of our business and say to you openly why we have come here from the East on this journey to your country. A long time ago there were noble men, men of good speech, who promised so much good and help in truthful words from the King of Heaven. At that time there was a wise man, a man of experience and great wisdom—this was a long time ago—our ancestor there in the East.[35] There has never been since then a single man who spoke so wisely. He was able to interpret God's speech,[36] because the Lord of mankind had granted him the ability to hear the Ruler's words up above from down on earth. For this reason, this thane's knowledge and his thoughts were great.

---

[34] The reader, like Herod, may have noticed the absence of the traditionally required camels. Unlike the sheep who were missing from the shepherd story, I do not think that the absence of camels requires a sociological explanation. In the dominant Byzantine art of the period, the wise men are depicted walking on foot as they follow the star, generally wearing attire associated in the art of the Roman Empire, East and West, with the Persians. I do not know when the custom began in Europe of depicting the wise men as riding on camels, but they are so represented in England four hundred years later, at the time of the crusades.

Herod's shock in the *Heliand* is probably to be understood as surprise at the failure of traveling noblemen to be mounted on horses.

[35] This seems to be very much the creation of the author. It is not clear what figure might form the basis for this thought. Zoroaster might be thought of, but it is equally possible that this 'ancestor' of the people of the East, represents the fact that pre-Christian peoples had access to God's word, a thought not unwelcome to the Saxons.

[36] *he mahte rekkien spel godes.* The play on words is clear in the original Saxon: he could interpret God's spell (gospel), and this the author affirms outside the Hebrew religion and before Christianity. Thus, once again, the author is implicitly respecting the possibility of divine revelation in Germanic religion as well.

"When the time came for him to depart, to leave the earth and the throng of his relatives, to give up the comings and goings of men and to travel to the other light,[37] he told his followers, his heirs and his earls, to come closer, and told them truthfully in soothsaying, everything that came afterwards, everything that has happened since in this world. Then he said that a wise king, great and mighty, was to come here to the middle world; he would be of the best lineage. He said that it would be God's Son, and that He would rule this world forever, both the earth and the heavens, for days without end. He said that on the same day on which His mother gave birth to Him blessedly in this middle world, in the East there would shine a bright light in the sky such as we had never had before between the earth and the heavens nor anywhere else—never such a baby nor such a beacon! He ordered that three men of the people should go to do adoration—he told them to remember well that when they saw God's beacon journeying upward they should get ready immediately. He said that we were to follow it as it goes before us, in a westerly direction, over this world.

"Now this has all happened, it has come true by the power of God. The king is born, daring and strong. We saw His beacon-light shining cheerfully among the stars of heaven, and thus I know that the holy Chieftain powerfully placed it there Himself. Every morning we saw the bright star shining, and went toward it, following the beacon all the time over roads and through forests. The greatest of our desires was to be able to see Him Himself, to know where we should look for Him, the King in this empire. Tell us to which clan He has been born."

At that, Herod felt pain in his chest and in his heart, his mind began to reel, his spirit was worried. He had just heard it said that he was to have a more powerful king, of good clan, over his head, that there was a more fortunate person than he among his warrior-companions.

---

[37] Cf. I. Rauch. "Another Old English-Old Saxon Isogloss: (REM) Activity." *De Gustibus: A Festschrift for Alain Renoir.* Edited by J. M. Foley. New York: Garland (in press).

Then he called together all the good men in Jerusalem, the most learned and eloquent and those who truly held the most book-power in their breasts, and he asked them very carefully with words, that evil-minded man, the king of the people, where Christ, the greatest Man of Peace, was to be born in the earthly realm. The people then responded to him, men of truth, saying that they did indeed know that He was to be born in Bethlehem. "It has been put down thus in our books, wisely written, just as the soothsayers, very intelligent and learned men, spoke long ago by the power of God: it is from Bethlehem that the Herdsman of Hill-forts,[38] the beloved Protector of the Country, is to come to the light—the mighty Counselor who will rule the Jewish people and who will distribute His gifts generously throughout the middle world to many peoples."

Song 8

The three foreign warriors present their gifts to the Ruler's Child.

I have heard it told that immediately after the cruel-minded king said the words of his soothsayers to the foreign heroes, who were earls in their homeland and had traveled afar, he asked them when they first saw on the roads of the East the King's star coming, the sign shining down cheerfully from heaven. They did not wish to conceal anything from him and so they told him the truth. He then instructed them to go on their journey and to investigate the matter thoroughly about the coming of the Child. The king himself, the lord of the Jews, commanded the wise men very sternly, that, before they left the West, they let him know where he could find the Child himself. He

---

[38] *burgo hirdi,* an unusual image. Perhaps, visually, what the author is suggesting is this: As one looks at a hill-fort on the top of a hill, one sees a group of rounded thatch-roofed houses, and the mead-hall, surrounded by a palisade. He suggests it looks like nothing more than a herd of tawny animals enclosed within the posts of their corral. Christ he then sees as the herdsman of these corrals, the 'Protector of Hill-forts'.

said that he wanted to go there with his warrior-companions to adore the Child. (He was hoping, with the edge of the sword, to become the Child's murderer.)

But the ruling God thought about this: He [the Child] should accomplish more, do more in this world; His light must shine longer, making known the power of God.[39]

The sign then moved on, shining among the clouds. The wise men were ready to travel.[40] They decided to leave and go on, they were eager about their mission! They wanted to see the Son of God Himself. They had no other warrior-companions of their retinue with them; there were only three of them—they understood things, they were smart men, the ones bearing the gifts.[41]

Then they looked up to the high heavens, where they saw in their wisdom how the bright stars which had been created by Christ for His world, moved across the cloudy sky—they recognized God's sign. The warriors walked on after it, following faithfully—the Force helped them—until the road-weary men saw God's bright-shining beacon, the white light in the heavens, stand still. The bright star shone brilliantly over the house where the holy Child willed to live, where the woman, the maiden, was taking proper care of Him. The thanes' hearts became merry within them, they understood from the beacon-light that they had found God's Peaceful Son, the holy King of Heaven. They then walked inside the house with their gifts, those road-weary warriors from the East, and immediately recognized Christ, the Ruler. The foreign fighting men fell on their knees to the good Child and greeted Him in the royal manner.[42] They carried the gifts to

---

[39] In other words, the Christian God is depicted here as thinking about frustrating the normal procedure of fate, and then deciding to do it.

[40] *fusa te faranne*. The expression is interesting because it is also the one that the author uses of Christ when He is about to die on the cross: 'He is ready to travel.'

[41] This is unclear to me. Why is it so important to travel without an escort? Perhaps this has something to do with the practical, sociopolitical aspects of foreign travel in that time. Would a large retinue seem threatening, draw unwelcome attention?

[42] The Christ-Child in the *Heliand* is the King. The visitors from the East are wise men, noble warriors (as Herod recognizes immediately), but they are not made into the Three Kings of the later Middle Ages. This is perhaps because the title 'king'

Him: gold and incense as a sign of divinity, and myrrh as well. The men stood there attentively, respectful in the presence of their Lord, and soon received It [the Child] in a fitting manner in their hands.[43]

Then the Wise Men decided, road-weary as they were, to go home to the guest-hall. It was there, as they were sleeping during the night, that God's angel showed them in their sleep, in a dream, what the Chieftain Himself, the Ruler, wanted. It seemed to them that a man was telling them in words that they, the earls, should leave the place by another way when they went home, and that they should not go back to that loathsome man Herod again, that moodily violent king.

Then morning came shining to this world. The Wise Men began to tell one another their dream and they recognized the Ruler's word themselves—they had great wisdom in their hearts. They asked the All-Ruler, the high King of Heaven, that they might be able to continue to work toward His glory, to carry out His will. They said that they had changed their minds and their hearts that morning—for every morning![44]

Then the men traveled away again, the earls from the East, just as the angel of God had instructed them in words. They took another road, following God's directions. The messengers from the

---

might not have been one gladly recognized among the Saxons—their highest rank being 'chieftain' or 'lord'—and perhaps because the notion of making the Magi into the Three Kings had simply not yet begun in the church of Northern Europe in the ninth century.

[43] This beautiful if obscure line merits closer observation. The Wise Men have presented the gifts, they then stand devoutly and attentively in the presence of the Son of God, they then receive "It" in their hands. The *It* causes difficulty for translators, since the previous reference to Christ in the last sentence was to "Him" as "their Lord," thus requiring "Him" rather than "It" as the expected pronoun of reference. Using "It" is much more rich an allusion. Not only does it hearken back to the word "Child'" but it also makes, by suggestion, the whole scene into a beautiful allegory of the moment of communion in the Mass, when one receives "It." For in the ninth century the ancient practice of receiving the communion wafer in the hand was still current.

[44] The author is taking some liberrty here with the story of the Wise Men. His expansion of the text is no doubt well-intended preaching to his Christian Saxon audience to keep their change of heart for more than a day!

East, road-weary men, would never tell the Jewish king a thing about the Son's birth; rather they traveled on as they wished.[45]

Song 9

Herod orders his warrior-companions to behead all two-year-old boys around Bethlehem.

Soon thereafter the ruling God's angel came to speak to Joseph. The Chieftain's messenger told him in a dream while he was sleeping at night, that the slime-hearted king would come looking for God's Son, in order to kill Him. "You are to lead Him away from here to Egyptland, and live among those people with God's Son and with the good maiden, dwelling with their warriors, until word comes to you from your Lord that you may lead the holy Child, your Chieftain, back to this territory." Joseph jumped up from the dream in his guest-hall, and immediately obeyed God's command. The noble warrior, together with the virgin, started off on the journey away from there, and looking for other peoples across the wide mountains. He was determined to get God's Son away from His enemies.

Soon thereafter, Herod the king, enthroned in his realm, was informed that the wise men had returned from the West to their homeland in the East, and had taken another route. He knew that they did not want to report to him again in his throne room. His mind then became troubled; his mood worried. He said that those men did it to him, those heroes, to scorn him. As he sat there with so much pain and rage in his breast, he said that he had another idea, a better plan. "I know His age, the number of His winters, and

---

[45] The Wise Men, like Zachary, are used by the author to express the religious situation of the Saxons. The author seems to suggest that it is quite conceivable for those who come from religiously afar to 'receive the Child in the hand' while not wanting to have anything to do with the violent and moody intentions of the current king of the land. The prayer of the Wise Men after their vision in their sleep of the angel is entirely the author's insertion (Matthew's gospel has nothing of it), and turns the whole incident into a small and very appealing allegory of conversion for the Saxon audience.

therefore I can see to it that He never ever grows old on this earth, here in this realm."

Then Herod sent a strict command throughout his kingdom, ordering his warriors, as king of the people, to march. He gave the order that by the strength of their hand they were to decapitate the boys around Bethlehem, as many as had been born there who had reached two years of age. The king's warrior-companions did this horrible deed. Many a man was to die there in his childhood, innocent of any sin. Never before or since has there been a more tragic departure for young persons, a more miserable death. The women were crying, the many mothers who saw their infants killed. Nor were they able to help them. Even if she held her own boy, little and loveable, tightly in her arms, the child still had to give up its life—in front of the mother. They saw nothing evil, they saw nothing wrong,[46] the ones who carried out this outrageous crime. With the weapon's edge, they did an enormous work of evil, cutting down many a man in his infancy. The mothers were weeping over the violent deaths of their young children. Sorrow was in Bethlehem, the loudest of lamentations—even if you cut their hearts in two with a sword, nothing more painful could ever happen to them in this world, the many women, the brides of Bethlehem. They saw their children in front of them, men in their childhood, violently killed, lying in blood on their laps.

The murderers killed the guiltless innocents, and didn't think a thing about the evil they were doing—they wanted to kill mighty Christ Himself! But God in His strength had saved Him from their hatred. Earls, Joseph and his men, had led Him away from there by night to Egyptland, to the green meadows by the best earth, where a river flows, the fairest of streams, northward to the sea—the mighty Nile.

There God's Peace-Child lived willingly until fate removed Herod the king, and Herod thus left the sons of men, the mad comings and goings of human beings. His heir was then to have power over the

---

[46] There is nothing parallel to this thought in the gospel itself (Mt. 2: 16-18). It is the author's comment. Is he thinking of some Frankish behavior in the Saxon war, or is it a pastoral Christian comment?

region. His name was Archelaus, army commander of the helmet-wearers. He was to rule the warriors, the Jewish people, around Jerusalem.

Then word came to Egypt, to that honorable man Joseph. God's angel, the Chieftain's messenger, spoke to him and told him to take the boy back home to his country. "Herod the king," he said, "has left the light. He was always after the Child, always after His life. Now you can lead the Child back in peace to your family clan. The king is not alive—that arrogant madman of an earl!"[47] Joseph complied completely with this sign from God. They got themselves ready immediately, the thane and the girl; they both wanted to leave immediately with their Son. They were accomplishing bright-shining Fate, the will of God, as He had told them before with His words.

Song 10

Mary and Joseph find the holy Child at the shrine.

Joseph and Mary then returned to Galileeland, the holy household of the King of Heaven was at hill-fort Nazareth. The saving Christ grew up there among the people, He became full of wisdom, God's favor was with Him, and He was very much liked by His mother's relatives. He was not like other men with regard to goodness.

When He was twelve years old, the time had come for the Jewish people to worship their clan's God in Jerusalem, to carry out His commands. Inside the shrine in Jerusalem the Jews had assembled, a great crowd of men. Mary herself was there in attendance and had her Son, God's own Child.

---

[47] The extraordinary degree of emotional reaction in the text (greatly exceeding the biblical account) against King Herod, his self-centered motives, his killing without feelings of guilt, his ruthless use of his army, seems to point to another determined kingly figure, Charlemagne, reaction to whose ruthless, thirty-three-year 'war of conversion' against the Saxons may be fueling the fire of the author's feelings.

Charlemagne died in the year 814. The Herod story in the *Heliand* might lead one to speculate that the author was there when that fateful news traveled eastward and reached Saxony.

The earls performed the worship service there as commanded in their law, in accordance with their country's customs. The people then departed, the men going wherever they liked. The mighty Son of God stayed at the shrine, without His mother knowing anything about it. She thought He had left with the men, traveling with her friends. She found out the next day, that woman of noble lineage, blessed girl, that He was not among their companions. Mary then became deeply sorrowful; worry seized her heart. When she could not find the holy Child among the people, God's young maiden began to moan.

They decided to go back to Jerusalem to look for their Son. They found Him sitting there inside the shrine where wise and intelligent men read and learn in God's law how to praise the One who made the world in human words. There He was, sitting in the midst of them, the mighty Child of God, the all-ruling Christ, and they did not recognize Him at all—and they were supposed to be in charge of the shrine!

With great interest He was asking them questions in wise words. They were all amazed that a young man, a child, would ever be able to say such words with His mouth. The mother found Him there, sitting in their company. She greeted her Son, a wise man among the people, and spoke to Him in these words, "How could You give Your mother such worry, dear, that I, poor sorrowful woman, would have to go asking for You among these hill-fort people?" Then the Son replied to her in wise words. "What? You knew very well," He said, "where I belong and where I by rights would want to be—where My mighty Father is the Ruler!"

The people, the men at the shrine, did not understand why He spoke words like that with His mouth. Mary retained it all—she concealed in her heart whatever she heard her Son say in wise words.

Joseph and Mary then decided to leave Jerusalem, they had the Son of the Chieftain in their retinue. He was the best of sons, the best of those who have ever been born as a baby from a mother! They loved Him with a clear mind; and God's own Son was very humbly obedient to His clan-relatives and parents.

He did not want to reveal His mighty strength to mankind so soon in His childhood, nor let them know that He had such power and authority in this world. Therefore He decided to wait for thirty years among the people, as was proper, before He wanted to give them any indication or let His companions know that He was Himself the Chieftain of the human race here in the middle world.

The holy Son of God had contained His voice and His wisdom and knowledge that was beyond all, as well as His incredible mind, so that no one could discern from His speech nor from His words, that He had such wisdom, that the thane had such thoughts. Instead of that, He, very properly, awaited a clearer sign. But the time had not yet come that He was to tell the whole middle world about Himself, when He was to teach the people how they were to have faith, how to carry out the will of God.

Many people in the country knew, however, that He had come to the light, but they were not able to be sure that they recognized Him until He himself wanted to tell them.

Song 11

John announces Christ's coming to Middlegard.

John had been growing up from his youth in a wasteland. There were no other people there except all-ruling God, Whom he was serving alone in that place. The thane left behind the crowd of people and the community of human beings. There in the wasteland, the Word of God, the divine voice of God, came to him powerfully and told John that he was to announce Christ's coming and powerful strength throughout this middle world. He was to say truthfully in words that the heaven-kingdom, the greatest of delights, had come to those heroes' sons, to people, to the soil of that country. John was very willing to tell of such fortunate blessings.

He decided then to go to where the Jordan's water freely flowed, and there he made known every day to the people of that country that they could make up for their many evil deeds, their own sins, by fasting. "Become clean," he said. "The heaven-kingdom is approaching the sons of men. Now, in your hearts regret your own sins, the loathsome things you did in this light, and listen to my teaching, turn around in accordance with my words! I will gladly immerse[48] you in water, but I do not have the power to take away your sinful deeds, so that by the work of my hands you could be washed of your evil accomplishments."

"He, however, has come in His power to this light, to human beings, and has been standing in your midst (though you do not want to see Him), who is to immerse you, in your Chieftain's name, in the Holy Spirit. He is Lord over everything, He is able to free any human being whatsoever from his evil-minded sins—everyone who has the wish to be so happy in this world, that he is willing to carry out whatever orders the Child of God gives these people.

"I have come to this world on His mission, and I am to clear the road for Him. I am to teach these people how they are to hold on to their faith by having a clear mind,[49] and that they do not have to go to Hel's[50] realm, to the heat of that infernal place.[51]

---

[48] *gidopean* 'dip' or 'place in water'. The author takes poetic advantage of the Saxon use of 'submergence' or 'immersion' as the translation of 'baptism' (which in gospel Greek implies more 'to cleanse' than 'to immerse'). Later in this section he can thus describe baptism not only as cleansing by the Holy Spirit, but as immersion in the Holy Spirit.

[49] This sentence may contain the clearest statement of the author's intent in composing the *Heliand*, putting the gospel in Northern terms: so that the Saxons will be able to have a clear-minded grasp of their new faith. By clear-minded he indicates that they will not have to vacillate between their older Germanic beliefs and the new Mediterranean ones, but that they will hear the meaning of the new religion in their own terms. It seems the author tended to identify himself with the role of John the Baptist.

[50] *hellea* 'the region of Hel'. Hel was one of the three Germanic horror figures: the Wolf, the Serpent and Hel. The Wolf and the Serpent would devour Woden and Thor on the last day, the twilight of the gods. Hel was the monster daughter of the god Loki, the god of trouble-making and mischief, who also sired the other two monsters. The Wolf and the Serpent were to devour the two principal person-gods at the end, and Hel received into her horrible kingdom of darkness, graves, and snakes, any who were unfortunate enough to die of sickness or old age. (Those who died in battle were taken by Valkyries to heaven.) The poet here gives both the Northern and the Mediterranean visions of hell, one cold and damp, the other hot as an inferno.

"This makes mankind rejoice for many an hour: whosoever gladly forsakes evil crimes, the commands of the horrible one, whoever is transparently loyal to the all-mighty God up above, will stand in the good favor of the King of Heaven!"

Many of the earls and the people, when they heard this teaching, thought truly that he was himself the ruling Christ since he spoke so much wisdom in truthful words. That became known very widely to everyone throughout the promised land as they talked in their houses.

Then Jewish people came there from Jerusalem looking for him, emissaries from the hill-fort, and asked if he were God's Child. "The One of whom honest people said long ago, that He was to come to this world." John then spoke and answered the emissaries boldly, "I am not," he said, "God's Child, true Ruler Christ, but I am to clear a road for Him—my Lord."

The heroes, the earls, who were there on this mission, the emissaries from the hill-fort, asked, "If you are not God's Son, are you then perhaps Elijah who days long ago lived among this people? He is supposed to come back again to this middle world. Tell us what man you are! Are you one of the wise soothsayers who were once here? What are we to report to the people truthfully about you? Never before has another man like you come to this middle world with such great deeds. Why are you performing immersions among the people if you are not one of the prophets?"

John the good had his clever answer ready. "I am the fore-messenger of my Sovereign, my dear Lord. I am to bring the land and the people into order according to His will. From His speaking to me I have a strong voice, even though many people here in this wasteland do not want to understand it."

"I am not the slightest bit like my Chieftain. He is so powerful in His deeds, so great and mighty (that is known to many in this world), that I, even though I am His personal servant, am not worthy to untie the straps of the shoes of so powerful a Chieftain! He is

---

[51] *fern.* This is the other word for hell, obviously borrowed from the Latin *infernum* 'the lower regions'. It is curious that in both English and German the Germanic word for this place has won the contest for survival in the language (*hell*, *Hoelle*), but the flame-filled Latin concept has won in the imagination.

that much greatly superior to me. There is not a single emissary on earth who is His equal, nor will there ever be in this world. Keep that as what you want and what you believe; your minds will long be merry when you forsake the power of Hel and the company of the loathsome ones, and seek for yourselves God's light, the home up above, the eternal realm, the high meadows of heaven! Do not let your minds doubt!"

Song 12

Christ the Chieftain is immersed in the Jordan by His loyal thane John.

Thus spoke the young man, by God's teaching, in order to inform mankind. Many of the sons of Israel were assembled there at Bethany. The king's warrior-companions came there to John, people coming for instruction and to receive their faith.

He immersed them every day and reproved them for their deeds, the will of the evil creatures, and praised the word of God, his Lord, to them. "The kingdom of heaven," he said, "is getting ready for any man who thinks of God, and who wants to believe in a clear way in the Healer, and carry out His teaching."

It was not long before it happened that God's own Child, the dear Chieftain's Son, came to him from Galilee, seeking immersion. The Ruler's Child had grown so much that He now had thirty winters among the people in this world. Now He wanted to come to the river Jordan where John was devoutly immersing many people all day long.

The moment he saw his Chieftain there, his dear Lord, his mind became merry, for this was what he wanted. John, that very good man, then spoke to Christ in these words, "You have come to my immersion, my Lord Chieftain, greatest man of the people; I should be coming to Yours, since You are the most powerful king of all!"

Christ Himself, the Ruler, told him truly not to say another word like that. "You know that it is proper for us," He said, "to fulfill all laws whatsoever from this point forward, according to God's will."

John stood there every day, with his own hands immersing the great mass of people in the water, in the best of all baths, including ruling Christ, the lordly Heaven-King—and John bent his powerful knee in prayer.

Christ came up radiant out of the water, the Peace-Child of God, the beloved Protector of people. As He stepped out onto the land, the doors of heaven opened up and the Holy Spirit came down from the All-Ruler above to Christ—It was like a powerful bird, a magnificent dove—and It sat upon our Chieftain's shoulder,[52] remaining over the Ruler's Child.

Then there came Word from heaven, loud from the skies above, and greeted the Healer Himself, Christ, the Best of all kings, saying that He Himself had chosen Him from His kingdom, and that He liked His Son better than all the human beings ever born, and that He was the most loved of all His children.

John had to see and hear all of that there; that was God's will. Soon thereafter John made it known to human beings that they had a mighty Lord right there. "This is," he said, "the King of Heaven's Son, the one All-Ruler—to this I wish to be a witness in this world. The Word of God, the Chieftain's voice, said it to me when He told me to immerse people in water. It was at that time that I truly saw the Holy Spirit coming with power to this middle world from the meadows of heaven to find one individual man. 'That,' the Voice said, 'will be Christ, the dear Chieftain's Son. He will immerse people in the Holy Spirit and heal the evil deeds of many men.'"

"He has the power of God to take away the sinful crimes of any person. This is Christ himself, God's own Child, the Best of men, Security against the enemy. Well, it should make you be in a joyful mood in this world, that it was granted to you in your lifetime to see the country's Guardian himself."

---

[52] *uppan uses drohtines ahslu* 'upon our Chieftain's shoulder'. This subtle change from the original gospel text (in which, as in the following phrase in the *Heliand*, the Dove remains 'over' the Lord) effects a powerful iconographic change. Jesus is depicted here in the manner of Woden who always had the bird(s) of consciousness and memory on his shoulder. Cf. *The Saxon Savior*, Ch. 5.

"Now may many a soul have a quick and easy journey, when God wills it, unburdened with sins and freed from evil deeds—the many souls who desire to live loyally with their friends and to believe firmly in Ruling Christ. What a great credit it will be then to any man who does these things out of enjoyment!"

Song 13

The Champion of mankind fights off the loathsome enemy.

Thus I have heard it told that John praised his Lord Christ's teaching to every man of the people, telling them that they could win the greatest of good things, blessed eternal life, the kingdom of heaven. The good Chieftain Himself, the Son of the Ruler, after the immersion went out to the wild country.[53] The Chieftain of earls was there in the desert for a long time. He did not have any people with Him, no men as companions, this was as He chose it to be.[54]

He wanted to let powerful creatures[55] test Him, even Satan, who is always spurring men on to sin and malicious deeds. He understood Satan's feelings and angry ill-will, how Satan first deceived the earth people in the beginning through sin, how he misled the

---

[53] *uuostunnea* 'wild country, wasteland, wilderness'. It is not immediately clear to the modern reader just what this term would have suggested to the Saxon reader (or listener). It does not seem to signify the desert sands that are implied in the following line. The *wostunnea* is no doubt the Germanic analog to the scriptural desert wilderness. Its exact nature is not made clear, perhaps deliberately, until the first lines of the fourteenth song when we learn that at the end of the forty days Christ emerged from the forest!

[54] The author is gradually remaking the scene of the temptations of Christ into a Germanic challenge to trial by single combat.

[55] *wihti* 'creatures' or 'beings'. The contest is depicted as single-man combat, with Satan as the champion of the evil creatures, and Christ as the champion of the human beings.

couple, Adam and Eve, with lies, into disloyalty[56] so that the souls of the children of men would go to Hel after their departure.

God the Ruler wanted mightily to change that, He wanted to grant to these people the high heaven-kingdom, and for this reason sent them a holy messenger, His Son. This caused Satan a great deal of pain in his mind—he did not want to grant the kingdom of heaven to mankind. He wanted to deceive the mighty Son of the Chieftain with the same things with which he cunningly deceived Adam in days long ago so that Adam became loathsome to his Chieftain. He deceived him with sin—now he wanted to do the same thing to the healing Christ.

Then the Ruler's Child hardened His heart and stiffened His mind against the blasphemer—He wanted to win the heaven-kingdom for people.

The Guardian of the Land, the Chieftain of Mankind, was fasting for forty nights, eating no meat. For that entire time the evil creatures did not dare to approach Him[57]—the evil-minded [serpent[58]] enemy—nor speak to Him face-to-face! Satan thought He was simply God, the mighty One, without anything of human nature, simply the holy Guard of Heaven. But when He let Himself feel hunger and, because of His human nature, began to want food

---

[56] *untreuua* 'disloyalty'. The original sin in the book of Genesis is reinterpreted in the *Heliand* not so much as an act of disobedience to a command but as an act of disloyalty to one's sovereign lord.

[57] The author gives a new twist to the forty days of the fast. It is not that 'forty days' is a commonplace of the Old Testament, but rather that the power of Christ even at fasting is so great that the forces of evil did not recognize Him and were afraid to approach a person of such supernatural ability, for fear He must be the Almighty God.

[58] *nidhudig* 'hate-minded'. This adjective would seem innocent enough until one recalls that it is the name of the horrible Serpent, the snake of the dark underworld that in Germanic religion is eternally devouring the hidden roots of the cosmic tree of life, and is locked in an unending, verbal single combat of taunts with the eagle of heaven who nests in the crown of the tree. The Serpent's name is *Nidhogg*. Christ is thus contending in single combat in this retelling of the story of the temptations with a very powerful enemy, an ultimate enemy in the old as well as the new religion.

after forty days, then the enemy came closer, the murky[59] causer of harm, thinking now for sure that He was simply a man. Satan spoke to Him then in his words—the spear-enemy greeted Him.

"If You are God's Son," he said, "Why do You not command these stones to become bread?—if You have the power, Best of all those born, heal Your hunger!" Then the holy Christ responded, "People," He said, "the children of men, cannot live by simple bread, but they are to live on the teaching of God in this world and they should do the works proclaimed aloud by the holy tongue, by the voice of God. Human life for any people whatsoever is to want to do what is commanded by the Ruler's Word."

Then the horrible enemy came closer and began to try another way of tempting his Lord. The Peace-Child of God suffered the will of the evil one, and granted him power, so that Satan could test His mighty strength. He allowed the people-hurter to lead Him to Jerusalem, to the shrine of God, looking down on everything, and set Him down, up there on the highest of all houses. The evil one said to Him mockingly in a mighty voice, "If You are God's Son," he said, "glide down to earth! It was written long ago in books, that the all-mighty Father has commanded His angels that they are to be Your guards on any of Your ways, and to hold You in their hands. Well?—You are not allowed even to hit Your foot against a rock, or a hard stone!"

Then the holy Christ, the Best of all ever born, spoke back, "It is also written in books," He said, "that you should not maliciously tempt your Lord and Master. This is no accomplishment to your credit."

He let the people-injurer take Him on a third journey up onto a high mountain. There the perdition-leader let Him look and see over all the population of the world, enjoyable possessions, as well as the realm of the world with all the things for more beautiful tasks which this earth contains. The enemy then spoke to Him and said that he would grant Him all that magnificence, the high princely kingdoms, "if You will bow to me, fall at my feet and have me as lord, and pray

---

[59] *mirki* 'murky'. This attribute seems to carry overtones of the dark realm from which Grendel and his mother come in *Beowulf*.

at my lap. Then I will let You enjoy all these possessions which I have shown You."

Now the holy Christ did not want to listen any longer to this loathsome word, and so He drove him away from His favor, He brushed Satan away. Soon after, the Best of those ever born spoke. He said that one should pray to the all-mighty God up above, and that the many noble thanes seeking God's favor should very devoutly serve Him alone, "There is the help that reaches to every man." Then the malicious destroyer, in a very worried mood, went away from there; Satan, the enemy, returned to the valleys of Hel.

Afterward a great crowd came down from the All-Ruler above to Christ, God's angels, who were to render service to Him. They were to care for Him when it was over, serving Him with humility. This is the way one should serve the God of the Clan, the King of Heaven, in accord with His graciousness.

Song 14

Christ, the mighty Chieftain, chooses
His first warrior-companions.

The happy Child of God remained for a long time in the deep forest until the time came when He felt He would rather make known His great strength to people. He then left the protective cover of the woods, His desert dwelling,[60] and made His way back to the company of earls, to the great crowds of people, to the comings and goings of men.

He went to the shoreline of the Jordan. There John found Him, God's Peace-Child, his Lord, the holy King of Heaven. When John saw Him walking along there he said to his followers, the heroes, "That is the Lamb of God who will take away evil sin, the crimes of

---

[60] This is not a contradiction but rather another striking example of the author's poetic technique of placing the Semitic scriptural concept (alone, in the desert) in parallel to its equivalent Germanic meaning (alone, deep in the forest).

mankind, from this wide world—the great Chieftain, the Strongest of kings!"

Christ, God's own Child, then set off for Galileeland, journeying to His friends, to the place where He was born and beautifully raised. There He, the most powerful of kings, told His clan relatives in words how they should repent of their own sins. He told them that they should make themselves regret their many injurious deeds and chop down the evil they had done. "Now has come to pass what the ancients said long ago when they promised you Heaven's kingdom as your help. It has now come to you through the power of the Rescuer.[61] You can enjoy it from now on—anyone can who is willing to serve God and act according to His wishes!" Many of the people were delighted at this; the teachings of Christ were very sweet to the warrior-companions.

It was there He began to gather men to be His followers, good men to be His word-wise warriors. He walked along the shore of a body of water where the Jordan has created a sea on the border of Galileeland. There He found the brothers, Andrew and Peter, sitting by the stream at the place where they worked hard setting out[62] their nets on the wide waters as they fished in the current. It was there, on the seashore, that the Peace-Child of God Himself spoke to them and told them to follow Him.[63]

He told them that He would give them so much of God's kingdom. "Just as you catch fish here in the Jordan river, you will be

---

[61] *neriandan* 'savior, rescuer, someone who sustains life'.

[62] *thenidun* 'stretched out'. Apparently Saxon fishermen did not 'cast' their nets when fishing (as in the Sea of Galilee) but must either have staked the nets out in the current or used seining techniques. Peter and Andrew are described as sitting on the sand (a difficult position to cast nets from!); thus it seems they have staked their nets in the current. James and John are described as repairing nets cut open 'the night before'. The author seems to have been aware of night fishing with nets stretched between stakes (weirs) in the current.

[63] The constant emphasis on the water's edge as the place where Christ called His disciples leads the reader, or listener, to another level of meaning. By the seashore, or river, 'by the water's edge', is where many of the author's Saxons lived, and where he must have felt them to be called to be Christ's companions. Cf. *The Saxon Savior*, Ch. 4.

hauling in the sons of men hand over hand, so that many people can be led to the heaven-kingdom by your teaching." Both of the brothers became very happy over this—they recognized God's Son, the dear Lord. Andrew and Peter together left behind everything they had there by the water, all that they had come to own by the seashore. They wanted very much to go together with God's Son, to be His warrior-companions; they would receive a blessed reward. This is what all good people do who want to deserve the Lord's favor and carry out His will.

As they came farther along the seashore, they came across an old man and his two sons, James and John, young men, sitting by the sea. The father and his sons were sitting up on a sand dune. They were hard at work with both hands repairing and reweaving the nets that they had torn the night before on the water.

God's blissful Child told both of these young men to come with Him on the journey. James and John, very young men, both came along. Christ's word was so important to them in this world that there on the shore they left their elderly father alone by the flowing water—and all their possessions, nets, and nailed ships.[64] They chose the holy Christ, the Rescuer, to be their Lord, they felt a need to deserve His help. This is how all thanes feel, all warriors in this world.

Then the Ruler's Son decided to move on with the four. Christ chose the fifth at a market place—one of the king's followers, an intelligent man. His name was Matthew. He was in the service of the nobility, his duty was to accept in his hands taxes and tolls for his lord. He was a man of great loyalty and noble appearance. He abandoned gold and silver, many gifts and precious jewels, and became our Chieftain's man. A thane of the king chose Christ for his

---

[64] The nailed ships were a matter of professional pride in the North. The ships, as evidenced from Viking ship burials, were clinker-built (also called lapstrake), in which the planks overlapped each other. This made for a lighter, more easily rowed vessel, but one which required very extensive and very visible nailing along the edge of each strake or plank.

Lord![65]—a more generous jewel-giver[66] than his former chieftain in this world had ever been! Matthew chose the happier thing for himself, the more long-lasting support.

It became known to all the people, from hill-fort to hill-fort, that the Child of God was assembling companions,[67] and that He spoke many words of wisdom, demonstrated many brilliant truths, and worked many signs in this world. It was clear from His words as well as His deeds, that He was Chieftain, the heavenly Lord, who came to this middle world, to the light and the sons of men, to help people.

Song 15

The mighty Rescuer calls twelve to be His men.

He often made that very visible in that country, where He brilliantly performed so many signs, where He healed the crippled and the blind with His hands and cured many people of the worst diseases and sicknesses, long-term suffering, which the enemy inflicted upon the sons of men. The people came every day to the place where our Chieftain was with His retinue of warrior-companions, so that there was a great crowd of people there from many clans—though they did not all come with the same intent, nor did they all want the same thing.

Some were looking for the Ruler's Son—many of the poorer people needing food—so that they could get donations of meat and

---

[65] Presumably, the highest lord in whose service a warrior-nobleman could work would be the king. Matthew is depicted as seeing this particular Chieftain's service as of much greater import than royal service.

[66] *milderan meðomgebon* the translation is quite literal! Germanic lords and chieftains are often praised by the poets for generosity both with gold ('generous ring-givers'), and for unstinting liberality with alcohol to their guests in the mead-hall. (Mead is thought to have been a mixture of alcohol and honey.) Obviously, Christ has to equal the 'other' Germanic chieftains in virtue.

[67] *samnode gesiðos* 'was collecting warrior-companions'. The tone is almost as if He were gathering a picked group of His own for a special expedition or mission.

drink from the people in the crowd there, since there were many good thanes there who gladly gave their alms to poor people.

Some of them were of the Jewish clan, sneaky people.[68] They had come there to spy on our Chieftain's deeds and words, they had a sneaky attitude of mind and ill-will. They wanted to make Ruling Christ loathsome to the people so that they would not listen to His teaching nor act according to His will.

Some, however, were very wise men, men of intelligence and of worth before God, the elite among the people. They came to the teaching of Christ in order to hear His holy Word, to learn it and to do it. They had firmly grasped their faith in Him with devout minds. They became His thanes so that after their last days, He would lead them up to the greatest thing for a human being, God's kingdom.[69]

He gladly received so many of mankind, and promised them His protection for a very long time—as well He could do! There was a huge crowd of people assembled there around the famous Christ. He saw them coming together from every land and from all the wide roads, warriors from powerful peoples. The story of His fame had spread afar to many people!

Then He moved mightily up onto a high mountain—the most powerful Person ever born—and sat apart. He chose for Himself twelve good, loyal men to be the followers whom He, the Chieftain, wanted to have around Him every day from this day forward in His personal warrior-company. He then called them by name and told them to approach Him: Andrew and Peter, the two brothers, first, and with them both James and John—they were precious to God—He was generously disposed toward them. They were both by birth the sons of one man. God's Son chose them, good men to be His followers, many men, truly outstanding: Matthew and Thomas, the

---

[68] This is quite a change from 'those fighting men renowned for their toughness', the description of the sons of Israel given in the first song of the *Heliand*. This change reinforces the idea that there is a hidden polemic in the first song against imposed imperial government (Charlemagne's imposition of rule on the Saxons) which is left aside in this passage.

[69] The (not enormously subtle) implication occurs throughout the *Heliand* that the intelligent and wise, as well as the noble and those of no duplicity, come to Christ to be His thanes.

two Judases, and the other James who was His own cousin—they were born of two sisters and came from the same clan, Christ and James were good kinsmen.

Christ the Rescuer had brought the number up to nine loyal men, then He told the tenth to go join the warrior-companions—his name was Simon. He also told Bartholomew and Philip who was with him, loyal men, to leave the other people and to come up onto the mountain. Then the twelve walked together, fighting men headed for a secret council, to the place where the wise Ruler[70] sat, the Protector of many people, who wanted to help all of mankind against the oppressive force of Hel, the infernal power—to help anyone who wanted to follow the lovely teachings which He intended to explain to the people there with His great knowledge and understanding.

Song 16

The Chieftain's instructions on the mountain;
the eight Good Fortunes.

Then the warrior-companions whom He chose from among the people gathered closer around Christ, the Ruler and Rescuer. Wise men were very eager and willing to stand around God's Son, intent on His words. They thought and kept silent and wondered what the

---

[70] *radand* '[the] support-giving [One]' or '[the advice- (or counsel) giving [One]'. This is a participial construction parallel to the other three very common ones in the *Heliand*: *uualdand* '[the] ruling [One]', *neriend* '[the] rescuing [One]', and *heliand* '[the] healing [One]'. In the *Heliand* this construction clearly implies divinity and may therefore not have had parallels in Saxon secular language.

Does the structure come from Latin? Of the three equivalent Latin participles: *adjuvans, potens, salvans*, only the second, *[omni-]potens*, strikes one as being in such common usage in Jerome's New Testament and early ecclesiastical Latin as to have imposed itself upon the author. The nouns, on the other hand, *adjutor* 'helper' and especially *salvator* 'healer, savior' are of quite frequent occurrence. It seems therefore that these heroic-sounding and constantly repeated participial nouns in the *Heliand* are not Latinate, but may echo, instead, old forms used for the gods in Saxon and Germanic epics and prayers.

Chieftain of Peoples, the Ruler Himself, would want to say out of love for these people.

Then the Land's Herdsman, God's own Son, sat down in front of the men. He wanted with His talk to teach the people many wise sayings, how they could perform the praise of God in this world-kingdom. The holy Chieftain sat there in silence and looked at them for a long time with tender feelings for them in His mind and generosity toward them in His heart. Then He unlocked His mouth, and the Ruler's Son instructed them in words about many amazing things. Moreover, Christ spoke in wise words to the men whom He had picked to come to His talk, to those men who were of all the inhabitants of earth, of all mankind, the most precious to God—to them He spoke in soothsaying."[71]

He said[72] that those were fortunate here in this middle world who were poor in their hearts through humility,[73] "to them is granted the eternal kingdom in all holiness, eternal life on the meadows of heaven."

He said that those too were fortunate who were gentle people,[74] "they will be allowed to possess the great earth, the same kingdom."

---

[71] Soothsaying in the *Heliand,* or 'truth-telling' is fortune-telling. The twelve apostles hear their fortunes, those of mankind, in a private circle around Christ, just as Mary and Joseph did in the temple from Simeon and Anna in song 6. In the hands of the author fortune-telling becomes a very rich re-contextualization of the eight Beatitudes. They are made into an interesting revelation of mankind's (good) fortune, told by the Ruling God, the Fortune-teller.

[72] *quad* 'quoth He'. This verb solemnly introduces each one of the Beatitudes. It implies that these are the very words themselves spoken by the Soothsayer. *Quad* stands out by its exclusive use and repetition in this passage and in the absence of other common words for 'saying,' *seggian* and *sprecan*, to provide variety. This use of *quad* heightens the ritual and oracular feeling of the Beatitudes in the text, but frustrates any easy translation.

[73] 'Blessed are the poor in spirit, for theirs is the kingdom of heaven.' Mt. 5: 2-3.

[74] 'Blessed are the meek, for they shall inherit the earth.' Mt. 5: 4.

He said that those also were fortunate who cried here over their evil deeds,[75] "in return, they can expect the very consolation they desire in their Master's kingdom."

"Those too are fortunate who desired to do good things here, those fighting men who wanted to judge fairly.[76] With good things they themselves will be filled to satisfaction in the Chieftain's kingdom for their wise actions; they will attain good things, those fighting men who judged fairly here. Nor will any people want to deceive them with secrets when they are seated there at the banquet!"

"Fortunate as well are those who have kind and generous feelings within a hero's chest,[77] the powerful, holy Chieftain will Himself be kind and generous to them."

"Fortunate also are the many people who have cleaned their hearts,[78] they will see Heaven's Ruler in His kingdom."

He said that those too were fortunate "who live peacefully among the people and do not want to start any fights or court cases by their own actions,[79] they will be called the Chieftain's sons for He will be gracious to them, they will long enjoy His kingdom."

---

[75] 'Blessed are those who mourn, for they shall be comforted.' Mt. 5: 4-5. The Beatitude speaks of those who mourn in general, the author makes the object of mourning specific.

[76] 'Blessed are those who hunger and thirst for justice, for they will be satisfied.' Mt. 5: 6. This Beatitude is commonly understood as speaking of those who come seeking that justice be done. The author redirects it to his own audience, the warrior nobility in the hill-forts, whose task is to administer justice, and changes the beatitude into a blessing for those who hunger and thirst to judge justly. In so doing, he changes this and other Beatitudes from a blessing of a state of mind to a blessing calling for specific action.

[77] 'Blessed are the merciful, for they will have mercy shown them.' Mt.5: 7.

[78] 'Blessed are the clean of heart, for they will see God.' Mt. 5: 8. The subtle change from 'the clean of heart' to 'who have cleaned their hearts', encourages action.

[79] 'Blessed are the peacemakers, for they shall be called the children of God.' Mt. 5: 9. This must have been a sensitive one for the author, especially in view of his warrior audience. Still, he manages ingeniously to find common ground--there are some fights even warriors must not have enjoyed!

He said that fortunate too are the fighting men who wanted justice,[80] "and, because of that, suffer more powerful men's hatred and verbal abuse. To them is granted afterwards God's meadow and spiritual life for eternal days—thus the end will never come of their beatific happiness!"

So the ruling Christ had told the earls in front of Him the eight Good Fortunes. With them, anyone will always reach God's kingdom, if he wants to. If not, he will afterwards do without possessions and happiness for endless days, from the moment he gives up this world, the fate of life on earth, and goes to the other light—for better or for worse[81]—depending on how he treated people here in this world, just as Christ the All-Ruler said it there with His words, the most powerful of kings, God's own Son, to His followers.

"You too will also be fortunate," He said to them, "the people of this country will sue you in court cases and say repulsive things about you, they will make fun of you, and arrange to hurt you greatly in this world. They will punish you and cover you with verbal abuse and hostility, deny your teaching, and do great wickedness and harm to you because of your Lord. But let your minds always enjoy life, since in God's kingdom your reward is standing ready for you: every good thing, in full strength and diversity! That is given to you as payment, since beforehand you suffered hardship and punishment here in this world.

"Something worse will be given to those others, a more horrible thing, to those who had possessions here and were very well-to-do in the world. They used up their happiness here. They enjoyed it to the full here; in return those heroes will suffer with something more skimpy after their departure. They will weep over their misery, those who here before were joyful, who lived according to their every

---

[80] 'Blessed are those who are persecuted for justice's sake, for theirs is the kingdom of heaven.' Mt. 5: 10. Here the author reverses field and praises a passive state of endurance, and does not attempt to transform the Beatitude into a praise of action. The reason does not lie far from the surface. The author's reworking and elaboration of this Beatitude gives the reader (or hearers) a glimpse of his thinly disguised sympathy for the Saxons' situation vis-à-vis their Carolingian overlords.

[81] *so liof so led* 'whether dear or repulsive'.

desire, the ones who did not want to omit a single thing, no immoral idea or dirty deed, which their emotions spurred them on to. When their reward comes to them, evil hardship, they will look toward its end with grave concern. Those who so much followed the will of this world will become deeply worried in mind and in heart.

"Now, you are to reprove them for such evil deeds, and stop them with words, as I will now teach you, My companions, in true words, in soothsaying. From now on you are to become this world's salt, sinful men's salt, to heal[82] their deadly deeds, so that they, the people, can turn to better things, and cease from doing the enemy's work, the devil's deeds, and head toward the kingdom of their Chieftain.

"Thus you are to turn many of the people with your teaching toward following My will. If, however, any of you turns away from this and abandons the teaching which he is supposed to be doing, then he is like the salt which people scatter all over the beach, the sons of men kick it with their feet when they are on the sand. It is worthless. So it will also be with the man who is to tell God's word to human beings. If he lets his feelings doubt, so that he does not, with a clear mind, want to urge people toward the kingdom of heaven with his speech, nor to recite God's spell, but rather vacillates in his words, the Ruler will become extremely exasperated, enraged at him—and so also will the sons of men! He will be despised by all the peoples of the world, by everyone, if his teaching is worthless."

---

[82] *botian* 'make better'. The *Heliand* author transforms the salt analogy of the gospel from one of discipleship as having a 'taste-improvement' role for the world, to a medical one of 'with salt' seen in its other role as a (painful) antiseptic for improving the condition of wounds. The disciples are thus given a much more active (if more abrasive) role in the *Heliand*.

Song 17

The instructions on the mountain.

Thus He spoke wisely and told God's spell. The Guardian of the land taught His people with a clear mind. Heroes were very eager and willing to stand around God's Son, intent on His words. They thought and kept silent. They listened to the Chieftain of the People giving law to the nobly-born. He promised them the heaven-kingdom and said to the heroes, "I can also tell you, My companions, in truthful words, that from now on you will be, for the human race, this world's light, shining peacefully among men, over many peoples, bright and beautiful. Your great works cannot be hidden, nor the intent with which you proclaim them, any more than a hill-fort on a mountain, a high steep-sided hill, can be hidden with its gigantic works. So also your words and deeds cannot be concealed from human beings in this middle world. Do as I teach you: let your powerful light shine for people, for the sons of men, so that they understand your feelings, your works, and your will, and therefore they will praise the ruling God, the heavenly Father, with a clear mind in this light,[83] because He gave you such teaching.

"Nor should anyone who has light hide it from people, keeping it well concealed, but rather he should set it up high in the house so that all who are inside, the heroes in the hall, can see it together.

"So you should not hide your holy word from the people of this country, concealing it from mankind's heroes, but instead you should spread God's command high and wide throughout all this countryside, so that every one born will understand it and carry it out. Just as in the olden days when earls held the old law, very wise men spoke in words, so now I tell you all the more: just as it was commanded in the old law—each and every man is to serve God.

"Do not think for a moment that I have come to this world to destroy the old law, to chop it down among the people and to throw

---

[83] *an thesemu liohte*. This seems to be a deliberate pun by the author, since the phrase means 'in this light' both in the sense of 'in this world' and in the sense of the 'light' to be emitted by the disciples.

down the word of the prophets—they were truthful men, clear in their commands. Heaven and earth standing now united will both fall apart before even a minute bit of their words, in which they gave true commands to the people here, goes unaccomplished in this world. I did not come to this world to fell the word of the prophets, but to fulfill them; to increase them and to make them new again for the children of men, for the good of this people.

"It was written before in the old law—you have often heard word-wise men say it—whosoever in this world so acts that he steals another's old age[84] from him, robs him of his life, the sons of men shall put such a person to death. I now want to add more depth to this concept, to push it further: whosoever is hostile to another in his feelings, angry in his heart—they are all brothers after all, the blessed people of God, they belong to the clan, they are family relatives!—if someone, however, becomes so hostile to another in his feelings that he would rob the man of his life if he could do so, then he is already guilty, condemned to lose his life-spirit, receiving the very same sentence as the other man who by the strength of his hand robbed another earl of his head.

"It is also written in the law in true words, as you all know, that one should love his neighbor zealously in his heart, be kind to his relatives, be good to his fellow clansmen, be generous in his giving, be loving to each of his friends, and shall hate his enemies, resisting them in battle, and with a strong mind shall defend himself against their wrath.

"Now I say to you truthfully, with greater fullness for the people, that you are to love your enemies in your feelings, just as you love your family relatives, in God's name. Do a great deal of good for them, extend friendly loyalty to them with a clear mind—love versus their hatred. This is long-lasting advice for every man, this is how a person's feelings against his enemy should be directed. Then, you will have as your own, the gift that you can be called the Heaven-

---

[84] *aldru* lit. 'age, getting older'. The idea is that a murderer steals one's future time, the days of the future which would otherwise still have been allotted to one by time and fate.

King's sons, His happy children—and you cannot obtain anything better than that in this world.

"I would also like to say to you in all truth, to everyone born, that you cannot donate anything of your goods to God's house that would be worthy of His acceptance with an angry mind—or for as long as you are thinking anything hostile or vicious against another human being. You are to reconcile yourself with your opponent beforehand, talk out an agreement, then afterwards you may donate your treasures at God's altar; then they are worthy of the King of Heaven. You should serve God more according to His graciousness, following His will, more than other Jews do, if you want to own the eternal kingdom and see everlasting life.

"I shall also tell you that it is commanded in the old law that one earl must not seduce another man's woman, the other's wife, into immorality. But then I say to you in all truth that a man's eyes can quickly lead him off into murky evil behavior, if he lets his emotions goad him on so that he begins to yearn for someone who can never go with him. At that point he has already committed a sin himself, on his own, and chained the penalty of Hel to his heart. If, then, a man's eye or his right hand, or any other member of his body, wants to lead him off onto the path of evil, then it is better for any earl, any of the sons of men, that he remove it from his body and throw it away. It is better to come up to heaven without it than, with all his members intact, a man wend his way hale and hearty to the inferno, to the bottom of Hel.

"Human weakness dictates that no one should follow a close friend if the friend is going to urge him on to crimes, to court trials; it does not matter how closely he is related to him by clan, nor how powerful their family relationship is—if the friend is urging him to murder, pushing him to commit crime. It is better for him that he cast the friend far away from himself, avoid this relative, and not have any love for him, so that he will be able to go up to the high kingdom of heaven by himself, rather than that they both go together to the extensive tortures and hideous hardship of Hel's confinement."

Song 18

The instructions on the mountain.

"It is also written in the law in true words, as you all know, that all of mankind should avoid false oaths, that no one should perjure himself, since that is a great sin and leads people off onto the loathsome path. But I want to tell you that no one should swear any oaths at all, neither by high heaven—since that is the Lord's throne, nor by earth beneath it—since that is the Lord's bright footstool. Nor should any human being swear any oath by his own head—since he cannot turn a hair of it black or white unless God in His power decided to make it so. Earls should very much avoid taking oaths. Anyone who swears often, always gets worse, since he cannot control himself.

"I will now tell you in true words, that you are never to swear any oaths more serious and heavy to human beings than the ones that I most truly command you here with My words. If a man is on trial, let him tell the truth; say 'yes', if it is so, admit what is true; say 'no', if it is not so. Let that be enough for him. Whatever a man does beyond that, all comes to no good for the human race, since one earl will not believe the word of another because of [earls'] unfaithfulness[85] [to their word].

"Then I say to you also in truth, that it was commanded in the old law: whoever takes the eye of another man, separating it, or any other limb, from his body, he shall immediately pay for it with the same limb of his own. But now what I teach you is that you should not avenge wrongful deeds in that way, but that you humbly tolerate

---

[85] *untreuua* 'disloyalty, unfaithfulness'. This must not have been an easy teaching for the author to justify to the Saxons. The nobles of the warrior class among Franks and Saxons often legally 'proved' their innocence in court simply by swearing an oath that they were not guilty of the charge. The author makes the gospel passage intelligible by pointing out what must have been a fact under the system of Germanic law: if too many guilty earls establish their innocence through frequent false oaths, then the system will lose its credibility. An earl will not believe another's word of honor because of the frequency of incidents of *untreuua*. Thus the gospel system is presented as not only simpler, but as restoring faith in Germanic *treuua*.

all the evil and wrongs whatsoever that people do to you in this world. Let every earl do good and profitable things for the other man, just as he wishes that the sons of man do good for him in return. God will then be generous with him and with every person who desires to behave in this way.

"Honor poor people! Share your possessions with needy folk! Do not be concerned whether you will receive any thanks or repayment in this passing world; instead, think of your beloved Lord for compensation for your gifts; be aware that God, the powerful Protector, pays you for them, for whatever you do out of His love. If, despite that, you want to give your gleaming coins to good men through such people,[86] because you think to make more profit in return, then why would you expect any reward from God as repayment in this world for what is only transitory wealth?

"So it is with everything which you do out of love of other people. If you intend to get similar things back in return in both word and action, then why would our Ruler owe you anything for giving in such a way as to get back what you want in return? Give your possessions to the poor people who never pay you back in this world, and strive toward your Ruler's kingdom. When you are giving your alms to the poor man with your own hands, do not do it loudly! Do it for the man gladly and humbly and for God's appreciation. Then you will be able to receive wealth in return, the very lovely payment in the place where you will long enjoy its more beautiful profits!

"Whatever you give away in secret and with good intentions is valued by Our Chieftain. Do not brag too much about your giving, no one should do that, for then it will not be worth any return—miserably lost for the sake of the vanity of fame. It is before the eyes of God that you should receive the reward for good works.

---

[86] Though the *Heliand* advocates helping the needy, there is a distinct ambiguity in the work with regard to the virtue of the poor. See for example song 15, where the poor are portrayed as coming to the place where Jesus is teaching not so much in order to hear Him, but to take advantage of the generous crowd for donations. In this passage, people of means are simply described as 'good men'. This pattern may tell us something of the author's social background as well as that of his audience.

"I shall also command you that when you want to bow in prayer, and you want to ask the Lord for help, to free you from loathsomeness—from the crimes and sins that you yourselves have wrongfully done here—do not do it in front of other people! Do not tell it to everybody so that people will praise you for it and hold your action in high esteem, because then your prayer to your Chieftain goes lost for the sake of the vanity of fame. If you want to pray to the Lord and modestly ask His help—something you really need—so that your Victory-Chieftain will take away your sins, then do it very secretly. Your holy Chieftain in heaven already knows it Himself, since there is nothing in words or deeds that is hidden from Him. He then lets it all happen just the way you ask Him when you bow down to pray with a clear mind."

Heroes were very eager and willing to stand around God's Son,[87] intent on His words. They thought and kept silent. They needed very much to think about the many brilliant things that the holy Child had told them this first time in words. Then one of the twelve, one of the more intelligent men, spoke in reply to God's Son.

Song 19

The instructions on the mountain;
the secret runes of the Lord's Prayer.

"Our good Lord," he said, "we need Your gracious help in order to carry out Your will and we also need Your own words, Best of all born, to teach us, Your followers, how to pray—just as John, the good baptist, teaches his people with words every day how they are to speak to the ruling God. Do this for Your own followers—teach us the secret runes."[88] The powerful One, the Son of the Chieftain,

---

[87] This section repeats the beginning of the Sermon on the Mount and thus forms a frame closing off the first part of it.

[88] *gerihti us that geruni* 'teach us the secret runes'. The Beatitudes were God's *spel*, His soothsaying on mankind's future and present happiness; the Lord's Prayer is seen as magic runes which, when spoken with bowed head, are as powerful as any

had a good word ready right after that in reply. "When you men want to speak to the ruling God," He said, "to address the most powerful of all kings, then say what I now teach you:

Father of us, the sons of men,
You are in the high heavenly kingdom,
Blessed be Your name in every word.[89]
May Your mighty kingdom come.
May Your will be done over all this world—
just the same on earth as it is up there
in the high heavenly kingdom.
Give us support[90] each day, good Chieftain,
Your holy help, and pardon us, Protector of Heaven,
our many crimes, just as we do to other human beings.
Do not let evil little creatures[91] lead us off
to do their will, as we deserve,

Germanic charm or spell. They give immediate results, direct access through [the secret] words to the Power[s] of the other world--in this case, to the ruling God.

The *Heliand*, in song 1, treats the entire gospel as being special secret words of this same powerful magic, taught by the Creator Himself to the four evangelists. The Lord's Prayer, however, is the instance par excellence of magic words for the author, since the Instructor, the mighty Chieftain Himself, also made its length quite similar to that of parallel Germanic spells and prayers.

[89] *uuordo gehuuilico* 'in each word'. By adding this phrase to 'hallowed be Thy name', the author subtly makes this petition more active and more concrete, more demanding on the person praying. The phrase in the original is more of an abstract form of wish.

[90] *rad* 'support, advice, help'. The original 'give us this day our daily bread' may have been unacceptable to the warrior nobility. Thanes, however, did honorably rely on their overlord, their chieftain, for his support in time of war and danger. It appears to have been his main reciprocal responsibility to them in return for their pledge of loyal military service to him. God as 'Chieftain of the Human Race' is conceived of in the *Heliand* in this early feudal relationship. We render Him service, He in turn protects us from the hostilities of the enemy.

[91] *leda uuihti* lit. 'loathsome wights'. Little evil beings were held responsible for many of the bad things that happened to the human race. They can be seen attacking humans with sickness and suffering in the *Utrecht Psalter*'s illustrations. (Their descendants today, the medical profession might say, are less anthropomorphic but still repulsive and aggressive—if somewhat smaller—little creatures.)

but help us against all evil deeds.[92]

That is how you men should pray in your words when you bow in prayer to ask the ruling God to pardon the evil of mankind. If you are willing to pardon the violent crimes and sins that they do against you yourselves here, then the ruling God, the all-mighty Father, will forgive your enormous deeds of evil and many culpable acts. But if your emotions get too strong for you so that you are not willing to forgive other earls, other men, their wrongdoing, then God the Ruler will also not forgive you your grim actions—and you will receive His payment, the extremely loathsome reward that lasts a long, long time, for all the injustice that you did to others here in this light, since you did not reconcile yourselves with your fellow human beings over a problem before you departed on the journey from this world.

"I will also tell you in truth how you are to carry out my teaching. When you wish to do your fasting to diminish your bad behavior, do not let the multitude know you are doing it, avoid doing it in front of other men. God, the mighty Ruler, knows your intention, even if other people, the children of men, do not praise you. Your holy Father in the heaven-kingdom grants your reward on the basis of the humility with which you earls serve Him so devotedly among the people. You noble warriors, do not desire to acquire wealth unjustly; instead, work for God above for your pay—that is a greater thing than living in riches and worldly possessions here on earth.

"If you want to follow My words, then do not collect a great treasure of silver and gold here in this middle world, a treasure-hoard, because it turns to rust, thieves steal it, worms ruin it, the clothes get torn, golden wealth disintegrates. Do your good works,

---

[92] *ubilon dadiun* 'evil deeds'. Once again the author changes an abstract request, 'deliver us from evil', into one that is concrete, and one that demands action from the prayer. In addition, "Help us against all evil deeds" contains the rich ambiguity that it can be understood both as a request to the Chieftain for help against the evil deeds done against us by others, or it can equally mean a request for help against our own evil deeds.

collect a greater hoard for yourselves in heaven[93]—one made of much brighter coins—one of which not a single enemy can take even the smallest bit away from you! Your wealth stands ready for you in heaven: whatever good you heroes heap up by the contributions of your hands—your hoard! Keep your minds firmly set on this, because the emotions and thoughts of each and every human being, heart and mind, are where his hoard, his treasure, lies collected.

"Nor is anyone ever so fortunate that he is able to do both of these things in this wide world: both live richly on this earth, enjoying every worldly delight, and at the same time serve God with gratitude; rather he will always abandon one or the other of these two things: either the delights of the body or eternal life.

"Do not worry about your clothing, instead keep your thoughts firmly on God. Do not be emotionally concerned about what you are to eat and drink tomorrow, or what clothes you warriors are going to wear—the ruling God knows what those who serve Him well here need, those who follow their Lord's wishes. Look, you can truly understand that from these birds here in this world. They travel about in feather shirts, they cannot earn a single coin, yet God the Chieftain gives them help every day against hunger.[94] You men can also determine this in the case of your clothes by thinking about how the plants that are here out in the field are beautifully adorned, blooming brightly. Even Solomon the king, guardian of hill-forts, who had attained an enormous treasure, the largest jewel-hoard in one man's possession, with the choicest of goods and all clothing—even though he held power over all this country—he was

---

[93] The romantic notion of hidden treasure hoards, full of gold coins and jewels, robes of cloth-of-gold, must have been very popular in Germanic oral epic poetry. We know of it from the examples that were retained in written literature, for example, the treasure of the Nibelungs lost in the Rhine, and the hoard won by Beowulf at the end of his saga. In addition, recent burial-mound archaeology, for example at Sutton Hoo in East Anglia, has tended to confirm that there was a real basis for belief in hidden treasure hoards.

The author has transformed the hidden hoard, guarded usually by a dragon-serpent, into the heavenly 'treasure' of one's good deeds, guarded by God.

[94] God is depicted as having a Chieftain's relationship to the birds, supplying them with His help against any threat.

never able to get clothing for his body equal to what the plants standing here in the field are wearing so beautifully: the lilies with their lovely flower. They were clothed by the Ruler of the land from the meadows of heaven.

"He cares more, though, for this clan of heroes, He loves people much more, the human beings whom the Ruler created on this land in accordance with His desires. Therefore there is no need for you to be worried about your clothes. Do not be overly worried about your wardrobe, God will supply everything, help from the meadows of heaven, if you are willing to gain His favor through service. Always be concerned first about God's kingdom, and then act in accord with His good works, strive for more important things. The rich and powerful Chieftain will give you every good thing whatsoever, if you will follow Him in the way which I am saying to you here in true words."

Song 20

The instructions on the mountain.

"You should never pronounce even the slightest detrimental, unjust judgment on any man, since the judgment comes back on the same man who spoke unjustly of another. Then it is he who begins to worry about the penalty. Never let any of you men, when you are buying or selling here in the middle world, behave in such a way that you deceitfully give another man unjust measure. No matter which earl it is: what he did to others is what will come back to him—even if he prefers not to see his sins.

"I will also say to you where it is that you should guard yourselves against the greatest of evils, the greatest quantity of acts of wickedness: why should you have a talk with a man, your brother, to tell him that under his eyelash you have seen a tiny fleck of straw in his eye, when you are not willing to be aware of the huge beam, the hard and heavy tree, that you have in your eyes. Fell that tree in your own consciousness, think how you will get rid of it first, then the light will come shining through to you, your eyes will be opened.

After that, you will then be able to improve and heal the sight of your friend's eyes.

"Let each one here in this world be more conscious of the wrong things that he does than of keeping an eye on other peoples' crimes and sins—he has done more awful things himself. If he wants to do a good deed, he should first free himself from sins, separate himself from loathsome deeds. After that, he can be a help to heroes with his teaching, once he knows himself to be clean, safe, and secure from sins.

"Nor should you put your pearls before pigs, or strew your jewels, the holy medal around your neck,[95] before them. They will trample it into the muck and make it filthy in the dirt—they know nothing about cleanliness nor about beautiful jewels. There are many people like that here. They do not want to hear your holy word nor follow God's teaching—they know nothing about goodness, and have a powerful preference for empty words, useless things, over the God of Mankind's works and will. They are not worthy, then, to hear your holy word, if they are not willing to think about it in their minds, to learn it and carry it out. Do not tell them a thing about your teaching, so that you do not waste God's speech and many spells on people who are not willing to believe the words of truth.

"As you travel through this country you should also guard against the trickery of these people, so that the teachers of lies do not seduce you with words or actions. They come to you in such robes with the

---

[95] *helag halsmeni* lit. 'holy necklace, holy neckband'. I am not certain how to understand this. The author has added it to the gospel account, which mentions only the pearls. In ancient times Celtic and Germanic peoples had worn the torc around the neck. Small Thor hammers have been found which were worn around the neck into the time of the *Heliand* and beyond, presumably to ask for the god's help and protection. (Some of these hammer-amulets also had been manufactured with Christian crosses on the back, presumably 'just in case.') Was there some sort of cross medallion of similar size, similar to a bishop's pectoral cross, that had been given to Saxon converts, perhaps as a sort of good-conduct pass, during the times of the Frankish-Saxon war? If so, the author has inserted into the Sermon on the Mount an appeal from Christ to the Saxons not to throw away the holy symbol of their religion.

finest of jewels,[96] but they have deception in mind. You will recognize them immediately as soon as you see them coming. They speak wise words, but their actions are worth nothing, worthless are the thoughts of those thanes. For you know that wine-grapes do not grow on a stickerbush—nor do any of the finest fruits—and heroes cannot pick figs from a thorntree. You can certainly understand that a bad tree standing on the earth never gives good fruit, nor did God ever ordain that the good tree of the sons of men should bear bitter fruit. Each and every tree brings to this world the kind of fruit that comes from its roots, either sweet or sour.

"In their deepest thoughts and inmost feelings most of mankind believes that every earl reveals himself, telling you with his mouth what kind of feelings and thoughts are in his heart. He cannot disguise it. From an evil man will come malicious advice, bitterly negative speech, just what he keeps within his chest chained around his heart. His thoughts and his will always make themselves known in his words, and then his actions come traveling along behind.

"From the good man comes an intelligent and wisely thought-out answer, just as he always speaks in his words. Out of this man's mouth comes the treasure-hoard of feelings that he has around his heart (that is where the holy teaching comes from,[97] the very appealing word!) and his works following thereafter will thrive for the good of the people, and will be appreciated by many thanes. This is just what the Ruler Himself, God all-mighty, the Lord of Heaven, gives to good human beings, since without His help they would not be capable of accomplishing any good at all in words or in deeds in

---

[96] The familiar phrase, 'like wolves in sheep's clothing', is not used, even though it is one whose animal imagery must have been intelligible in the North. The substitution of impressive robes and jewels and the avoidance of sheep (as in the Christmas story), must have its reason in the class-consciousness of the thanes who must have been the intended audience of the *Heliand*.

[97] *thanan cumad thea helagan lera* 'from there comes the holy teaching'. A truly remarkable and gracious statement. The author locates the source of the gospel's teachings as having its roots in the goodness of the human heart.

this middle world. It is for this reason that all[98] of the children of men should believe in His power alone."

Song 21

The instructions on the mountain.

"I will also show you how there are two roads here in this light on which all the peoples of earth, the children of men, travel. One of them is a broad and wide highway. Many people take it, much of mankind, world-lusting warriors, because their feelings urge them into it. What is worse, this road leads people to where the heroes become lost—to Hel-land, where it is hot and black, terrifying inside. This road is easy for the sons of men to travel on, though it ends up as useless. Then there is the other road in this world, much narrower, not much traveled, few people take it. The sons of men do not like to walk it, even though it takes earls to God's kingdom, to eternal life.

"You take the narrow one, even if it is not so easy for human beings to travel on, yet it will be to the advantage of whoever goes on it to the end. That person will get his prize, the very long-lasting reward, and life everlasting—the wonderful comings and goings of living—forever. You should always ask the Chieftain, the Ruler, for you to take that road from the start, and for you to keep going on it all the way to God's kingdom. He is always ready to respond by giving to those who really ask Him, to the sons of men whenever they ask. Go look for your Father up in the eternal kingdom, you can find Him there, to your advantage thereafter.

"Announce your arrival there at your Chieftain's doors! They will open for you immediately, the gates of heaven will swing open, so

---

[98] By rooting the gospel in the hearts of good men, as a direct gift of God, rather than in any other more ecclesiastical structure, the author has created a very broad pastoral basis for appealing to the Saxons and, as he says, to all, to find the gospel acceptable and familiar to persons of goodness.

that you can walk into the holy light, into God's kingdom, and see eternal life!

"I will also tell you a true picture to give to all these people. Whoever wants to keep My teachings in his heart, and wants to think about them in his mind, and carry them out in this land, is doing the same thing as a wise man of knowledge and clear intelligence who chooses very solid earth as the site for his home, and constructs his walls upon rock where neither wind nor wave nor the water current can do any harm to it. There it will stand for him up on a rock, resisting all storms, because it was placed so solidly on rock. The site supports the house from below, defies the winds, so that the house does not have to yield.

"Every person, however, who does not want to hear My teaching, nor do any of it, is behaving like the unwise earl, the person of poor intelligence, who wants to set up his house on sand, by the water's edge, where the west wind, the waves in the current, and the ocean breakers beat it to pieces. Sand and pebbles are not able to help the house resist the wind, and so it will be thrown down there; it will fall apart in the water, since its timbers were not placed in more solid earth. On the other hand, the works of every earl who does what I say and keeps My commands holy, will prosper."

Then many of the huge crowd began to sense wonder in their minds. They heard the loveable teachings of mighty God. They were not used to hearing such things said in the past in their land, neither in words nor in deeds. Wise men, though, understood that He taught in this way, the people's Chieftain, in truthful words, because He had power—unlike all those who in former times had been chosen from among the people and clans to be teachers. There was no match for the words of Christ among men as He spoke in front of the crowd, up on the mountain, commanding.

Song 22

The instructions on the mountain.

He gave them two orders there. They were always to say His words on how one should get to the kingdom of heaven, the most extensive good, and also He gave them power so that they could heal the crippled and the blind—human weaknesses—many of the bed-ridden and those with severe sickness.

He also commanded them Himself, that they were not to accept payment from any person for this, no precious jewels. "Remember," He said, "where your craft, your knowledge and wisdom came from—and the power was given to you by the Father of all men—therefore, you have no need to buy it with any money, nor to pay for it with any jewels. So, have an attitude of generosity when you help human beings—teach the sons of men the long-lasting advice, something good that lasts. Criticize acts of wickedness, severe sinfulness. Do not let silver or gold—the beautiful coins—become of such worth to you that it comes under your control. It is not able to do you any good at all, nor bring you any happiness.[99]

"You earls, men, should not own more clothes than what you wear at the times when you have to go out in public. You should never spend a long time worrying about your meat, or about your food, since the people should feed their teachers. Indeed, what you say[100] to the people is worth support, worth a loving repayment. The worker is worth being well fed. The man who is going to care for so many souls and get so many spirits on the road to God's meadow is worth his porridge. It is a greater thing to care for many souls and to care about how to bring them to the heavenly kingdom

---

[99] The author is here perhaps casting a sideways glance at his fellow monks and their vows of poverty, rather than the Saxon thanes.

[100] An addition made by the author to stress the power and worth of the words of the teaching themselves. In Scripture (Mt. 10:10) the idea seems simply to be an appeal to a common proverb emphasizing ordinary fairness, 'the worker is worthy of his pay', or 'the laborer is worthy of his keep'. In the *Heliand*, it is not only the worker who is worthy—as in the following sentence in the song—but the divine Message, the secret runes that he reveals, that are worthy of support.

than to provide the bodies of the sons of men with porridge. For this reason people should dearly hold those in honor who show them the road to heaven's kingdom, who hold off the evil, harm-inflicting enemy, and who reprove acts of wickedness, severe sins.

"I will now send you off into this country like a lamb among wolves— that is how you will travel in the midst of your enemy, among many peoples, among unlike human beings. Keep your feelings opposed to them, stay intelligently face-to-face with them, just like the yellow snake, the colored serpent, when it becomes aware of its hated enemy, so that no one of the world-people can sneak up on you during the journey. You should take care that human beings are not able to twist the thoughts of your heart or your will. Be as truly against this, against their deceptive deeds, as one would be against enemies.

"Then you should also be like a dove in your actions. Have a simple, straightforward mind toward every earl, be generous spirited, so that no one comes to be deceived because of your behavior, tricked because of your sins.[101]

"Now you are to go on the journey, on a mission. There you will suffer many hardships among the people and pressures both many and diverse when you teach the people in My name. For that you will receive bad treatment and punishment before the kings of the world. Often you will stand in shackles in front of rulers because of My true Word, and you will endure both ridicule and insulting language—but do not let your minds doubt because of that, nor let your spirit give ground.

"There is no need for you to have any worry at all in your mind—when they order you out to come before the noble lords in the guest hall—about what you should then say to them face-to-face in good words spoken wisely. Success will come to you, help from

---

[101] This is a much more pointed treatment than in Matthew's gospel (10:16) where the serpent-and-dove analogy is given as a single line with no elaboration, 'Be as wise as serpents and as simple as doves.' It is tempting to think that the author may here be thinking of the precarious situation of the missionaries among the Saxons (and Frisians), which as even St. Boniface could have testified, did invite more than a little caution.

heaven, and the Holy Spirit will speak mightily from your mouth. Therefore do not be afraid of human beings' hatred, do not fear their hostility. Even though they have power over your life-spirit, in that they could take away the body's life by striking with the sword, they cannot do anything at all to the soul. Fear the ruling God, revere your Father, enjoy doing His bidding, for He has power both over people's life and over their body, as well as over the living soul itself. If you should lose your life-spirit on this journey because of the teachings, you will be able to find it again before the light of God, because your Father, holy God, will hold it for you in the kingdom of heaven."

Song 23

The end of the instructions on the mountain.

"Not everyone who here calls me Protector will come to heaven. There are many who want every single day to bow to the Chieftain and ask Him for help, but who are thinking of other things, of doing deeds of wickedness. Their words do them no good. The people who will come to the light of heaven and arrive at God's kingdom, are the ones who are glad to carry out here the works and will of the all-ruling Father. There is no need for them to call on God for help in many words, since God knows the feelings and thoughts, the words and the will, of every man, and He tallies everyone's reward on the basis of his works.

"When you are on the journey, you should be concerned about how you are going to complete your mission. When you are going through the countryside, all across the world, wherever the roads take you, the broad road to the hill-fort, always look right away for the best men in the population, and let them know what is on your mind in true words. If they are worthy, if they are happy to perform your good works with a clear mind, then be willing to live at the house with them and reward them well, pay them back with goodness, consecrate them in words to God Himself, and promise them sure peace, the holy help of Heaven's King.

"If, because of their own deeds, they are incapable of becoming so fortunate as to do your deeds and carry out your teaching, then leave those people quickly, travel on, away from that group. Your peace, returning, will go with you on your journey. Let them continue on in their sins and wickedness. You look for another hill-fort, another large population, and do not let a bit of the dust from a place where they do not want to receive you follow you on your feet. Shake it off your shoes, so that those people will be shamed, and it will become public knowledge how worthless their good will is.

"I will tell you in all truth: when this world comes to an end, and the Great Day comes upon mankind, on that day Fort Sodom, which because of its sins was burned to its foundations by the force of the flame, will have more peace and a more generous Protector than those men will have who are unwilling to do your word and throw you out.

"Whoever does receive you with a devout mind because of their spirit of generosity, such a person has carried out My will, and has received ruling God, your Father, the Chieftain of Mankind, the powerful Counselor, who is aware of every act of goodness. The Ruler Himself knows and rewards the good will of every man, whatever good a man does here—even if someone for the love of God willingly just gives a drink of water from a cold spring to heal the thirst of a needy man.

"These words will come true: it will not be a long time before a man shall receive his reward, the manifold payment, before the eyes of God, for whatever he has done because of love of me. Whoever denies Me to the sons of men, whatever hero denies Me in front of the warriors, I will do the same Myself to him in heaven, up there in front of the all-ruling Father and in front of all His angel forces, in front of that great multitude! Whoever of the sons of men in this world does not want to avoid the words, but instead says 'yes' in front of the human family, that he is My follower, I will recognize him in return before the eyes of God, in front of the Father of all mankind, when the great throng of mankind all walk to judgment before the powerful One, the All-Ruler. Then I will rightly be the gracious Protector of whoever hears My words and does the things that I have commanded up here on this mountain."

The Ruler's Son had truly taught the people how to praise God. He then let the people depart from that place. They went in every direction, crowds of humanity, journeying homeward. They had heard holy teaching, the word of the Heaven-King Himself. Whoever of the many members of the human race throughout this middle world is wiser in word and deed when he speaks, is one who heard the spell spoken on the mountain by the most Powerful of those born.

Song 24

The marriage feast in the guest-hall at Fort Cana.

Three nights afterwards the Chieftain of these people decided to go to Galileeland. He, God's Son, had been invited to a wedding. There a bride was to be given away, a beautiful maiden. Mary, the happy virgin, the mighty One's mother, was there with her Son. The Protector of People, God's own Child, went with His followers to the high house where the crowd of Jewish people were drinking in the guest-hall. He was there at the wedding too, and it was there that He made known that He had God's strength, Holy Spirit, help from the Father in heaven, the wisdom of the Ruler.

The warriors were merry, the people were enjoying themselves together, the men were feeling good. The servants went around pouring from pitchers, they had clear wine in steins and barrels. The conviviality of the earls in the drinking hall was a beautiful sight, and the men on the benches had reached a very high level of bliss, they were really happy! Then the wine ran out on them; the people had no more apple wine. There was not the smallest drop left in the house that the servants could still bring to the crowd. The vats were empty; the liquor was gone.

Now it was not very long before the loveliest lady, Christ's mother, found out about it. She went and spoke with her Child, with her Son Himself, and told Him in words that the hosts did not have any more wine for the guests at the wedding. Then she asked the holy Christ earnestly to arrange some help for the people, for the sake of their happiness. The mighty Son of God had His answer ready and said to His mother, "What is it to Me and you," He said, "what happens to these people's liquor, to these warriors' wine? Why are you talking so much like this, woman, admonishing me in front of all these people? My times have not yet come."

The holy virgin, however, trusted well in her mind that, even after these words, the Ruler's Son, the Best of healers, would help. Then the most beautiful of women told the servants, those pouring and those in charge of the wine barrels, all the ones who were serving the crowd, that they were not to let out a whit of the words or actions that the holy Christ would tell them to do for the people.

Six stone vats were standing there empty. God's mighty Child gave His orders very quietly so that a lot of people would not know for sure how He said it with His words.[102] He told those who were pouring to fill the vats there with clear water, and then He made the sign of the cross over it with His fingers, with His own hands—He worked it into wine! Then He ordered it poured into a drinking vessel, drawn off with a pitcher, and then speaking to a servant, He

---

[102] The author gives great weight to the words and actions of Christ by making it important in the text that no one learn these secret magic words! Since God's words create, as the author emphasized in song 1, they are performative words, and can act of themselves. It seems clear that the Saxon audience would love to learn (and use!) the formula for changing clear water into apple wine, and the author has to go to great lengths to explain how the followers of Christ do not know these powerful runes--both Mary and Jesus are made to take explicit means to see that the words and actions are kept quiet!

In making the transfer from Hebrew to Germanic, the author has had to understand Hebrew miracle (dependent on some divine intervention each time) as Germanic magic (dependent on powerful divine words and formulae). In medieval sacramental theology, transfer may have gone in the other direction as the sacraments, baptism, penance, the eucharist, in particular, may have been seen in this more northern light.

There is a prayer still said in the Roman Catholic Mass after the gospel has been proclaimed which reflects this Germanic attitude toward the miraculous/magical. *Per haec evangelia dicta, deleantur nostra delicta.* 'By the gospel having been said, may our sins be destroyed.' The prayer is in a rhyme form, and, like a spell, expects an action because of words said and, perhaps significantly, like the words of Christ at Cana, it is to be said quietly! Could this prayer-spell be a charming survivor from the *Heliand's* time of inter-cultural communication?

told him to give it to the most important person at the wedding, to put it right into the hands of the one who had the most authority over these people after the host.

As soon as he drank the wine the man could not contain himself from speaking, in front of the crowd, to the bridegroom. He said that it was always the best apple wine that every earl serves first at his wedding, "men's minds wake up with the wine, so that they start feeling ever more merry—drunk, they rejoice! Then, after that happens, one can serve the cheaper apple wine: that is the custom of these people.

"Now you, as host, have made your arrangements for the crowd in a most amazing way! You ordered your servants to bring the worst of all your wine to these folks and to serve it first at your wedding. Now your guests are full, the whole wedding party is very drunk; they are all intoxicated. Now you have ordered the loveliest of all apple wines brought out that I have ever seen lifted anywhere in this world. This is what you should have given to the guests earlier today; at that time, every one of us would have received it with gratitude!"

After those words, and after they had drunk this wine, many a thane became aware that the holy Christ had performed a sign there inside the house. They had more trust in His protection after that, more confidence that He had the power and authority of God in this world. It became widely known to the Jewish people throughout Galileeland how the Chieftain's Son, right there in their country, had changed water to wine. That was the first of the wonders which He performed there in Galilee for the Jewish people as signs.

There is no one who can tell, no one who can say for certain, what the wonders were that were done afterwards among the people, as Christ the Ruler taught the Jewish people in God's name all day long. He promised them the kingdom of heaven and He protected them against Hel's oppression with words. He told them to look for God's attention and eternal life—that is where there is the light of souls, God's comings and goings, daylight, the glory of God! There many a guest lives most happily—they are the ones who kept obedience to the Heaven-King's command well in mind here.

Song 25

At hill-fort Capharnaum, God's Child of Peace heals
a household lad of a commander of a hundred men.

When He left the wedding, Christ, most Powerful of kings, decided
to go to Capharnaum, the great hill-fort, with his followers. His
forces of good men, His happy warrior-company, assembled in front
of Him. They wanted to hear His sweet and holy word.

A commander of a hundred men, a good man, then approached
Him, and asked the Holy One earnestly for help. He said that he
had long had a frail cripple among the members of his household, a
sick person in his house. "Not a single man is able to heal him with
his hands. Now he needs Your help, my good Lord." Then the
Peace-Child of God spoke to him, replying immediately and saying
that He would come there and would rescue the child from this
affliction. At that the man come closer to Him, leaving the crowd
behind, to exchange words with the mighty One. "I am not worthy,
my good Lord," he said, "that You should come to my house or enter
into my hall, for I am a very sinful man in both what I say and do.
I believe that You have power, that You can work his cure from
here, my Lord Ruler. If You say it with Your words, then his
sickness will disappear immediately, and his body will become whole
and restored, if You give him Your help.[103] I am an officer, I have
attained sufficient property and prosperity for myself. Though I am
under the command of a noble king, I have a troop of earls, loyal
fighting-men of the army, who are so obedient to me that they do not
fail to do a whit of the words or activities which I order them to do
in this territory. They march off, they carry out my orders, and they
come back loyally to their lord and master. Even though I have
extensive property and plenty of people, fight-minded warriors, at my

---

[103] As in the miracle at Cana, Jesus is depicted as capable of Germanic magic.
In Scripture the Centurion says that Christ is capable of healing the boy at a distance
('Lord, I am not worthy that you should come under my roof, but only say the word
and my servant will be healed') in the *Heliand* this power is made quite explicit by
adding the word *hinana* 'from here'.

residence, I do not dare to ask You, God's so holy Son, to walk to my house, to go into my home, because I am so sinful. I know my wrongdoings."

Then Christ the Ruler spoke, the Man spoke to His followers and said that He had not found anyone among the Jews, the descendants of Israel, like this man—no one in this country who believed more clearly in God and in heaven. "Now I want you to listen to what I am going to tell you here in true words: there are still many foreign peoples from the East and the West, many of the clans of men, who are to come together, the holy people of God, in the kingdom of heaven. There they can rest in the lap of Abraham, of Isaac himself, and of Jacob too—those good men—and can enjoy welfare and happiness, a life of pleasure, good life in God's light!

"Then many of the Jews, the sons of this kingdom, will be robbed, deprived of these glories, and will lie in dark valleys at the farthest ends of the infernal regions. There you will hear those heroes lamenting, there they continually bite their teeth in their anger. There the guest rages in pain and the fire is greedy—the hard hellish torture, hot and dark, black eternal night—the reward for sins, for wrathful wrongdoing, paid to whoever did not have the desire to save himself before he gave up this light, before he wended his way from this world.

"Now you may go on your way, if you will, and return to your house. At home you will find the young man healthy. He is in good spirits! The boy is cured just as you asked Me. It all happened because you have faith firmly fixed in your mind." The officer then said his thanks to the Heaven-King, to the all-ruling God, in front of the people for helping him with such a problem. What he wanted had been happily granted to him.

He then set out from there on the journey, and willingly went to where he had his property, his house and his lands. He found the boy, a man in his childhood, healthy. Christ's words were fulfilled! He had such power to perform signs, that no one on this earth can tell or count all the famous deeds He did by His own strength in this middle world, all the wonders He worked, because everything, heaven and earth, is under His command.

Song 26

Christ the Rescuer raises the dead son
of a widow outside Fort Naim.

Then the holy Christ decided to keep on traveling. Every day the all-mighty, good Chieftain did loving things for the people. With words He taught the people God's will, and He always had many followers with Him as warrior-companions, the people of God, a powerful force of men from many peoples, a holy army. His help was good, He was generous to human beings.[104]

At that time God's Son, the Rescuer, was coming with this noisy crowd to the high hill-fort at Naim. (There His name was to become famous among mankind.[105]) Christ the Rescuer walked powerfully toward it until He, the Best of all healers, was close to it. At that moment they saw people bringing out a corpse, a lifeless body. They were carrying it out the hill-fort's gate on a stretcher, it was a very young man. The mother was walking behind the corpse, her heart was grief-stricken, she was beating herself with her hands, lamenting and crying over her child's death—the poor woman. It was her only child. She was a widow, she had no more joy except for this one son, he was all that was left to her of happiness and delight—until fate took him from her, the great Measurer's doings. A crowd of the fort people followed as they brought the young man on the stretcher to his grave.

The Son of God became filled with compassion and spoke to the mother. He told the widow to stop crying, to stop lamenting over the

---

[104] The image of Christ here is that of a powerful Germanic chieftain or king, by ancient custom making the rounds of his territory with his retinue of warrior-companions, the 'royal progress' of later centuries.

[105] This remark is a commonplace form from Germanic epic poetry. The *Nibelungenlied's* poet-author was still using the technique four hundred years later. The author inserts such remarks into a text not so much to assert his presence in the story, or to alienate participation in the plot (in Brechtian style), but to give a sense of the fatedness of the happenings that occurred to the hero of the story. The author's voice becomes a sort of vehicle for a later time's all-knowing hindsight, and, in the *Heliand*, a vehicle for making Christ into a Germanic hero.

child. "You will see power here, the work of the Ruler, a favor will be granted to you here, consolation, in front of these people. There is no need for you to mourn over the life-spirit of your boy." Then He walked up to the stretcher, and the Chieftain's Son touched him with holy hands,[106] and spoke to the hero, telling the young man to get up, to rise up from his resting place. The young fighter sat up on the stretcher—his spirit had come back into his chest by God's power, and the man began to talk to his relatives. Then Christ the Healer gave the young man into the hands of his mother. Her heart was consoled, the woman was full of happiness that such a favor was granted to her. She fell at Christ's feet and praised the people's Chieftain before the crowd, because He had protected a life-spirit so dear to her against the workings of the Measurer.[107] She understood that He was the mighty Chieftain, the holy One who ruled heaven, and that He could help many, all earth peoples.

Many began to be aware of the wonder that had happened among the people; they said the Ruler Himself had come in power to make many wise, and that He had sent a great wizard[108] to them

---

[106] Scripture has that He touched the stretcher (Lk.7:13-14). In the Saxon text, the pronoun refers to the boy. The touching of the dead 'with holy hands' in a Germanic context (taboo in a Hebrew one) seems to add a much more magical tone to the scene, parallel to the changing of water into wine in the author's reinterpretation of the Marriage Feast at Cana.

[107] *metodigisceftie* '[god-] the Measurer's doings or decisions'. Fate is again made responsible for the timing, in this case inconsiderate timing, of the young man's death. As in the Zachary story, the author does not deny the power and activity of fate and time in this world, but shows the gospel as saying that Christ is more powerful.

[108] *uuarsago* lit. 'truth-sayer, soothsayer, wizard, fortune-teller'. This Germanic religious concept is used by the author as the equivalent for the biblical 'prophet'. *Uuarsagos* must have stood very high in respect in Germanic religion since not only the *Heliand* but also the very conservative literal translation of the day, the Old High German *Tatian*, uses an equivalent word, *wizago* for 'prophet'. From the *Heliand* context it seems that a *uuarsago* had two functions, that of person of wisdom, seer, and that of person of magic, wonder worker—both of which are attributed here to Christ.

Because of these two functions, 'soothsayer' might be too minimal a translation of *uuarsago* in this passage of the *Heliand*; more accurate, it seems, is 'wizard'!

in the kingdom of the world, One who had done such a great favor for them there.

Then many an earl was seized on the spot by terror, the people became frightened, when they saw the boy's own life-spirit looking at the light of day, the life-spirit which death had already taken from him when he died on his sickbed. He was healthy once again; the young child came to life.

This became known everywhere among the descendants of Israel. By the time evening came, there were assembled at the place all the sick people, people with crippled hands and legs—every single sick person living in the area was being brought there. They were coming to Christ, coming to the place where He with His great power was helping them and healing them, and then letting them go on their way wherever they wished—healed.

One should praise His work and appreciate His deeds, for this reason: He is the Chieftain Himself, the mighty Protector of Mankind—of any persons who believe in His words and in His works![109]

Song 27

Christ commands the wind and the sea.

So many people were coming from every foreign people to the place of Christ's honor, to such powerful protection, that God's Son wanted to take a trip out on the sea (it is on the border of Galileeland) with His followers—the Ruler out on the waves of the sea! He told the other people to travel on ahead and decided to get into a boat with a small number to get some sleep. The rescuing Christ was worn out with His journeys.

---

[109] This last paragraph is a doxology, and reflects the ancient liturgical practice of completing public prayers with a brief glorification of God. Many of the *Heliand's* 71 songs end with a form of doxology, usually of a mixed sort. The praise of God is combined with a moral admonition to the Saxon audience not to vacillate, 'to believe and not to doubt'.

The weather-wise warriors hoisted up the sail, and, keeping the wind aft, they ran before it over the ocean swells,[110] until the Ruler and His crew came to the middle. Then the weather began to increase in strength, the storm wind rose, the waves grew, thickening darkness rushed in, the sea began to move, the wind battled the water! The men were worried, the ocean was so angry, not one of the men thought he had much longer to live. It was then they woke up the country's Guardian with their words and told Him about the strength of the storm, and asked the saving Christ graciously to protect them from the water. "Otherwise we are going to die here in the sea in terrible pain!"

Then He Himself arose, the good Son of God, and spoke to His followers, He told them not to be a bit afraid that the storm was gaining on them. "Why are you so afraid?" He said, "you are still not sure in your minds, your faith is still too little. It will not be long before the waves will be quieter, and the weather will be beautiful." Then He spoke to the wind and also to the sea itself, and He told both of them to behave themselves more calmly. They carried out the command, the Ruler's word. The storm winds died down and the sea became tranquil. Then the people who were with Him began to wonder, and some said it with their own words, what kind of a more powerful human being He might be, that both the wind and the waves obeyed His word of command.

The Son of God had saved them from peril, the boat glided onward, the high-horned ship.[111] The heroes made land, they gave praise to God, glorifying His great strength.

Many persons came to God's Son. He gladly received anyone who came there with a clear mind looking for help. He taught them their faith and He healed their bodies with His hands. It did not matter how badly hurt by sickness the person was. Even if Satan's deceitful followers had a man in their hands with all their hostile

---

[110] The author knows his seamanship, and in this and other marine passages, inserts accurate nautical details to let the North-Sea audience know that Christ and Peter could also handle a boat.

[111] *hoh hurnidskip.* The boat is therefore something of a Viking-style longboat, with high curving stem- and sternposts.

endi oc thinoro uuordo so self alloro barno best · that thu us bedon

leres uugoronthine so Iohannes duot diurlic doperi dago gehuui

licas is uuerod mid uuordun · huuo sie uualdand sculun godan gro

tean · do thinun iungorun so self gerihti us that gerim

Thohabda eft the rikeo garu san aftar thiu sunudrohtines · god

uuod angegin · Than gi god uuillean uueros mid iuuuon uuordun

uualdand grotean · allaro cuningo craftigoston · than quedad gi

so ic iu leriu · Fadar isusa firihobarno · the isan them hohon himi

larikea · Geuuihid si thin namo uuordo gehuuilico · Cuma

thin craftag riki · Uuerda thin uuilleo obar thesa uuerold al so

sama an erdo · so thar uppa ist an them hohon himil rikea · Gef

us dago gehuuilikes raddrohtin thegodo · thina helaga helpa ·

Endi alat us hebenes uuard managoro mensculdio · al so uue

odrum mannum doan · Ne lat us far ledean letha uuihti so ford

an iro uuilleon so uui uuirdige sind · Ac help us uuidar allun ubi

lon dadiun · So sculun biddean thangi te bede hnigad · uueros

mid iuuuom uuordun · that iu uualdand god ledesa lite an leut

cunnea · efgi than uuilliad alatan liudeo gehuuilicun thero

sacono endi thero sundeono the sie uuid iu selbon hir uureda ge

uuirkeat · than alatid iu uualdand god · fadar alamahtig firin

uuerk mikil managoro meni sculdeo · Ef iu than uuirdid

iuuua mod te starc thatgi ne uuilleat odrun erlun alatan uue

ron uuamdadi · than ne uuil iu oc uualdand god · grim uuere

fargeban · ac gi sculun is geld niman · suido ledliclon · telanguru

had been crippled for so many days that he did not have any power at all over his body.

There were so many people there though, that they were not able to bring him before God's Son. They could not force their way through the throng to tell Him about such a needy sick person. The healing Christ went inside into a hall. A mob formed around Him in there, a great crowd of people. Then the men who had long been carrying the weak crippled man, bearing both him and his bed, began to talk about how they could get him in front of the Son of God, through the people inside to where the ruling Christ would Himself catch sight of the man. Then those warrior-companions walked up to the place, they lifted the sick man up with their hands and climbed up on top of the house. They cut open the hall from above, and let him down with ropes into the shrine[113] where the powerful One was, the strongest of kings.

When He saw the man coming down through the rafters of the house, Christ understood that these men in their minds and in their feelings had a powerful faith in Him. He then spoke before the crowd, and said that He wanted to free the sick man from his sins.

Then, in answer to that, people spoke to Him, hostile-minded Jews[114] who were spying on the words of God's Son. They said that that could not be done, the forgiving of sins, except by God alone, the Ruler of this world. The Ruler of the world had His answer ready. "I am doing this," He said, "for this man who lies here so sick in

---

[113] *rakud* '[Germanic] temple'. This is another Germanic word the author uses for 'temple' (the first was *uuiha*). The literal Old High German translation steers away from such accommodation and simply adopts the Latin *templum*. The word *rakud* is of uncertain provenance. A guess: *rak* may be the same word as in the Old Norse *ragnar* 'the ruling ones, the gods'; *ud* may be the same word as the Saxon *od* 'property.' If so, *rakud* would simply mean 'god's property.'

[114] In the *Heliand* there is no distinction, or even mention made, of the various religious groupings of the Jews. Where Scripture attributes a given word or action to the Pharisees or the Sadducees or the Scribes, the *Heliand* simply groups them together as 'the Jews.' No doubt the author would have been hard pressed to find any effective Germanic equivalents for these groups that would have contributed to his epic.

The disadvantage, however, of this no doubt necessary simplification is that the Jewish people have to be depicted as uniformly hostile to Christ.

terrible pain in this hall, to make seeable that I have power to forgive sins as well as to heal sick people—and I do not even need to touch him!"[115]

The great Chieftain then spoke to the sick man who was lying there lame and told him to stand up, in front of the people, completely healed. Then He told him to put his bed clothes on his shoulders and carry them on his back. He carried out the command immediately, in front of the warrior-companions, and walked out of there restored, leaving the house hale and hearty.

A great number of the pagan men, warriors, were in amazement. They said that the Ruler Himself, all-mighty God, had given Christ greater power, strength and knowledge than any other of the sons of men. The Jewish people, however, did not want to recognize that He was God, nor to believe His teaching, they fought Him in a dirty way and waged war on His words. Thus they loaded weariness onto themselves, a miserable reward, one that still will last for a long time, for they did not want to hear the teachings which Christ, the King of Heaven, was making known everywhere all over this world.

He let them see His works and deeds every single day, He let them hear His holy word which He spoke to help human beings, and showed them so many mighty signs in order that they would be able to trust His teaching more—and believe in it. He freed so many a body from deadly illness and made it better, He gave the life-spirit back to the dying. The hero who was all ready to make the journey to Hel—him Christ the Healer by His own mighty power revived after death, letting him continue enjoying happiness in this world.

---

[115] The author adds the idea of 'and I do not even need to touch him.' This inserted remark confirms the probable importance of touching for Germanic magic. In this passage the *Heliand* shows Christ's superior magical powers to that of Germanic wizards—all He has to do is speak His 'magic' words, if He wants, and the magic/miracle occurs (as at the Creation) with no further ado!

Song 29

The story of the earl who sowed good seed.

And so He healed the legs and hands of the crippled, and made those who were blind better: He let them see the eternally beautiful bright light of day. He absolved from sins, the grim deeds of mankind. The Jews, however, loathsome people, did not ever get better in their faith in the holy Christ, but they kept a hardened attitude toward Him, they fought very strongly against Him. They did not want to understand that the enemy fiends had ensnared the Jews into doing their will by means of their [Jewish] faith.

Nor was the Chieftain's Son ever the laxer because of this; rather He said in words how the Jews could come to heaven's kingdom, taught across the countryside, and turned so many of these people to Him with these words, that a very great crowd was following Him.

The Son of God said much to them in pictures; thus they could not understand within their breasts, comprehend in their hearts, until the holy Christ would explain it by His own power to the crowd of earls in open words, and tell them what He meant.

Once, an enormous crowd of people thronged around Him. They felt a great need to hear the Heaven-King's words of solid truth. He was standing on the shore by the water and, with such a large crowd, a whole clan of thanes, He did not want to teach them up on the land, and so the good One, His followers with Him, moved closer to the water and got into a boat. He told them to scull it away from the land so that all these people would not crowd in on Him.

Many a warrior-thane stood there by the water where Christ the Ruler spoke and taught all those people. "My warrior-companions! I would like to tell you how an earl began to sow good wheat grain on the ground with his hands.[116] Some of it fell on top of hard

---

[116] This sentence is interesting since it may reveal something more about the culture of the addressees of the *Heliand*. The author carefully removed any possible association implied between his earls and sheep-herders in the Christmas story. He feels comfortable, however, about having an earl sow seed with his own hands. It seems that the warrior class to whom the epic is addressed must have been warrior-

rock, it had no earth in which it could grow and take root and be supported and sprout, and so the wheat that was lying there on the rock was lost. Some of it fell on land, on noble soil, and right away began to grow happily and take root, thriving merrily—so good was the soil with a lordly fertility![117]

"Some of it, again, fell on a road, hard-packed from many feet: the tread of horses' hooves and the footsteps of heroes. It had some soil there and so the wheat grain sprouted and began to grow on the roadway. But then the constant coming and going of travelers destroyed it, the birds pecked and ate it, so that none of what fell on the roadway survived to be of use to the owner. Then some of it fell that day where there were many thorn thickets. It had soil there, and so it came up, sprouted and took hold. But weeds grew up there in abundance and prevented its growth. The forest cover had overwhelmed it from the start, and it was not able to grow to be fruitful since the thornbushes had crowded it out."

The companions of Christ sat there; the word-wise warriors were silent. They were deep in wonderment about the images with which God's Son undertook to tell such a wise spell. Then one of the earls bowed to the gracious Lord and began with great reverence to ask Him, "You have power, holy Chieftain," he said, "in heaven and on earth, above and below, You are the All-Ruler of human spirits, and we are your followers, devoted to You in our hearts. Good Lord, if it be Your will, let us hear the meaning of Your words here, so that we will be able to let it be known after You among all the Christian people. We know that true pictures emerge from Your words and we have a terrible need in this country to understand from You Your words and Your works—since it all comes from such wisdom!"

---

farmers (and 'weather-wise' coastal fishermen).

[117] Two modifiers in the passage look suspiciously like pious puns aimed at giving a message to the people on the shore/the Saxons: the soil is "noble" and its fertility is "lordly".

Song 30

The explanation of the story.

Then the Best of men replied to him with this answer, "I did not intend in any way," He said, "to keep my deeds concealed, neither the words nor the works. You will know it all, my followers, for the Ruler of this world has granted to you that in your minds' feelings you are to know the secret mystery, the runes of heaven. Other people are to be taught the commands of God in images, pictures.

"I will certainly tell you here and now what I meant, so that you will be able to understand my teaching better throughout this territory. The seed about which I spoke to you is the Word itself, the holy teaching of the Heaven-King, as one should spread it over the middle realm, all across this world. People are different in their attitude of mind. Some people have feelings so hard-hearted and mean-spirited that it can never happen that such a person would act according to your words or would want to begin to carry out My teachings. So, all My teaching is lost there; God's message and your human words are lost on the evil man, just as I was saying to you before: the wheat on top of the stone died, for when it sprouted, it found no place to take root. It is all lost: the speech of noble men and the message of God, everything that has been taught in words to the evil man. What is worse, to the displeasure of God and to the delight of the evil ones, the man has chosen to journey among the enemy toward the embrace of the fire. From that moment onward, the thoughts of his breast will add heat to the flames!

"Never teach My doctrine any the less in your words because of this. If there are many earls like that one on this earth, there is also the other human being, the man who is young and intelligent—good-hearted—wise in his words and who understands your spells. He thinks about them in his heart and he listens there very intently, and then steps closer. In his heart he accepts God's bidding, he learns it and does it. His faith being so good, he calculates how he could convert the other man, the wicked one, into feeling pure loyalty to the King of Heaven.

"God's command, the loving faith, then spreads out widely in this man's heart—just as the wheat does as it sprouts in the soil where it has good ground, and where fate favors it with good weather, rain and sun, so that conditions are perfect. This is what God's teaching does day and night in the good person. As the devil walks far away from him (the evil little creatures), God's protective care comes powerfully nearer and nearer, night and day, until the teaching brings about two things in the man: the teaching that comes out of his mouth becomes a blessing to the sons of men, and he himself becomes God's. And so by his attitude of mind, he has exchanged this earthly moment for a part of the kingdom of heaven, the greatest possession. He is traveling to the realm of God's power free of bad deeds.

"Faithfulness is such a good thing for every man, no treasure-hoard of gold can be compared to such faith! Keep on being kind and generous teachers of mankind!

"Warrior-heroes are so different in their attitudes of mind. Some resist violently, they have ill-will and a vacillating mind. They are full of fakeness and wicked deeds. Then, one of them begins to think as he is standing there among the people, listening with rapt attention to God's teaching, that he would willingly like to follow it from now on. God's teaching immediately begins to attach itself to his mind—until the moment when once again some useful wealth and someone else's property come into his hands. The evil little creatures lead him off as he gets caught up in his desire for possessions; his belief burns out. It did him little good to have ever had it in his heart, if he was not willing to hold on to it.

"That corresponds to the grain that began to sprout alongside the road, growing in the soil. It was killed by people's coming and going—exactly what the serious sin in that man's mind does to God's teaching, if one does not watch out for it well. Otherwise, sin will throw the man down to the bottom of the infernal regions, to hot Hel, where he will be of no further service to the King of Heaven, but the enemies will punish him painfully.

"Always keep on teaching with words in this land![118] I know the minds of the peoples, the different feelings and attitudes of mankind, the different ways. . . [119] Some people's whole mind and concern is more on how they can hold onto their hoard than how they can accomplish the will of the King of Heaven. Because of this, God's holy will cannot grow there, even though it may attach itself and send out roots—wealth crowds it out. It is the same as the weeds and the thornbushes that entangle the wheat and prevent it from growing—that is what wealth does to a human being. It puts his heart in chains so that the man cannot think and pay attention to the thing he needs most: how he can work it out during the time that he is in this world that he will possess the kingdom of heaven for eternal days thereafter, thanks to his Lord, with wealth so endless that no man in this world could ever realize it.

"No thane here can think so broadly in his mind, nor can the heart of man contain or really know, what good things the ruling God has gotten ready, everything that stands prepared for each human being who loves Him here, for each person who takes such care of his soul that he will be able to sail to God's light."

Song 31

The story of the wheat and the weeds.

So He taught them in words. There was a great crowd of people standing around God's Son, they listened to Him as He told them in images and pictures about the way things are in this world. He told them about a nobleman who sowed pure wheat in his field with his

---

[118] This repeated exhortation to continue teaching no matter what happens to some of the 'grains' is the author's. He inserts it three times in the parable, each time putting it into the mouth of Christ. No doubt it reveals the difficulty of missionary labors in Saxony, and shows as well that part of the intended audience of the *Heliand* was those monks who were spreading the Word in the North. This strong exhortation seems to have something of the spirit of Ansgar, who was working during this period for the conversion of the northern Saxons and Scandinavians.

[119] One-half of a line is missing here from the manuscript.

hands; he was hoping to get beautiful growth and a bountiful harvest. Then his enemy went out afterwards with a vicious mind, and sowed ray-grass, the worst of all weeds, all over it. Then they both grew, the wheat and the weed. At this point his field men came back to the house and told their lord, thanes speaking to their sovereign, in straightforward words, "How is this? You sowed nothing but wheat, good lord, and wheat alone, on your field, but now each earl can see nothing more than weeds growing there! How could that have happened?"

Then the noble man replied directly to the earls, the lord to his vassals. He said that he could well understand it. An enemy had sowed the field after him with vicious weeds, "So that I would not enjoy the bounty of the harvest, and not have a successful growth." Then the lord's friends spoke to him, his followers replied and said that they were willing to go into the field in full strength and remove the weeds from there, pulling them up with their hands. Their lord spoke again to them, "I do not want you to weed it," he said, "because you cannot avoid or prevent yourselves, though you do not intend it, from trampling down a great deal of the sprouting wheat under your feet as you walk. From this moment on, let both of them continue to grow until harvest comes and the grain is ripe in the field, ready in the soil. Then we will all go to it, pulling the weeds up with our hands. We will cleanly separate out the wheat, gather it together and put it in my hall. We will keep it there so that no one can do anything to it. Then we will take the weeds, tie them up in bundles and throw them onto bitter fire, and let the hot flames of the ever-hungry fire haul them away."

Many earls stood there, the thanes were silent, wondering what the famous, mighty Christ could mean, wondering what the most powerful Son wanted to signify with these images. They therefore asked the good Chieftain to unlock this holy teaching for them so that from now on the people would be able to grasp it. Their Lord spoke to them again, the famous, mighty Christ. "That is the Son of Man," He said, "I myself am the one who is there sowing, and these blessed human beings who hear Me well and do My will are the pure wheat grains. This world is the field, mankind's wide farmland. Satan himself is the one who sows such wicked teaching afterwards.

He has ruined so many of these people that they do evil, they behave according to his will. Even so, they are to continue to grow here, those humans who are damned, just as the good do, until the forces of Mutspell,[120] the End of the World, come upon mankind. At that time every single field in this kingdom will be ripe and the sons of men will follow their decreed fate.[121]

"Then the earth will fall apart—that will be the hugest of all harvests!—and the bright-shining Chieftain above will come with His angel forces, and all the people who ever saw this light will come together and they will at that time receive their reward, a bad one or a good one. God's angels, the holy guards of heaven, will then go and separate out the clean men and gather them together, and put them into the infinitely beautiful, high light of heaven, and the others they will put down in the bottom of Hel's realm, throwing the evildoers to the surging fire. Bound up, they will there suffer the pain which the bitter flames inflict; the others, the riches of the heavenly kingdom where they will shine like bright suns! This is the reward men receive for their good deeds.

---

[120] *Mudspell* or *mutspell* is a concept from Germanic religious mythology. *Mutspell* is the force of Heat which will come from the South at the end, and will participate in the twilight of the gods, *ragnarok*. When Woden and Thor have been destroyed by their enemies the Wolf and the Snake, and have killed them in return, then, at the very end of the battle when all the gods and monsters are dead, the forces of Heat will cast fire upon the earth, killing all the human race, and destroying the earth. The flames will reach up to heaven, and as the end of world comes and all thinking beings, human and divine, disappear, the natural elements will rule again.

(It should be mentioned for completeness' sake, that there is also a tradition that the world tree preserves life, and from it the cycle begins again.)

[121] *regangiscapu* 'the ruling [Ones'] decisions, fate'. The parable does indeed lend itself to a certain predestinationist reading, and the *Heliand* author takes advantage of that appearance to bring in Germanic fate, as the 'weeds' march off to follow their necessary fiery fate, and those who are 'wheat' fulfill their heavenly destiny.

In actuality, though, the *Heliand* author is careful not to describe the 'weeds' as being poor souls, predestined from the beginning by their very nature for the furnace. He describes the weeds as meaning Satan's teaching. In this sense, it would have to be 'misgrown wheat' that goes to the furnace, and this the author would be excessively hard put to contrive. His main effort seems to have been to intertwine the Christian Day of Judgment with Germanic religion's *Mutspell*, the fiery twilight of the world.

"Whoever has wisdom and a thoughtful heart, any earl who can hear with his ears, let him be concerned, in the deepest feelings that are within him, about how he will answer to God the Powerful on that renowned day for all the words and works which he did in this world. That is the most terrifying of all things, the most frightening to the sons of men, that they will have to speak with their Lord, men with their good Chieftain. At that moment every single human being would gladly be free of wrongdoing, of all dirty business. Every one of the human race should worry about this beforehand, before he gives up this light, if he wishes to have eternal honor, the high heavenly kingdom and the gracious kindness of God."

Song 32

The grim-hearted Jews of Galileeland attempt to throw Christ off a cliff.

I have heard it told that the Chieftain's Son, Himself, the Best of all sons, described in pictures what there was in the world-kingdom among mankind that was similar to the heaven-kingdom. He said that often little things can be lighter and rise up very high. "The kingdom of heaven behaves in the same way. It is always greater than anyone in this world thinks of it. There is also work that is like the kingdom of heaven. When a man throws his net into the ocean, fishing in the sea, he catches both good and bad fish, he tows them up onto the beach, landing the catch, and only then sorts them, picking the good ones and putting them on the sand, and letting the others go back to the bottom, back to the wide waves. This is what God the Ruler will do with the sons of mankind on the renowned day. He will bring all the earth-people together, He will pick out the clean for the kingdom of heaven, and let the damned go to the bottom of the fire of Hel. And there is no warrior-hero among men who knows any equivalent to the pain which earth-people receive there in the inferno. There is also no equivalent reward that a man can find to the riches and happiness which the Ruler distributes, which God Himself grants to every human being who behaved himself here in such a way as to be able to make the journey to the heaven-kingdom, to the long-lasting light."

Thus, in His wisdom He taught them. People were coming there from all over Galileeland to see God's Son. They did it because of wonderment over where such words could be coming to Him from, spoken so intelligently, so that He could always soothsay God's spell, and say it with such power. "He belongs to the clans here," they said, "by family relationship. His mother is here with us, a woman from these people. All of us here know [Him], we are quite aware of His ancestry and we know His clan. He grew up here among these people. Where could this wisdom of His have come from and such greater power than other people here have?"

So the local men did not approve of Him. They said foolish things to Him, they looked down on Him, the holy One. They did not want to listen to His message. Nor in return did He want to show them many images or pictures, brilliant signs, because of their unbelief. He knew their doubting minds, their bad-will. He knew that there were no other people among the Jews as grimly hostile and hard-hearted as the ones from Galileeland. Holy Christ was born there,[122] the Son of God, but despite that they did not want to devoutly receive His message. Instead the local people, the warriors, began to plot among themselves how they could inflict the greatest pain on the powerful Christ. They called their fighting-men together, their warrior-companions. They wanted to accuse Him of sins and evil intentions. His word was of no use to them nor His brilliant spells, and so they began to discuss among themselves how they could throw such a strong man off a cliff, over a mountain wall. They wanted to take the life of the Son of God.

He came out happily together with the people; he had no fear in His mind. He knew that not the slightest harm or injury could be done to Him in His godlikeness by human beings, by the Jewish

---

[122] No doubt the author is thinking here of "born and raised" with the emphasis on "raised" and is not ignoring Bethlehem. It is perhaps just a standard way of saying that Nazareth is Christ's home.

people, before His time had come.[123] Together with the people He climbed up the rocky hill until He came to the place where they intended to throw Him down over the wall, to fell Him to earth, so that He would lose His life-spirit and His aging would come to an end.

But there, up on the mountain, the minds of those earls, the bitter thoughts of the Jews were dissipated, so that not one of them had such a grim, hostile spirit nor such evil will, so that none of them could recognize the Ruler's Son, not one of them knew Him nor could tell which one there was He. Thus He could stand among their warriors and walk through the center of their crowd, moving through their people.[124] He gave Himself this peace,[125] the Protector, against the crowd, and set off from there going, through the midst of the enemy's people. He went where He wanted to, the Ruler's Son, the strongest of kings, to a wilderness. He had the power to choose where in the land He would most like to be, where in this world He would like to stay.

---

[123] No reason for Christ's lack of fear is given in Scripture. The author has added (citing from the Cana incident) that nothing can happen before fate and time decree it. These Germanic elements are added into the scene as a reason for Christ's confidence.

[124] Jesus is here depicted as a Germanic wizard. He dissipates the minds of His enemies so that they cannot recognize Him, he walks among the hostile enemy warriors with an impunity that must have made every ninth-century listener envious. This elaboration is a nice touch by the author. The scriptural account he was working with is extremely plain: '. . . they took Him up to the brow of the hill their town was built on, intending to throw Him off the cliff, but He passed straight through the crowd and walked away' (Lk 4:29-30). The *Heliand* also sees to it that Jesus actively takes Himself up the hillside, He is not brought there.

During the Passion, the devil will don a Germanic invisibility cape to be present in Pilate's house, in an incident similar to the above. Christ, however, does His wizardry in the *Heliand* by His own power.

[125] 'Peace' here perhaps in the sense of victory after this short skirmish with hostile warriors.

Song 33

John the soothsayer is beheaded.

John, God's serving-man, was at that time traveling on another road with his followers. He gave the people long-lasting counsel, telling them to do good and to abandon evil, treachery, and murder. Many good people were fond of him.

He went to see the king of the Jews, the commander of the army, at his house. The king had been named Herod after his parents, and was a man of violent anger. He was living with the woman who had been his brother's bride and female property until his brother departed for another place, exchanging worlds. Then the king took the woman to be his queen. She had had children born to her by his brother.

John the good began to criticize the wife. He said that it was repulsive to God the Ruler to do this—to take one's brother's bride to bed and treat her as a wife. "If you are willing to listen to me and believe my teaching, then you should no longer keep her as your own, and avoid her in your feelings! Never have that kind of love for someone, do not bring such serious sins upon yourself!"

After these words the woman's mind began to worry. She was afraid that John would move the king with his speeches and wise words to abandon her. She then began secretly to plot many harmful things against John and told her fighting-men, her earls, to capture the innocent man and to lock him up in prison in irons, chained hand and foot. They were afraid to take away his life-spirit because of the people, all of whom were friendly to him, knowing that he was very much both good and God's. The people held him for a soothsayer— as well they might!

Then, in the course of the year, the time came, as calculated by wise men of the people, when the Jewish king had been born, had come to the light. It was the custom of the people that this [birthday] should be celebrated by every earl together with the Jewish people. A huge crowd of men were assembled there in the guest-hall; the army leaders were there in the house where their lord was on his royal throne. Many Jews came to the guest-hall, they were in a merry mood with joy in their hearts. They saw their ring-giver there in his happiness!

Clear wine was being carried to the drinking hall in pitchers; the servants who were pouring were hurrying back and forth with golden goblets. There was loud playfulness in the hall, the warrior-heroes were drinking! This made the country's herdsman [the king] in his joy and pleasure think what more he could do for the people's enjoyment. He then ordered his brother's child, a high-spirited young girl, to come out to where he was sitting on his bench, tipsy from the wine, and he spoke to the woman. He greeted her in front of the men, and asked her insistently if she would begin some entertainment for the guests, something beautiful there in the drinking hall. "Let these people see how you have learned to bring many people on the benches to a state of bliss! If you fulfill my request and do what I ask in front of these warriors, I will truthfully promise you here, in the open in front of these people—and I will keep my word—that I will give you afterwards as a present, here in front of my ring-receiving friends, whatever you ask me for! Even if you ask me for half of this realm, my kingdom, I will still do it, and in such a way that not a single fighting-man will be able to change it with his words—it will be done."

That so inclined the maid's spirit and mind toward her lord that, within the house, she began an entertainment in the guest-hall of the type customary among the people of that country, common among those peoples. The playing girl moved vigorously throughout the house—many a mind and many emotions were filled with pleasure! When the maiden had earned the thanks of the king and of all the earls, the good men who were in the house, she wanted to have her reward—right there in front of the crowd. She went to talk to her mother and asked her full of curiosity what she should request of the guardian of the hill-fort. Her mother advised the girl in accordance with her own desires and told her that she should ask for nothing else in front of the men but that she be given John's head, there inside the hall, separated from its body.

It was painful to all the people, painful to all the men's feelings, when they heard the maiden saying that. So it was also to the king. He could not make what he had said into a lie, he could not bend his words. Therefore he told his men-at-arms to leave the guest-hall and take the life of the man of God. It was not long before they brought the head of this great man to the hall, and there gave it to the young girl, the maiden, in front of the crowd. She took it out to her mother.

That was the end-day of the wisest of all men who has ever come to this world, whom any queen has borne as a child, whom any woman has borne to an earl—allowing always ahead of him for that one Person whom the virgin bore, the maiden who never knew man-warrior in her lifetime—for thus the ruling God from the meadows of heaven had powerfully determined him to be by the Holy Spirit. No one, not a single man, was ever to equal him, neither before nor after.

Earls hurried around John, his many followers, blessed warrior-companions, and they buried him, his precious body, in sand. They knew that he had to go on the blissful journey to the light of God, to the dear comings and goings with the Chieftain, in the home up above.

Song 34

With five loaves and two fishes the Chieftain of human beings feeds a great throng of earls.

Then the warrior-companions, John's followers, decided to go away from there, sadness in their feelings, holiness in their life-spirits. Their lord's death was their great sorrow. They set off to find the Ruler's Son, the powerful Christ, in the wild country, to let Him know of the good man's departure and how the Jews' king had cut off the head of the greatest of human beings by the edge of the sword. The Chieftain's Son did not want to say anything hurting, He knew that John's soul was being kept in holy protection against the haters, and in peace against enemies.

Then the fame of the Best of teachers spread over the country-side in the wilderness. People gathered; clansmen journeyed to Him. There was great desire among them to know about His wise words.

In the same way, He too, the Chieftain's Son, had a great desire to lead a gathering of warrior-companions like that to God's light, to bring them to happiness.

All day long the Ruler taught many people from far and wide until in the evening the sun sank to its resting place. Then His twelve warrior-companions went to God's Child and told their good Lord of the hardship in which the earls lived thereabout, saying that the people living in this barren land needed His help. "They cannot begin to do anything here because these heroes are oppressed by hunger.[126] Now, good Lord, let them go to find places to stay. There are many well-populated hill-forts nearby. There the people will find food for sale in the villages."[127] Then the ruling Christ, the people's Chieftain, spoke in reply and said that it was not necessary "that they leave My dear teachings because of lack of food. You give these people enough to eat so that you have them willing to stay here."

Philip, a man of experience, had his answer ready. He said there were so many people there in the crowd that "even if we had food here ready to give to them, the greatest amount of food that we could buy with the sum of two hundred silver pieces, it would still be doubtful whether each one of them would get something—so little would that be for all these people!" The Protector of the Country then spoke; the Chieftain of human beings asked them with great interest what they had there by way of meat and food. Then Andrew spoke, answering in his words, in front of the earls, and said to the All-Ruler Himself that in their warrior-company they only had "five loaves of barley bread for our travels, and two fishes. What can that do for this crowd?"

The mighty Christ spoke to him, God's good Son, and ordered that the crowd be divided up and separated, and that the multitude of earls should sit down on the ground, the enormous throng, on the

---

[126] The author seems anxious to provide reasons to excuse nobles asking for bread. The scriptural reason is merely that the crowd has come a great distance.

[127] *uuikeon* 'homes, village, settlement' borrowed from the Latin *vicus*. Presumably what is meant is the cluster of farmers' and tradesmen's homes located near the foot of a hill-fort.

green grass. Then the Best of those born spoke to His followers and told them to go and bring out the bread and the fishes. The people waited quietly; the enormous company of warriors sat. At the same time the Chieftain of Mankind, the holy King of Heaven, hallowed the food by His own power, broke it with His hands, gave it out to His followers, and told them to bring it to the people and divide it among them. They obeyed their Chieftain's order, and to everyone gladly brought His gift, His holy help. It grew between their hands[128]—there was food for every single person! The great crowd came alive with pleasure, the people who had come together there from far and wide had happily eaten their fill!

Then Christ the Ruler told His followers to go and see to it carefully that none of the leftovers were lost. He ordered them to collect them once the crowd of mankind had eaten their fill. There was such food, bread, left over there, that they collected twelve full baskets. That was a great sign, a great act of God's power, since the number of men, the number of people gathered there, not counting women and children, was five thousand!

All those people understood in their feelings that they had a mighty Lord. They praised the Heaven-King, they said that never would a wiser wizard[129] ever come to this light who would have more power with God here in the middle world or a more sincere mind. Everyone was saying that He was worthy of all wealth, that He should possess the kingdom of earth, the broad earth's world-throne! "After all, He has such wisdom, such great power with God."

The men all thought it would be good to elevate Him to the highest ruling position, to choose Him to be king. That was something not at all worthy of Christ, since He had worked the

---

[128] *It undar iro handun uuohs.* Scripture says nothing specific about how or where the multiplication of the loaves and fishes took place. This charming addition by the author turns the scene into magic!

[129] *uuisaro uuarsago* 'wiser truthsayer, wiser soothsayer, wiser wizard'. In view of the beautifully magic depiction of the miracle, it seems to me that 'prophet' is inadequate as a translation for the *Heliand's* magic-working *uuarsago*. It is misleading to take the very word (in its Greco-Latin form) which the poet is attempting to transfer from a Hebrew to a Germanic context, and to translate the Germanic word into English by its Hebrew equivalent, rather than seeking a Germanic one.

kingdom of this world, earth and heaven up above, into being by His own power,[130] and had afterwards preserved the earth and its population (though some people did not believe this—angry enemies), so that everything is already under His rule: the power of kingdoms and of [the] empire,[131] the assembly of all mankind! Because of this the holy Chieftain did not want to be raised to any lordship by the speech of human beings nor to the name of King of the World. He also did not want to start any further verbal strife with those people, and so He moved on to where He wanted to go, up into the mountains. The Son of God fled the overheated, presumptuous talk, and told His followers to sail across a sea, telling them where they were to go to meet Him.

Song 35

The mighty Child of God and good Peter
walk on water.

The people departed for places all over the country, the great crowd scattered, since their Lord, the most powerful Person, the Ruler, had decided to go up into the mountains.

There on the shore by the water Christ's warrior-companions, the twelve whom He Himself had chosen, assembled out of their good loyalty. Nor did they have any doubt—they would gladly sail over the

---

[130] The passage uses the same verb as in the changing of the water into wine at Cana. Here the verb *giuuarhte* 'worked' is used to describe the act of creation (as opposed to transformation) by combining it with 'into being'. The description of God as 'working the world into being' makes the whole world into an act of God's magic!

[131] Though 'kingdoms' is plural and invites the plural 'empires', the *Heliand* deliberately uses the singular and speaks only of one *kesurdom* 'empire'. This entire passage once again seems to represent a delicately pointed protest against human authorities (those of the Holy Roman Empire) attempting by their words and decisions to make the kingdom of Christ into something awarded by their human authority to Him, an unjustifiable attempt to make their political actions His.

As in his description of the Incarnation as being entirely of the Spirit, the author's concept of the kingdom of God is also completely spiritual.

sea in God's service. They let the high-horned ship cut through the swift current, the bright waves and the clear water. The light of day departed, the sun went to its rest. Night wrapped the seafarers in fog. The earls daringly kept on sailing over the waters. The fourth hour of the night had come—Christ the Helper was guarding the wave-riders—and the wind began to blow powerfully. A great storm arose, the waves of the sea roared against the bow stempost! The men fought to steer the boat into the wind—their minds were in panic, their emotions filled with worries. The lake-sailors began to think that they would never make land because of the violence of the storm.[132]

Then they saw the Ruler Christ Himself walking on the sea, traveling on foot. He did not sink into the seawater because His own power was holding Him up. The men's minds began to be fearful as well as their emotions—they were afraid that the great enemy might be doing this to them as a deception. Then their Chieftain spoke to them, the holy King of Heaven, and told them that He was their great and powerful Lord. "Now you should be steadfast and courageous, do not be fearfulminded, be brave! I am the Child of God, His own Son, and I will defend you against this sea and protect you from the ocean waves."

Then in reply one of the men called overboard to Him. It was that very worthy man, Peter the good—he did not want to suffer pain, to feel the water's power—"If You are the Ruler," he said, "as I think You are, good Lord, then tell me to walk to You across this seaway, dry across deep water, if You are my Chieftain, Protector of many people."

Then mighty Christ told him to come over to Him. Peter was ready immediately, he stepped down from the bow stempost and strode off, walking toward his Lord. The water held the man up by

---

[132] The author displays a great deal of nautical competence in this section. He knows about North-Sea fog (there is none in the biblical account), he accurately describes the high-horned, Viking-type ship and its sailing characteristics, he even knows about the danger of this type of vessel being swamped if its low sides come broadside to the waves, thus the apostles fight to keep the high bow stempost facing the oncoming waves.

the power of God until in his emotions he began to feel the fear of deep water as he watched the waves being driven by the wind. The waves wound around him, the high seas surrounded the man. Just at that moment he began to doubt in his mind. The water underneath him became soft and he sank inside a wave, he sank into the streaming sea! Very soon after that he called out quickly, asking earnestly that Christ rescue him, since he, His thane, was in distress and danger.[133]

The Chieftain of peoples caught him with His outstretched arms and asked him immediately why he doubted. "Listen—you can be confident and know for a fact that the power of the water in the sea, the lake's undercurrent, was not able to prevent you from walking as long as you had faith in Me firmly in your mind! Now I am going to help you, rescue you from this peril." Then the holy, all-mighty One took him by the hand and all at once clear water became solid under his feet, and they went together on foot, both of them, walking, until they climbed on board the boat from the sea. And then, by the bow stempost, the Best of those who have ever been born sat down. At that moment, the broad waters and waves became calm and the lake-sailors arrived at the shore. Together they made land, coming through the water's onslaught. They thanked the Ruler, they praised their Chieftain in words and in deeds, they fell at His feet and spoke many words of wisdom. They said that they knew very well that He was Himself the Son of the Chieftain and that He had authority over the middle world and that He was able to be a help to every human being's life-spirit—just as He had done for them out on the lake against the onslaught of the water.[134]

---

[133] Peter calls on Christ's feudal bond as Chieftain to a thane (liege-lord to a vassal, in the later Middle Ages) with its obligation on the lord to render help to his warrior-vassals. The thanes had done their part earlier in the scene when they showed loyalty by gathering at the shore and sailing according to orders.

[134] The author has carefully restructured this scene so as to place Christ in the center of a frame. The storm in scripture begins suddenly, the *Heliand* author introduces a calm before the storm to parallel the calm after it. Within the storm he has Jesus and Peter walking hand-in-hand back to the boat—something that he has beautifully placed in the middle of his compositon. See *The Saxon Savior*, Ch. 4.

Song 36

Christ the Ruler heals the daughter
of a woman from a foreign clan.

Christ the Ruler then set out away from the sea, the Son of the Chieftain, the only Child of God. Foreigners came to Him, they came to meet Him. From far away they had heard tell of His good works and that He said so much in wise words. He had a great desire to do something for such people so that they would always serve God gladly and so that many of the clans of mankind would be under obedience to heaven's King.

Then He crossed over the Jewish border and went to Fort Sidon. He had His warrior-companions with Him, faithful followers. There a woman of another nationality approached Him. She was of noble birth, of the Canaanite clan. She asked the mighty Chieftain, the holy One, that He give her His help. She said that harm had been done to her, that she was worried about her daughter. She said that her daughter had been seized by sickness. "Evil creatures have confused her, her death is at hand, the evil ones have taken away her mind. Now I beg You, my Lord Ruler, Son of David, that You free her from this sickness, mercifully ward off the evil injurers from such a poor girl."[135]

Christ the Ruler did not yet give her any answer. She went after Him, following Him determinedly, until she came to His feet and spoke to Him weeping. Christ's followers asked their Lord to be kind and generous in His attitude toward the woman. The Chieftain's Son had his answer ready and spoke to His warrior-companions. "I am to take care of Israel's hereditary clansmen first, to see that they have a proper attitude toward their Lord. They need

---

[135] The request for aid would have been familiar to any chieftain or lord in the audience. Any noble who was subject to an overlord had the right to ask that lord for help against any attacking enemy. By casting the evil creatures who cause disease as unjust aggressors, the author manages both to make any lord or chieftain present feel how helpless he would be in this case, and to show how great a feudal lord Christ is.

help! The people are lost; they have abandoned the Ruler's word; the warriors have doubts; people are driven by evil thoughts; nor do the earls of Israel want to listen to their Chieftain; warrior-heroes do not believe in their Lord—even though it is from here that help is to come for all the foreign peoples!"

Zealously the woman kept asking Christ the Ruler in her words to feel kind and generous toward her so that she would be able to continue to enjoy her child and to have her well again. Then the Lord spoke to her, the Great and Powerful. "No man has the right, no human being has the right, in order to do a good deed to take the bread away from his children, depriving them against their will, and let them suffer the horrible pangs of hunger in order to feed his dogs with it." "That is true, Ruler," she said; "what You are soothsaying with Your words is true; but listen, often inside the hall, underneath their lords' tables, puppies go around well-fed from the scraps that fall down from their lord's board."

At that, God's Child of Peace heard what the woman wanted, and spoke to her in His words. "It is well, woman, that you are of such good will! Great is your faith in the strength of God, the Chieftain of peoples. Everything will be done concerning your daughter's life just as you asked Me."

The girl was soon healed just as the holy One promised in words of unshakeable truth. The woman rejoiced that she would be able to continue to enjoy having her child. Christ the Healer had helped her, He had snatched the girl away from the power of the enemies, warded off the evil injurers.

The Ruler traveled on, the Best of those born, coming to another hill-fort, one very densely settled by the Jewish clan, southern people.[136] There, I have heard it told, He spoke to His warrior-

---

[136] Throughout the following passage the twelve apostle/warrior-companions, through the narrator, are made to speak of Jews as somewhat 'foreign' to them ("southern people"). The author thus cleverly lets the reader/hearer imply that the twelve must be something different: perhaps "northern people"--Saxons?! The author takes full advantage of this pericope's concentration on the question of identity--to Saxonize. Though the overt message of this passage in the *Heliand*, as in Scripture, is the identity of Christ, the covert message is the spiritual identity of the companions of Christ.

companions, the followers whom He in His goodness had picked out, men who gladly stayed with Him because of His wise speech. "I shall ask all of you, My followers, with words—what does this great population of Jewish people say about what man I am?" His friends happily answered Him, His followers. "The Jewish people, the earls, are not of one mind. Some say that You are Elijah, the wise soothsayer who was here long ago, a good man among these people. Some say that You are John, our Chieftain's dear messenger, who once immersed people in water. Every one of them says in their words that You are one of those noble men, the soothsayers, who have always taught these people here in words, and that you have come again to this light to instruct this people."

Then the ruling One, Christ, spoke again. "Who do you say that I am, my followers, good men of the people?" Simon Peter, not disconcerted, answered immediately, one man speaking for all—he was a man of great courage and careful thought, his Commander was very fond of him—.[137]

---

[137] This very important line introduces the two central songs of the *Heliand*. The author has marked this verse very distinctively by making it—a creation of his own—a run-on line between songs 36 and 37. This is the sole instance in the whole of the *Heliand* of two songs being so united. The endearing content of the verse emphasizes the role of Peter in a way designed to elicit from the Northern listener a more comfortable identification with the faithful soldier Peter and, concomitantly, with his recognition of Christ.

The author has created his usual triptych to emphasize the good thane's recognition: song 36 (second half) introduces the question and has Peter prepared to speak for all; song 37, Peter confesses the nature of Christ and is glorified with authority over souls; song 38, Christ is glorified on the mountain with Peter. The structure is very similar to that of the scene of Christ and Peter walking together on the water in song 35, which thus proleptically reinforces the effect of the togetherness of Peter and Christ in 36, 37, 38, the confession and transfiguration. It can be argued (and has been) which of the above instances constitutes the precise center (and thus intent) of the author. I prefer to see the three instances: the question, the confession, the transfiguration, as an ascending movement, in which Peter is seen as receiving first power, and then beatific vision in reward for his faith.

Song 37

Peter, the best of thanes, is given power
over Hel's gates.

"You are the true Son of the Ruler, the living God, who created this light, Christ, King forever! All of us, Your followers, want to say that You are God Himself, the Greatest of healers." His Lord answered him, "You are fortunate, Simon son of Jonah, you could not have become aware of that yourself, or decided on it in the thoughts of your heart, nor could any human being's tongue have told you that in words. No, the Ruler Himself, Father of all the sons of men, did this for you, so that you spoke so forthrightly and deeply with your Chieftain. You will receive a precious reward for this—you have clear faith in your Lord! Your convictions are like rock, you are as solid as hard stone—the sons of men will call you Saint Peter—on top of that rock my great hall will be built, the holy house of God, and there His family will happily gather.

"Hel's gates will not be able to hold out against your great strength.[138] I give you the heaven-kingdom's keys, so that, after Me, you will have all authority over the Christian people. All men's spirits[139] will come to you. You have great power: whomever[140] of the nobly-born you wish bound here on earth will have two things

---

[138] Another transformation of Scripture from passive to active. The biblical metaphor is visually and militarily difficult to comprehend: "the gates of hell will not prevail against you," since gates in the North are associated with defense and are not capable of offensive ability (though they are in the Old Testament). In one stroke the author both makes the metaphor intelligible and changes it from passive to active: the gates of hell will not be able to hold out against your offensive strength.

[139] *gestos* 'spirits' [Eng. cognate 'ghosts']. Presumably the souls of the dead is meant (not consciences). The author might have preferred to use *seolas* 'souls', but love of alliteration seems to have forced his hand in this line: *[kumad alle te thi]/ gumono gestos; thu haƀe grote giuuald.*

[140] The *Heliand* changes the neutral form of "whatever you shall bind . . ." (*so waz* and *quodcumque* in the literal *Tatian*) to "whomever you shall bind." Peter is thus given authority not to make and cancel laws and obligations that bind, but like a feudal chieftain he is visualized as having personal authority over men, to bind or free them.

done to him: heaven will be locked to him, and Hel will be open, the burning fire. Whomever you wish to unbind once again, taking the manacles off his hands,[141] for him heaven stands unlocked—eternal life in the greatest of worlds on God's green meadow.

"With this gift I wish to reward you for your faith, but I do not want you yet to tell these people, the great crowd, that I am mighty Christ, God's own Son. The Jewish earls are still to bind me, though innocent, to torture me at Jerusalem by inflicting astonishing pain with the weapon's edges; with the spear-point to see to it that I age no more, with its sharp edges to take away my life.[142] From death I will rise up to this light by our Chieftain's power on the third day."

At that, the best of thanes, Simon Peter, became very concerned, his mind was worried. The fighter spoke to the Lord in secret. "Never will God, the powerful Ruler, want You ever to suffer such great pain from these people, nor is there any need of it, holy Chieftain." Then his Lord, the great, powerful Christ, answered him—He was deeply fond of Peter. "What, now it is you, best of thanes, who are against my will!"[143] You know the ways of these peoples, the human race; you do not know the power of God which

---

[141] The author interprets the biblical power of legally "binding and loosing" more physically than in Scripture, envisioning Peter as having the authority to make prisoners of souls and/or to let them go free.

[142] This astonishing description of the passion and death is done in terms which, though they do not contradict the biblical crucifixion details, can be heard through Germanic ears much more easily as the death of a captured warrior-chieftain. Torture was done in the ninth century by cutting ribs open "with the weapon's edge" as is known from Viking exploits against the Saxons in England. Prisoners were often killed with the spear or lance, since that weapon was sacred to Woden, to whom prisoners were often "dedicated." The *Heliand* and its reader/listeners would have found the incident of the lance penetrating the side of the prisoner Christ particularly intelligible and moving to them.

This emotional insight in the *Heliand* may be the first instance of the curious fascination with the crucifixion lance which continued during the later Middle Ages, for example in *Parzifal*, even when the Germanic origin of the interest eventually had come to be forgotten.

[143] The author has made the tone of Christ's reply to the author's favorite character much milder and friendlier than the one in Scripture: "Get thee behind me, Satan!"

I am to carry out. I can tell you this much in truthful words, that here among the people there stand many of my warrior-companions who will not die, will depart from here, before they see heaven's light, God's kingdom."

Then, soon after that, from among His followers He picked Simon Peter, James, and John, the two men who were brothers, and with these warrior-companions set out to go up on a mountain on their own—the happy Child of God and the three thanes. The Chieftain of peoples, the Ruler of this world, wanted to show them many wonders and signs so that they would trust better that He was the Chieftain's Son, the holy King of Heaven.[144] They climbed along the mountain face over rock and slope until the warriors came to the place near the clouds which Christ the Ruler, King most powerful, had chosen, the place where He wanted, by His own power, to show His followers His divinity—bright-shining vision!

Song 38

On the mountaintop the Son of God gives off bright light.

As He bowed down to pray up there, His appearance and clothes became different. His cheeks became shining light, radiating like the bright sun. The Son of God was shining! His body gave off light, brilliant rays came shining out of the Ruler's Son. His clothes were as white as snow to look at. Then, after this, a wonderful thing was

---

[144] This sentence is significant since it is the author's insertion and again reveals his intent. His two verses provide an explicit motivation for the Transfiguration, and, for added strength, they are placed in the mind of Christ. In Luke's gospel (9:28-29), in the Latin *Tatian*, the motive for Christ's going up on the mountain with the three is simply *ut oraret* 'so He could pray.' The Transfiguration itself happens as an accident of His praying. In the *Heliand* the Transfiguration is quite deliberate and it is the prayer that is accidental to the situation. Christ transforms Himself 'by His own power', *that sie gitruodin thiu bet, that he selƀo was sunu drohtines* 'so that they (the warrior-companions) could trust better that He Himself was the Son of the Chieftain'.

seen there: Elijah and Moses came there to Christ, to exchange words with One so powerful! There was a beautiful conversation, good words among men, as God's Son willed to talk there with the famous men. It became so blissful up on the mountain—the bright light was shining, there was a magnificent garden there and the green meadow, it was like paradise![145]

Peter the steady-minded hero then spoke up, addressed his Lord and said to God's Son, "This is a good place to live, Christ All-Ruler, if You should decide that a house be built for You up here on the mountain, a magnificent one, and another for Moses, and a third for Elijah—this is the home of happiness, the most appealing thing anyone could have!"

Just as he said that word, the air parted in two,[146] a cloud of light shone with a glistening glow and wrapped the good men in brilliant beauty. Then from the cloud came the holy voice of God; and the voice said to the heroes that this was His Son, the One He loved most of all the living, "I love Him very much in my heart, You should listen to Him—follow Him gladly!"

Christ's followers could not stand up to the brilliance of the cloud and the Word of God, His mighty strength, and they fell forward—they did not think their life-spirits would live much longer. Then the Protector of the land went over to them, the Best of all healers touched them and told them not to be afraid of Him. "Nothing at all of the wonderful and amazing things you have seen here will hurt you." Then the men again came back to their senses, their courage restored, confidence in their chests. They saw God's

---

[145] *gard godlic endi groni uuang, paradise gelic*. As he did in the case of hell, the author combines the Hebrew and Germanic imaginative visions of paradise: the beautiful garden of the book of Genesis and the green meadows of Valhalla.

[146] This phrase is also used in the Christmas story as the angels speak to the horse-guards. The parting of the air to let the "other light" shine through to the middle world is used by the author to form a giant triptych of his whole gospel epic. The light of the other world shines through the clouds in the Resurrection scene as well, at the end of the epic. The Transfiguration is thus made into the center of the whole composition—and the familiar and welcome image of a beam of sunlight shining down through an opening in the clouds of Northern skies, is hallowed by the author, and made into an icon of divine intervention.

Child standing there alone; that other light though, heaven's, was hidden.

Then the holy Christ decided to go back down the mountain. He ordered His followers afterwards not to talk among the Jewish people about the sights they had seen "before I myself get up most gloriously from death, arise from My rest. After that you can go and recount it, tell the story throughout the middle world to many peoples—all over this wide world!"

Song 39

Christ pays the king's head-tax to an arrogant thane.

Christ the Ruler then went back in His power to Galileeland to visit His relatives and the home of His clan. There He spoke of many things in brilliant images, and the Child of God did not conceal from His happy warrior-companions the sorrowful tale, but rather told all His good followers openly how the Jewish people would subject Him to astounding torture. This made wise men very concerned, their minds became troubled, sorrowfulness encircled their hearts. They heard their Lord, the Ruler's Son, telling in words what He was willing to endure among the people of this clan.

Then ruling Christ, the man from Galilee, set out for the Jewish hill-fort community of Capharnaum. When they arrived, they found an arrogant king's thane[147] there among the people. He said that he was the fully empowered legate of the noble emperor Caesar.[148]

---

[147] The Latin *Tatian* (from Mt. 17:23) simply has *qui didragma accipiebant* 'those who were collecting the half-drachma [the half-shekel temple tax]'. The *Heliand* not only manages to change the plural to the singular, and common tax-collectors to a thane, but also changes the unfamiliar Jewish temple tax to an imperial tax paid to Caesar, one the Saxons could more familiarly loathe!

[148] *adalkesure* is difficult to express literally since it means both 'noble Caesar' and 'noble emperor'. In both cases it is clearly a reminder, once again, of the Carolingian empire, and enables Saxon identification with this scene to be more realistic.

After that he addressed Simon Peter and said that he had been sent for the purpose of reminding each and every man of the head-tax which everyone had to pay as revenue to the imperial court. "No man has the slightest hesitation about immediate payment of the tax in their choice jewels, except for your Master alone, who has not done it! My lord will not like that very much when it is made known at court to him—the noble emperor, Caesar!"

At that, Simon Peter went to tell it to his Lord. Ruling Christ was already aware of this in His mind—not a single word can be concealed from Him, He knows every man's thoughts. He then ordered His famous thane, Simon Peter, to cast a hook into the sea. "The very first fish that you catch," he said, "haul it out of the water and open its mouth. From between its jaws you will be able to remove golden coins. With them you will be able to satisfy the man who has come looking for us by paying My taxes and yours."[149]

He did not have to say another word or have to give any further orders. The good fisherman, Simon Peter, cast his hook into the waves of the sea and using both hands hauled up a fish out of the water. He opened up the mouth and from between the jaws took out golden coins. He did everything just as the Son of God had instructed him in words.

So it was revealed there through the Ruler's great power how every man should very willingly pay the debts and taxes he is assessed to his worldly lord, and do so gladly! No one should ignore his lord or think poorly of him in his feelings, but rather everyone should be kind and generous in his attitude toward his lord—and serve him humbly. In doing this, a man can carry out the will of God and also have the respect of his worldly lord.[150]

---

[149] More than in the Bible, this sentence brings Christ and Peter close together by associating them as together in adversity. The addition of "the man who has come looking for us" is the author's own delightful touch, which makes the incident seem curiously modern.

[150] The *Heliand* poet has here expressed what would become another ideal of the High Middle Ages: to achieve a harmony of godliness and worldliness, to deserve the respect of God and king, even while living in a less than perfect Christendom.

The author never encourages Saxon rebellion in the *Heliand*. In the Sermon on the Mount he eliminated all references to "I have come to bring a sword, to set

Song 40

Forgiving;
The young man with the great treasure-hoard.

This is what the holy Christ taught His good followers, "If any man does anything sinful against you, then take that warrior aside by yourself, and advise him of it in secret and set him right with words. If he proves himself to be unworthy of this by not listening to you, then take some other good man with you and criticize his grim handiwork to him—saying it in wise words. If after this he does not regret his harm-causing sin, then let other people, many of them, know about his wrongdoing. He will find it easy to begin to regret what he did, to rue it in his mind, when he hears about it from many warriors—people are aware of it, and censure him in words for his evil deed. If however he still will not deviate from his course, and scorns all these people, then let the man go, treat him like a heath-dweller,[151] let him be repulsive to you in your mind, avoid him in your emotions, unless it should happen that the kind and generous God, the lordly King of Heaven, as the Father of all the sons of men, again grants him help.

Then Peter, best of all thanes, asked his Commander, "How often, beloved Chieftain, should I forgive people who have done something vicious against me? Should I forgive the sin of their wicked behavior seven times before I wreak the vengeance their viciousness deserves?" The Guardian of the Country then answered

---

brother against brother . . ." His sympathies, however, remain with the Saxons, as is gently shown in the first half of this pericope: Christ and Peter being pursued by the emperor's tax-collecting thane! Instead of rebellion, he seems to see this hearers as being hounded like Christ and, like Peter, to be mystically associated with Christ. Then too, Saxon lords listening to the *Heliand* in their drinking halls might also not have been amused to find the singer disparaging taxes to one's "worldly lord!"

[151] *hedinen* 'some one who lives out on the heaths, a heathen'. Heath originally connoted wasteland, and later came to mean the scrub vegetation on it. A 'heath person' is therefore someone who lives away from the farming and fishing communities, and is deemed ignorant and backward. Christian urban prejudices made this the word for a 'nonbeliever' in Germanic, analogous to *pagan* in Romance speech.

him, God's Son speaking to the good thane, "I did not say anything to you about seven, as you are saying—as you just uttered with your mouth—but I will add more onto it: seven times seventy times you are to forgive someone's wicked sins! I want to teach you this in words of solid truth. After all, I gave you the great power to be the lordliest of my family of so many of mankind; therefore you are to be kind and generous[152] to people, be gracious to them!"

Then a young man who was there came up to Christ the Teacher[153] and asked Jesus Christ: "Good Master," he said, "what things should I do so that I bring myself to the heaven-kingdom?" The young man had attained all wealth and possessions and owned many a jewel-hoard, although he had a kind and generous heart in his chest. God's Child spoke to him. "What are you saying about 'good?' Not a single person is that, except the One who created the All—the world and its loveliness! If you have the desire of traveling to the light of God, you should obey the holy teaching, what is commanded in the old law—that you not kill, nor commit perjury, stay away from the adulterous bed, from giving lying testimony, from fighting and stealing. Do not be too stubborn-minded, do not hate or be hostile, do not commit armed robbery, avoid all envy. Be good to your parents, your father and mother, and be loving to your friends, gracious to those near you. Then you will enjoy yourself in the heavenly kingdom! If you wish to possess it, follow God's teachings."

The young man then answered, "I have done everything that You are now teaching me in wise words," he said, "and I have left none of it out, from my childhood." At that moment Christ began to look at

---

[152] *mildi* 'kind, generous'. The argument is that since Christ put Peter in a position of lordliness, he should then practice the virtue expected of a feudal lord: that he be *mildi* to his subjects.

[153] *lereand* '[the] teaching [One]'. This is another of the titles given to Christ in participial form. This form, as with the other examples, cannot have come from Latin where the noun *magister* is extremely common in the gospels for 'teacher', and the participial form, *magistrans*, is, to my knowledge, unevidenced. In addition, the noun *lero* 'teacher' exists in Old Saxon, but the author clearly prefers the participial form *lereand* for Christ. The roots of the usage must lie hidden in the oral tradition of the Germanic religious past.

him with His eyes. "There is still one thing missing of your good works. If you have the desire of serving your Lord all the way, you should take your treasure-hoard and your wealthy possessions and sell all of it, all your precious jewels, and order it to be distributed to poor people—after that you will have a hoard in heaven! Then come, bring yourself[154]—to Me; follow My footsteps and you will have peace ever after."

The words of Christ made this very young man deeply sorrowful. There was pain in his mind and an uneasiness in his heart. He had attained many jewels and possessions. He turned and went away from there. There was no lightness within his heart; in his feelings there was a heaviness.

Christ the All-Ruler looked after him and at that moment said to His followers who were there present that it was not easy for a man of wealth to come up to God's realm. "It is easier to get an elephant—even though it is immeasurably large—to slip gently through the eye of a needle—even though that is extremely narrow—than for the soul of the wealthy man to be able to get to heaven, a person whose mind and a person whose will were here completely turned to world-coin, and who had no awareness of the power of God."

Song 41

The story of the rich man and the beggar.

Simon Peter, the highly honored man, answered Him and asked the beloved Lord, "What will we receive as reward," he said, "as good repayment? To be Your followers, we abandoned property and inheritance, farmsteads and families, and chose You to be Lord and followed Your footsteps. What advantage will this bring to us, what lasting reward?" The Lord of People said to him, "When I come to

---

[154] A beautiful spiritual play on the verb of the young man's original question, how to get [gehalan] to heaven, answered by: by having gotten [gihalden] one's self (not one's possessions)—to Christ. The pun nicely suggests that attaining heaven now, and bringing one's de-secularized person to Christ, are equivalent.

sit," He said, "in great power, on that Awesome Day when I shall determine the verdicts for all earth peoples, you yourselves will be sitting with Your Chieftain, and you will be in charge of the cases. You will give verdicts for the noble Israel-folk in accordance with their deeds. That is how you will be honored then! Let me tell you this in soothsaying: whoever so acts in this world that he leaves his beloved family seat because of love of Me, he will receive a repayment here of ten times tenfold—if he does it with loyalty, with a clear mind.[155] And, beyond that, he will also have heaven's light, eternal life lying open to him."

After that the Best of those born began to speak in images. He said that once, a long time ago, there was a rich man among the people. "He had gathered together a great deal of wealth and buried treasures, and was always wearing gold and good clothes with beautiful ornamentation. He had great quantities of goods on his property. He sat down for a banquet meal every single day! He had a wonderful life sitting there in bliss on his benches! Now there was also a beggar-man there with a crippled body. Lazarus was his name. Every day he lay there, outside the front door, where he knew the rich man was inside with his guests enjoying a feast, seated in his hall at a banquet. The poor man always waited outside, feeling miserable. He was never allowed to come in, he was never able to persuade anyone to bring out to him some of the bread that fell down from the table under their feet. It never did him any good to be there, nothing good ever came to him from the important man whose house it was— except that the man's dogs went to the poor man and licked his body

---

[155] This is one of the clearest instances of what the author means by his continually repeated phrase 'with a clear mind' *mid hluttru hugi*. He sets the phrase in parallel to 'with loyalty' *mid treuuon*, and thus he paints an 'unclear mind' as a mind of uncertain or divided loyalties, one that is hedging its bets by avoiding a 'clear' commitment of feudal loyalty to its Christ-Chieftain and secretly remaining a thane to other religious chieftains. Christ is made here, in this sentence, to call on the Saxons as their feudal lord, and ask them for undivided, 'clear-minded' loyalty as a condition for their being enthroned with Him.

wounds as he lay there suffering hunger—not a bit of help ever came to him from the influential rich man.[156]

Then, I have heard it told, the poor man was informed powerfully of the decisions of the sovereign fates,[157] of his end-day, by a very severe sickness—he was to give up the comings and goings of men. God's angels received his life-spirit, and led it away from there so that they could place the poor man's soul on Abraham's lap. There, from now on, he would always be happy.

Then the decisions of fate[158] came also to the rich man, the fateful moment,[159] when he left this light behind. Evil creatures lowered his soul down to black Hel; they sank it into the inferno just as the enemy fiends desire, they buried him in their horrible homeland! From there he could look up and see where Abraham was, living in pleasure, and where Lazarus sat blissfully on his lap, receiving his shining reward for all his poverty. The rich man, lying hot in Hel, called up to Abraham from down there, "Father Abraham," he said, "I desperately need you to be kind and generous to me in your feelings—my limbs are in this blaze! Send Lazarus to me so that he can bring me some cold water in this inferno. I am burning alive, I am hot in this Hel! I need your help now, so that he can put out the fire on my tongue with his little finger. My tongue

---

[156] *rikeon manne* '[politically] powerful man'. The inclusion of the word *riki* may be to prevent the parable's being restricted in interpretation only to the very wealthy few of the warrior-nobility. Many thanes who might decline being described as *odag* 'rich', might still feel quite at home being described by the more ambiguous *riki* 'powerful'.

[157] *reganogiscapu* '[the] sovereign [ones'] doings, workings, decisions'. The Fates decide on and cause the moment of death; in the world of the *Heliand*, terminal illness does not cause death but merely informs the man that their decision has been made. This is the text of the London manuscript *C*.

[158] *uurdegiscapu* 'fate's workings, decisions, doings'. Putting such pre-Christian expressions into the mouth of Christ as He tells a story, makes them far less pagan and threatening, and serves to reassure the Saxons that, at the very least in story, there is a Christ-acknowledged place for fate and time in His worldview.

[159] See *The Saxon Savior*, p. 54, note 3.

has its sure sign now: horrible punishment for its malicious advice, its evil speeches[160]—I am now receiving my reward for all of it!"

Abraham answered him (he was the ancestral father), "Remember in your heart," he said, "what wealth you had in the world. All your joys, every happiness which was going to be given to you, you tore through! You used them up on earth! Lazarus endured pain in the light, he had many setbacks and sufferings in the world. Because of that he shall now possess wealth and live in luxury; you shall suffer the flames, the burning fire. Nor can any messenger for you be sent from here to Hel. The holy God has made it firmly so with his outstretched arms. No thane can travel there through the darkness which is so thick between us."

Then the earl spoke again to Abraham from hot Hel and asked for help. He asked that Abraham send Lazarus to the world of the comings and goings of men, "So that he can tell my brothers there how I am burning and suffering pain here. There are five of them among the people of our clan. I am afraid that they may also incur guilt and will also be sent here to me for punishment in this insatiable fire!"

Old father Abraham replied directly to him and said that they always had people of God in the land, Moses' commandments, and the words of the many soothsayers. "If they are willing to abide by them, they will never have to go inside Hel. They will never journey to that inferno, if they do what is commanded them by those who read the books for human instruction.[161] If they are unwilling to do this, they would also not listen to a man who rose right up from death. For as long as they are in the world let them choose for themselves in their feelings which of the two they think it is sweeter to attain, so that afterwards they will have evil or good."

---

[160] This concept continued into the twentieth century in popular Catholicism. The part of the body that had done the most sinning would do the most burning in hell!

[161] No doubt a reference to the missionary monks who came to Saxony from the British Isles and who were famous for traveling with their books in wagons. In the biblical account there is mention only of Moses and the prophets, not of book readers. The *Heliand* shows deep respect for learning and the learned.

Song 42

The story of the workers
who came late to the vineyard.

The Best person of all who have been born taught the people in light-filled words; the mighty Chieftain spoke to mankind in many images.

He said that a good man began in the morning to gather men. "He was the head of a household and promised the men very handsome pay as wages. He said that he would give every one of them a silver piece. Many men assembled at his vinyard, and he assigned them their work early in the morning. Some also arrived later in the morning, some came to work at noon, some came there at none[162] (that was the ninth hour of the long summer day); some came even later at the eleventh hour. Then evening arrived and the sun went to rest.

"Then this chieftain of earls commanded his supervisors that each of the men should be paid his wages for the hard work. He instructed them first to pay the people who had arrived last for work, and in his words ordered that the men who had arrived first, willing to work, should be given all their money at the end. These men were quite convinced that more pay would be given to them because of their hard work, but then everyone was given the same.

"That made all the men hostile and angry who had arrived first. 'We came here in the morning,' they said, 'and today we endured very much here: tasks of hard labor, hours of immeasurable heat, the sun's burning rays. Now you are giving us no more money than you give the others who were only here for a while working for you.' The head of the house had his answer ready, he said that he had never promised them any more pay than that for their work. 'Listen,' he

---

[162] In ecclesiastical usage, 3:00 PM, one of the monastic canonical hours; one of the ancient Roman hours. It may seem unusual to find a monastic expression in the *Heliand*, but it is consistent with the author's style: in the following sentence the Germanic equivalent (or, in this case, definition or explanation) is given in parallel.

said, 'I have the right[163] to give all of you equal pay in return for the value of your work.'"

Christ the Ruler, however, meant something more when He spoke to the human race in His words about the vineyard, and how the earls came to work there at different times: this is how the sons of mankind go from this world to the great light, to God's meadow. Some begin soon in their childhood to get themselves ready, they have the spirit of the chosen—good will! They avoid the affairs of the world and do not pursue its delights, and their bodies cannot lure them into immorality. They learn wisdom, God's law, they pay no attention to the will of the hostile evil ones, and they continue to behave thus while they are in the world, alive in this light, until the evening of their lifetimes comes to them. Then they set off on the road that leads upward. There all their hard work will be rewarded, paid back with good in God's kingdom. This is what is meant by the earls who started working hard in the vineyard early in the morning and who stayed at it continually until evening.

Some also came at midmorning, they were late and had wasted the morning hours of the workday. Many fools do this, crazy people. In their youth they enjoy chasing after many things—they learn disrespectful and nasty speech, and many dirty words—until their time of childhood passes away. After their youth, God's favor happily admonishes them in their hearts and they then turn for the better in words and works, and lead their lives in this manner until their years come to an end. They will be rewarded in God's kingdom for all their good works.

Some men abandon their wickedness, their serious sins, in midlife. They turn to happier things, and by God's power begin to do good works. They correct their malicious language and feel regret in their minds for their bitter actions. Help comes to them from God so that they can keep their faith as long as their lives last. With that faith they depart and receive their wages, the good reward from God—and there is no gift any better!

---

[163] *giuuald* 'authority, power'.

Some begin still later on, when they have become more aged, when their lifetimes are almost over. Then their evil deeds begin to be hateful to them in this world as God's teachings talk to them in their feelings. They become more kind and generous in their attitudes, they proceed on to the end in goodness, and receive repayment, the high kingdom of heaven, when they depart from here. They receive the same wages as the ones who came to work in the vineyard at none, at the ninth hour of the day.

Some get to be so very old that they do not want to correct their sins, but instead add on every possible evil to them—until their evening comes near, and their lifetimes and pleasures are worn out. Then they begin to dread the punishment, their sins put them in a worried mood, they think of the grim things they did for as long as they enjoyed youth. Nor are they able at this time to make up with other good deeds for the evil things they did so cruelly, and so they beat their breasts every day with both hands and weep bitter tears. They cry out to the holy Chieftain, the mighty One, to be kind and generous to them. Nor does He let their mood of despair last any longer, so merciful is He who rules over everything. He does not want a single earth-man denied his desire! The Ruler Himself gives them the holy kingdom of heaven and they receive His help ever after.

All of mankind are to receive honor there, even though they never come at the same time. The powerful Chieftain wants to reward all people—every single person—who embrace faith here. One heaven-kingdom is what He gives to all people, to all human beings, as their wages.

That is what mighty Christ meant, the best Person born, when He spoke in that image of how workmen came differently[164] to the vineyard, and yet each one received full wages from his lord. So also

---

[164] *mislico* 'unevenly, unequally, in an un-alike way'. The word opens the interpretation of the parable to an even broader reading.

shall the sons of men receive the same wages from God, the loveliest of rewards, even though some of them come late![165]

Song 43

Christ tells His loyal followers about His future torture and death; the curing of the blind men outside Fort Jericho.

He asked His good followers, the twelve, to come closer—they were the most loyal men on earth to Him—and told them one more time what hardships lay before Him. "And there can be no doubt about it," He said. He said that they should journey to Jerusalem, to the Jewish people. "There everything will come to pass, it will happen among that people, just as wise men said about Me long ago in their words. There, among that powerful people, warrior-heroes will sell Me to the leaders. My hands will be tied, My outstretched arms will be put in irons.[166] I will have to endure very much there; I will have to listen to many words of scorn and insult, mockery and threat. They will subject Me to unbelievable torture with the weapon's edge. They will take My life. I will rise up from death and come back to this light by the Chieftain's power, on the third day.

---

[165] By ending this song with this lovely and humane verse, the author betrays his concern for his Saxon late-comers. Not just old age, but also simple chronology has let others come earlier than they to be workers in Christianity's vineyard. Our harmony-loving poet excluded some of the most famous of the parables from his gospel--'the Good Samaritan' and 'the Prodigal Son,' possibly because they contain scenes of unresolved social and familial conflict. Here in the last song before the beginning of the Passion and Death narrative, he sets a tone of hope and reconciliation.

[166] *fadmos uuerdad mi thar gefastnod.* By using the ambiguous *gefastnod* 'chained, fastened' for the description of putting Christ's arms in irons, the author manages not only to depict Christ as a prisoner of war but also to suggest the Crucifixion at the same time.

"I did not come to these people so that the sons of men would have hard labor because of Me, that they would do service for Me. I will not ask them for that nor demand it, but rather I will be useful to them, I will humbly do service for them, and for all these people I will give my soul. With My life I will free mankind—the many people who have been waiting for so long for My help." Then He traveled onward—the Chieftain's Son had a determined mind and a happy heart—He wanted to go to Jerusalem to teach the Jewish people happiness. He was very well aware of their attitude of ill-will, grim hatred and deep hostility. The throng moved on toward hill-fort Jericho. God's Son was there in the midst of the crowd.

Two men were sitting there by the roadside; both were blind. They had great need to get better, to be healed by Heaven's Ruler, for they had long been without light, they had suffered a long time. The two men heard the masses of people coming by and soon asked with great curiosity what powerful person was the leader of that group of people; the two men fated to total blindness asked what man of the nobility was at their head. A warrior-hero answered them and said that Jesus Christ from Galileeland, the Best of all healers, was the leader and was traveling with His people. Both of the blind men became very joyful-minded when they learned that God's Son was among the crowd of people. They called out loudly with their words to the holy Christ, they begged Him to be willing to help them. "Chieftain, David's Son, be kind and generous to us in Your deeds, save us from this awful condition—just as You do for so many among the human clans! You are good to many people, You help and heal!"

Then the crowd of warriors began to fend the two off with words, saying that they should not yell so loudly at the ruling Christ. The blind men did not want to pay any attention to that, and instead continued to call out more and more loudly over the crowd of people. The Healer stood still. The Best person ever born commanded them to be brought to Him, conducted through the crowd. He spoke to them wisely and kindly in front of the crowd of people. "What help do you want to have from Me?" He said. They asked the holy One if He would open their eyes for them to this light so that they would be able to see the comings and goings of people, the radiant sunshine, and the bright, beautiful world.

The Ruler did it. He touched them with His hands and gave them His help. The eyes of both blind men were opened by the power of God so that they could recognize earth and sky, light and people. They gave praise to God and reverence to our Chieftain for being able to enjoy the light of day! They both set off with Him, following His footsteps. The favor they requested was granted to them, and the fame of the Ruler's deed was made known widely, to many men.

Song 44

The author explains the meaning
of the cure of the blind.

That was a powerful picture that was presented there where the blind men were sitting by the roadside. They were enduring suffering, they were deprived of the light. What that picture means, though, is this: they are the sons of men, all of mankind. The picture is of how mighty God Himself in the beginning made two, the couple, Adam and Eve. He gave them the road to up above, the kingdom of heaven; but then the hateful one, the enemy with his deceptions and deeds of wickedness, came near to them. He tricked them with sin into abandoning the eternally beautiful light. They were thrown out into a much worse place, this middle world. Here, in darkness, they toiled at hard human labor. They had won a journey into exile, they had lost wealth and happiness. They forgot God's kingdom, they were in service to the hateful sons of the enemies.[167] They were paid for their labor with fire in hot Hel. Human beings' minds were blind in this middle world, since they never recognized the mighty

---

[167] The misery of the human race is described not only with the traditional metaphor of exile, but also with a more military one of being in exile and having human behavior seen as forced labor for the enemy—not the enemy of the nation, but the enemies of the whole human race. This metaphor is, of course, not such a radical departure from Mediterranean biblical tradition as it may seem. Satan does mean legal adversary or enemy.

God, Heaven's Lord, who made them with His hands, worked them out according to His will. This world was then so pushed away, forced into darkness, into hard human toil, into death's valley, that they sat there by the Chieftain's road, lamenting, begging God's help.

The help could not come to them, however, until ruling God, the mighty Chieftain, would send His own Son to this middle world to unlock light to the sons of men and to open up eternal life to them so that they would be able to recognize the mighty All-Ruler, God the Powerful.

I can also tell you,[168] if you are willing to listen and think—so that you will recognize the Healer's power, how His coming was a help to many—what many things the Chieftain Himself meant by these actions, and why the great hill-fort in Judea built with walls is called Jericho. It is named after the moon, after that bright luminary which can never avoid its phases' times:[169] thus, every day, it is either waning or waxing. That is what human beings do in this world, the middle realm. The sons of mankind come and go in sequence, the old die, then the young who come after will wax older—until fate[170] takes them away.

---

[168] This is the first place where the author addresses the audience, marking the importance of this story for the meaning of the *Heliand*. He repeats his direct address again when he finishes the explanation of the story of the cure of the blind men and says, "Listen now. . . ." Since this sort of speaking to the audience in the epic tradition was omitted at the beginning of the *Heliand*, and first occurs at this moment, one is particularly touched at this point to have the author say *you* to the reader/hearer. Not only must the author feel that this incident depicts movingly the human condition; but, esthetically, light itself is what the author used to generate the *inclusio* or frame-structure of the whole story from the shining light of Christmas to the light of the Resurrection with the beaming light of the Transfiguration at the center. In addition, light occurs throughout the narrative, especially since the author favors using the word for 'light' for 'world'. What story in the whole gospel could have been more moving to him as he thought of himself and his Saxons—and his epic—than the scene of two by the roadside begging to be able to see 'the light'.

[169] *tidi* 'times' here also 'phases'. This is the strong pre-Christian element in the *Heliand* in its astronomical form. Time is irreversible, above divinities, the moon must go through its phases. It is curious that the plural is used not only here, but also at the wedding feast of Cana where Christ also is made to say 'my times have not yet come.'

[170] *uurd* 'fate, becoming'.

That is what God's Son meant, as the good One traveled on, leaving the hill-fort of Jericho. He meant that the blindness of human beings could never be cured so that they could see the bright infinitely beautiful light until He Himself took on human nature, flesh and body, here in this middle world. The sons of men became aware of this in this world. Those who previously, in punishment, had been sitting here in sin, deprived of sight, enduring the darkness, realized that the Healer had come to help these people. Christ, the Best of all kings, had come from heaven's kingdom! They were immediately able to recognize His footsteps.[171] Those men then called out so much to the mighty God that the Ruler felt kindly disposed because of it. But then the very serious sins which they themselves had committed held them off, prevented belief. Still, these sins could not hold off the two people from what they wanted, and so they called out loudly to the ruling God until He cured them; then they could see unending life, eternal light, open to them—and could journey on to the bright-shining home.

That is what the blind men signify who were calling out loudly to the Son of God there by Fort Jericho to grant them light in this life by a cure. Then, the great number of people who were fending them off with their words (those who were traveling along the road ahead and behind), they represent what wicked sins do to mankind in this middle world.

Listen now, to what the blind did once they were cured and could see the sunlight! They decided to set off together with their Chieftain, they followed His footsteps, and spoke many words of praise for the land's Herdsman! This the sons of men still do all over this wide world, once ruling Christ has enlightened them with His teachings and given eternal life to them, God's kingdom, the high

---

[171] This verse shows the complexity of the author's thought. In the actual story he has just related, the blind men have to ask who the leader of the throng is; they do not, in the manner of blind people, recognize His footsteps. This touching verse, therefore, is not just a moving allusion to how the blind "see," but also a deeply pertinent allusion to *Genesis* 3:8, where Adam and Eve, after they have sinned, without seeing Him, hear the sound of God's footsteps as He walks in the Garden in the cool of the evening.

heavenly light (and His help to reach it), to good men—to anyone whose actions show that he would like to follow His road!

Song 45

Christ enters Fort Jerusalem
and foretells its fate.

Then Christ the Rescuer, the holy One, came near to Jerusalem. Many people of good will there were glad to come and meet Him. They received Him with honor and they strewed the road before Him with their clothes and with plants—with bright flowers and with tree branches from the beautiful palms—covering the earth of the entire path that God's Son wanted to take to the famous hill-fort. The crowd of people surrounded Him happily, and in their joy they started singing[172] a song of praise. They thanked the Ruler that David's wise Son had Himself come there to their people. Then Christ the Good, the Ruler, looked at Jerusalem. The Best of men looked at the hill-fort's wall and at the dwellings of the Jews, the high-horned halls, and at God's house—the most beautiful of all shrines.

At that moment, inside Him His thoughts welled up against His heart,[173] the holy Child could not prevent Himself from weeping. Then in sadness He spoke many words of regret—His mind was in pain. "Woe to you, Jerusalem," He said, "that you truly do not know

---

[172] *ahof* lit. 'lifted up'. This verb, *ahebbian*, means to lift up one's voice in song, to begin to sing. It is significant that this is the same verb used in the first song of the *Heliand* in reference to the four evangelists. Their task from God was described as *that sea scoldin ahebbean helagaro stemnun godspell that guoda* 'that they should begin to sing, intone, the good God's spell with their voices.' It is of course also the very task the *Heliand's* author set himself.

[173] More prosaically: what He knew (about the future) came into conflict with what He loved.

the workings of fate which are going to happen to you in the future,[174] how you will be surrounded by a powerful army and besieged by cruel-minded men, the enemy forces. Then you will nevermore have peace or protection among men. Against you they will bring many spearpoints and swordblades, the words of war.[175] Your population will be devoured by the flames of the fire. They will devastate these villages, they will bring these high walls to the ground. Not a rock will stand upright, no stone on top of another, and these settlements around Jerusalem will become a wasteland of the Jewish people, because they do not recognize that their future[176] has come to them. Moreover, their minds are in doubt; they do not know that the Ruler's power is visiting them."

The Chieftain of human beings then set off with the crowd for the bright-shining hill-fort.[177] As soon as God's Son went inside Jerusalem with the throng of people, He was walking with His

---

[174] In this powerful verse and in the following discourse Christ acts both as soothsayer and as God, aware of what fate will do. The word for fate used here, *wurd*, is reinforced by a double repetition of its verb of origin, *uuerden* 'to become, to happen', in the verse, giving the utterance a strong ritual character. The adverb *noh* 'yet, still' is also repeated, giving it a strength that indicates that this fate is coming unalterably toward the city. . . . *thea uurdegiskefti, the thi noh giuuerden sculun, huo thu noh uuirdis behabd heries craftu* . . . '. . . the workings of fate, which are going to happen to you in the future, how you will be surrounded by a powerful army . . .'

[175] *orlegas uuord* 'words of war, fate'. This is a particularly sinister expression, since the word for war used here, *orleg* or *orlag*, also means 'fate' or 'doom'. Combined with the author's brilliant touch suggesting that the spearpoints and swordblades are the "words" of war, the author presents us with the remarkable poetic realization that even warfare has 'magic' words, performative words, which when properly 'spoken,' produce, by themselves, their fatal effect.

[176] *tidi touuardes* lit. 'future times'. This is a more fate-oriented description than in the New Testament, where Jerusalem is described as being unaware of 'her time' or of 'the time of her visitation'. The plural, *tidi* 'times', is also the form used in the *Heliand* when Christ replied to His mother at the wedding feast of Cana, 'my times have not yet come'. Jerusalem has missed her future.

[177] There is no mention of the jackass or the foal of the donkey on which Jesus rides into Jerusalem in the New Testament. Presumably what was a gentle allusion to Jewish kingship in Scripture would have meant something altogether different to Saxon warriors' sense of humor.

warrior-companions, the greatest of all songs began; loud voices began singing holy words as many people praised the country's Guardian, the Best person ever born. The fort was in an uproar; its people began to be afraid and soon asked who that was who was coming there with the people, with that mighty throng. Someone answered them and said that it was Jesus Christ from Galileeland, the Rescuer from Fort Nazareth, the wise soothsayer, who was coming to help the people.

It made the Jews who had been hostile to Him before think unkind thoughts and feel painful emotions to see that the people were singing so many songs of praise to Him, glorifying their Chieftain. In a furious mood they went to have words with the ruling Christ. They asked Him to tell His warrior-companions to be silent and not to let the people praise Him so much with their words. "It is loathsome to these people," they said, "to the hill-fort people." The Son of God replied, "If you interfere with them," He said, "not permitting the sons of men ever to glorify the Ruler's power here with their words, then the hard rocks and solid boulders would shout it out before the people! It could never be acceptable that His praise is not to be spoken anywhere in this world."

Then He went into the holy shrine, the house of God. There He found many Jews, a different kind of people, gathered—they had chosen this site as their business place. They were buying and selling all manner of things. Money-lenders were sitting inside the shrine; every day they had their loan-money ready to give. That was completely repulsive to God's Son. He drove them out of there, away from the shrine. He said it would be a much better thing for the sons of Israel to come there to pray, "To ask for help in My house, to ask that the victorious Chieftain take away their sins rather than to come here to a legal assembly[178] of thieves, the perverted

---

[178] *thingstedi* 'assembly place'. The humor here is that the Germanic 'thing' is the official law-making assembly, the opposite of any criminal assembly.

people who practice usury, plain injustice![179] You Jewish people never show any respect for the house of God!"

Thus the powerful Chieftain cleaned out the shrine, the holy house. There He was a help to many of mankind who had heard tell of His great power far away and had come traveling over long roads. Many of the weak and crippled were healed at the shrine, many of those whose hands were hurt and the blind were cured. God's Son did that for the people who wished it, since everything that concerns these peoples' lives and lands is under His authority.

Song 46

Christ praises the small gift to the shrine of the woman fated to poverty; He advises thanes to pay the emperor's taxes.

He stood there in front of the shrine, Christ the Ruler, the beloved Guardian of the country, and noted the mindset and will of the people. He saw many people bringing jewels to that famous house, making donations of silken cloths and precious ornaments. Christ the Chieftain watched all of that wisely.

Then a widow also came, a woman fated to poverty. She went to the altar and put two bronze coins in the treasury. She was a person of uncomplicated mind, of good will. At that, the ruling Christ spoke to His followers and said that she had brought a much

---

[179] Medieval Christian law and custom forbade Christians from taking interest on loans (thus, as a side effect, making borrowing money difficult). Jews, however, were legitimately able to practice usury (to take interest on a loan), and were thus both needed by Christians and, as is obvious from the text, despised by them—for a practice that a Christian normally initiated!

In the biblical accounts of this scene in the Temple (see, for example, *Mt.* 21: 12-17) Christ's anger is over buying and selling in the Temple, but there is no specific mention of usury, nor any description of the practice as *unreht enfald* 'plain injustice'. The *Heliand* author has brought the incident, by introducing the condemnation of usury, into close contact with the actual, if contorted, feelings of his own times. [Usury in modern usage, of course, has come to mean charging excessive interest.]

greater gift than any other son of mankind. "Whenever people of property bring presents here, many jewel-hoards, they leave more at home of the wealth they have won. This woman did not do that. She gave to this altar all the wealth she had won; she left no other wealth home in her house. Her gift is worth more to the Ruler because she did it with such a will for this house of God! For this she will be repaid with the very long-lasting reward—for having such faith!"

So I have heard it told Christ the Ruler, Chieftain of Mankind, taught wisdom with words every day at the shrine. People stood around, the great Jewish people, they listened to the good and sweet words He spoke. Some of the men in the crowd were very fortunate in that the words started to stay in their feelings. They learned the teachings which the country's Guardian, the Chieftain's Son, taught entirely by images.

To some again the Ruler's message, the teachings of Christ, were very loathsome. All of those who were highest in the leadership, the princes of the people, were opposed in their minds to those teachings. They thought out verbal traps for Him, and they brought in a troublemaker from the leading man, a thane of Herod, to help them. He was present, standing there with evil intent. He wanted to overhear their conversation to see if his people could capture Christ and put Him in chains and leg and arm irons—the sinless One!

Then he and his bitter-minded warrior-companions, evil adversaries, strode up to Christ to speak words with God's Son.[180] "Well now," they said, "You are a law-speaker. You teach all peoples a great deal of truth; and for You it is something unworthy to conceal anything from a man because of his authority. On the contrary, You always say what is right; and You lead the warrior-company of mankind along God's road by Your teachings—not a person among

---

[180] The Scribes and Pharisees are remade into Germanic warriors challenging Christ to combat. The combat is clearly kept verbal, however; there is no attempt to put a sword into Christ's hands. The author manages to make rabbinic disputations about the application of the law into Germanic challenges, but does not alter the subject matter of the disputation.

the people can find anything to blame You with. Now we will question You."

"Mighty Commander, what right does the emperor of Rome have to look for tax payments to himself from this clan here and to determine every year how much money we are to pay as a head-tax?[181] Say what You think about this, what is Your attitude? Is it right or not? Advise Your fellow countrymen well, we need Your teaching." They wanted Him to say no to it, but He was well able to recognize their bad faith. "Why are you pretending to tell the truth," He said, "and tempting Me so boldly? It will do you no good, you deceivers, to try to catch Me through deception!"

He asked that the coins be brought out in order to look at them, "the ones you owe for that payment." Jews took out a silver piece. Many looked and saw how it was minted. In the middle of the front face was the emperor's image—that they recognized well!—, the picture of their lord's head.

Then the holy Christ questioned them about who the person was of whom the stamped image had been made. They said that it was the emperor of the world from Fort Rome, "who has authority on earth over this entire realm." "Then I will tell you Myself in all truth," He said, "that you give him what is his—give the world-lord his money; and give the ruling God what is His—and that should be your souls, your human spirits!"

The Jews' intentions were ruined by what He said. The wicked troublemakers could not win with words (that was what they had wanted—to entrap Him), because God's Child of Peace defended Himself against their hostile attacks, and, in return, told them the

---

[181] This is the third time that a head-tax has been introduced into the *Heliand*, the first in song 5 where Joseph and Mary face the carefully writing tax scribes on their way to Bethlehem, the second in song 39, where Peter and Christ are accosted by the arrogant tax collector. The author clearly shows his sympathy for the taxed, but again, as in song 46, advises payment of the head-tax.

It seems clear from this repetition that some Carolingian head-tax is in the background—one liable to an annual tax hike! It may also be significant in this regard that in this song, as in song 39, there is no mention of Jewish religious authorities, and the questioners are kept secular.

truth-spell, even though they were not so fortunate as to be able to accept it so that it could be of benefit to them.

Song 47

Christ the Champion protects the life-spirit
of the woman caught in adultery.

They would not leave off, however, and instead they ordered a woman brought out in front of the people. She had done something wrong, a crime pure and simple—the woman had been caught in adultery. She was under the death penalty, the sons of men were to take away her life-spirit and end her days. That is what was written in their law.

Those bold and twisted people began to ask Him with their words what they should do with this woman, whether they should torture her to death or leave her alive—what would His verdict be after such a deed? "You are aware," they said, "that Moses commanded these many people in truthful words, that any woman found in adultery forfeits her life, and that people are to throw heavy stones at her with their hands. Now you can see her standing here caught in sin—say what You want done!" These opponents of His wanted to trap Him in His words. If He said that they should let her live her life in peace, then the Jewish people would say that He was contradicting their ancestral law, the law of the land. If He told them to take the young woman's life right there before the people, then they would say that He did not have the kind and generous attitude of heart which God's Son should have. In this way they intended to punish holy Christ for His words, no matter which of the two verdicts He pronounced before the people.

Christ the Chieftain knew very well their attitudes and feelings, their hostile intentions. He spoke then to the people, to all the earls. "Whoever of you is without evil sin," He said, "you go up to her yourself, and you be the first earl to throw a stone at her with your hands." The Jews stood there silently in thought. Not a single thane could think of any reply to what Christ had said. Each man was thinking of his own sins, his evil-mindedness. None of them was so sure of himself that after these words he would dare throw a stone at the woman. They left her standing alone there inside, and the fiercely hostile Jews went out of there, one after the other, until there was not a single one of the enemy left who wanted to take away the woman's life-spirit and bring an end to her days.

Then I heard it told that God's Peace-Child, the Best of all persons, asked her, "Where did the Jewish people go," He said, "your opponents who accused you here to Me? Did those people who wanted to torture you horribly and take your life do any harm or injury to you today?" The woman spoke to Him in reply and said that because of the Rescuer's help no one had done any harm to her to repay her for her crime. Then Christ the Ruler, Chieftain of human beings, spoke again. "I too will not hurt you in any way," He said, "leave here hale and well, take care after this in your mind not to become sinful in this way ever again."

The holy Son of God had helped her, He protected her life-spirit.[182] The Jewish people stood there as evilly determined as they had been at the beginning, viciously pondering how to wage verbal war against God's Peace-Child.

The people were divided in two over their faith. The little people were much gladder to obey the word of God's Son (they strove for right much more than the powerful people did), they held

---

[182] In this song Christ has acted as a Germanic "champion," defending an accused person by taking up cause in combat. This method of reaching a verdict, or of settling a battle before the armies attacked each other, was a part of ancient Germanic custom and law. Charlemagne himself used it whenever he could not determine which of two parties was telling the truth in a legal case.

Furthermore the author has expressed the dishonorableness of the Pharisees in Germanic terms. Though it is one person whom the authorities have brought in to act as troublemaker and to challenge Christ (see previous song), when he advances on Christ for honorable single-man combat, the troublemaker comes with his warrior-companions. Christ never uses or is made to mention His, but wins the unfair fight anyway, and the *fiundes folk* 'enemy forces' withdraw. In the High Middle Ages this scene might have been read with delight as Christ the word-wise Warrior who rescued the damsel in distress (albeit brought on by herself)!

Him for their Lord, even for King of Heaven, and were glad to follow Him.[183]

Then God's Son went inside the shrine. A great number of people, an enormous throng, surrounded Him. He stood in the middle of the crowd and taught the people with words of light in a loud voice. Many a thane stood in silence, they were all ears, as He invited the people, anyone there might be suffering from thirst, "Let him come every day to Me to drink," He said, "from the sweetwater spring! I can tell you, whoever here among the people, sons of men, firmly believes in Me, from him will flow—from his body—a living flood, running water welling up powerfully, from him will come the waters of life! These words will come true, they will be done for any person here who believes in Me!"

What the ruling Christ, high King of Heaven, meant by the water was the Holy Spirit, He meant how the sons of men were to receive the Spirit, light and insight, and life forever, the high kingdom of heaven and the graciousness of God.

Song 48

Dissension over Christ's teaching; Martha and Mary send for Him; Thomas accepts a warrior's fate.

Then the people began to quarrel over the teachings and words of Christ. Arrogant Jews stood there, their feelings were running high, they were saying very insulting things and holding Him up to ridicule. They said that they could hear quite well that evil little creatures, hateful things, were speaking out of His mouth, "since He teaches evil," they said, "with every word!" However there were other people

---

[183] This paragraph is an insertion by the author. It serves as a justification for the presence of both very positive and very negative characterizations of the Jews in the text. On the other hand, the fact that the division is explained in sociological terms rather than moral ones suggests very strongly that this paragraph is intended as comment on the success and lack of success of the missionary effort in Saxony.

who said, "How dare you criticize the Teacher! Life's words are what come powerfully from His mouth! He does many wonderful things in this world, and those things are not done by the power of the hateful enemies, otherwise they would never be of such benefit; on the contrary, they come directly from God the All-Ruler, from His power! You can recognize that easily by His true words that He has authority over all the earth."

At that, the opponents wanted to capture Him there on the spot and throw stones at Him—if they had not been afraid of the many men there and been intimidated by the crowd of people. Then God's Peace-Child spoke. "I have shown you so much good from God Himself," He said, "in words and in works. Now you want to punish Me here, throw stones at Me and take away my life, because you are hard-hearted." Then the people spoke back to Him, the hostile opponents, "we are not doing it because of Your works," they said, "[it is not because of them] that we wish to end Your days, but rather we are doing it because of Your words, because You say such unholy things, because You praise Yourself so, and say such evil that You pronounce in front of these Jews that You are God Himself, the mighty Chieftain!—and You are only a man like us who comes from this clan!"

Christ the All-Ruler did not want to listen any longer to the Jews' reprimands and hostility, and so He went away from the shrine across the Jordan River.[184] He had His followers with Him, His fortunate warrior-companions, the ones who were always glad to live with Him. He went to other people and there the Chieftain did as He was accustomed—He taught the people who wanted to believe in His holy words. They always do good for anyone who accepts them into his feelings!

Then, I have heard it told, messengers came there to Christ from Bethany. They told God's Son that they had been sent there with a message by the women, Mary and Martha, the lovely maidens, very

---

[184] The author almost seems to assume that the temple is close to the river. This may either be a simple mistake or an indication that perhaps Saxon temples were located near rivers. We know that the Irminsul which Charlemagne destroyed was near the headwaters of the Lippe.

beautiful women. He knew both of them. They were two sisters for whom He had feelings of love before because of their attitude of kindness and good will. They were now truly sending for Him from Bethany, because their brother Lazarus was bedfast and they did not think that he would live. They asked holy Christ the All-Ruler to come and help them.[185]

As soon as He heard them speak about the man who was so sick, He answered immediately and said that Lazarus's sickness would not bring him to die. "The glory of the Chieftain will be accomplished there instead," He said, "the sickness will not put him in any kind of danger." The Chieftain's Son stayed there two nights and days.

The time had come nearer when He would go back to Jerusalem to show them the power He had. The Chieftain's Son told His warrior-companions that He wanted to go back over the Jordan to the Jewish people. His followers immediately responded to him, "Why are you so keen, my Lord," they said, "to go back there? It was not so long ago that they intended to punish You for Your words—they wanted to throw heavy stones at You. Now You are determined to travel back to those people where You have plenty of enemies—arrogant earls looking for a fight!"

Then one of the twelve (Thomas was his name, he was an excellent man, the Chieftain's devoted thane) said, "We should not criticize His action or obstruct His will in this matter, we should continue on, stay with Him, and suffer with our Commander. That is what a thane chooses: to stand fast together with his lord, to die with him at the moment of doom. Let us all do it therefore, follow His road and not let our life-spirits be of any worth to us compared to His—alongside His people, let us die with Him, our Chieftain![186]

---

[185] This is a change from Scripture. The author turns the request into an appeal from the sisters for Christ to help *them*. In the New Testament the emphasis is on Christ's love for Lazarus, and the sisters' message is correspondingly simpler and more direct: *quem amas infirmatur* 'the man whom you love is sick' Jn. 11:3 (*Tatian*).

[186] This very important speech by Thomas introduces the entire recasting of the Passion and Death in Germanic 'last-stand' military terms. The *Heliand* has expanded the brief laconic statement of Thomas given in Scripture in Jn. 11:16: "Thomas, called the Twin, said to his fellow disciples, 'Let us go, that we may die with Him'." The fact that all the disciples will run away except John does not complicate matters for the

Then our decison and doom will live on after us, a good word among men!" And so the followers of Christ, nobly born earls, came to a simple decision—to their Lord's delight![187]

Then holy Christ told His warrior-companions that Lazarus had fallen asleep from the sickness. "He has given up this light, he is asleep on his sickbed. Now we will go on the journey and awaken him so that he can see this world again, see the light as a living being. Then, when that is over, your faith will be stronger from then on.

God's good Son set off from there, crossing over the river, until He and His followers, the Son of the Chieftain Himself and His warrior-companions, came to Bethany where the two sisters, Mary and Martha sat in painful mourning. Many Jewish people from Jerusalem had gathered there. They wanted to console the women with words so that they would not lament the loss of Lazarus to such an early death. As soon as the Guardian of the Country approached their property, His arrival was announced—God's Son, who was so strong, was outside the hill-fort. The two women felt great happiness when they learned that the Ruler, God's Child of Peace, had come to them.

Song 49

**By decree of holy fate, God's Son is able
to raise Lazarus from the grave.**

The women had the greatest of pleasures, the coming of the Chieftain and hearing Christ's words. Lamenting and mourning, Martha went to exchange words with the mighty One and spoke to the Ruler with grieved mind. "If You, my Lord," she said, "had been nearer to me, Best of rescuers, it would not have been necessary, good Healer, for me to suffer such bitter pain and suffering in my heart. My

---

author, for Germanic epics may have used disloyalty frequently as the tragic flaw of a thane as we see in *Beowulf*. Cf. *The Saxon Savior*, pp. 97-103.

[187] Another plea to Saxon warriors, no doubt, to follow Christ without wavering.

brother Lazarus would not now be dead, gone from this light, he would still be able to be alive, filled with life-spirit! However, my Lord, I clearly believe in You, Best of teachers—whatever You wish to ask of the bright-shining Chieftain, He will give You immediately, God All-mighty will honor Your request!"[188] Christ the Ruler said in answer to the woman, "Do not let this darken your spirits within you. I can tell you truthfully that there is no doubt that your brother, by divine command, by the power of the Chieftain, will rise up from death—in his body." "I believe all this," she said, "that it will come to pass when this world ends and the Great Day comes over mankind, he will rise up from the ground on doomsday[189] when everyone of the human clan will be revived from death and rise up from their rest by the power of God." Then the powerful, all-mighty Christ said to the women plainly that He was Himself the Chieftain's Son, both the life and the light of that rising up of the sons of men.[190] "Never will anyone die or lose his life who believes in Me. Even if human beings bury him down deep and cover him over with earth, he is none the more dead because of that: the body is buried, the life-spirit is preserved, the soul is hale and well!"

The woman answered Him straight way with her words. "I believe," she said, "that You are the true Christ, God's Son. It can be recognized clearly and known from Your words that You, by decree of holy fate,[191] have power over heaven and earth!"

------

[188] The staccato tone created by short phrases and the constant insertion of honorifics is the *Heliand* author's way of creating a sense of desperate pleading which will not hesitate to engage some flattery in its cause. It also suggests the speech of someone unable to speak except in short bursts, someone sobbing.

[189] *domes daga* 'judgment day'.

[190] The author has expanded the simple biblical reply of Christ to Martha, "I am the resurrection," to include his favorite images, life and light. He uses Christ as a causal nexus rather than an identity. Instead of 'I am the resurrection and the life' the *Heliand* says 'I am the life-force that causes resurrection and the light (world) to then come.'

[191] *thurh thiu helagon giscapu.* In her enthusiasm Martha seems to have slipped back into Germanic religion, saying that Christ rules thanks to the power of fate. This phrase can be interpreted as showing that the *Heliand* author really is a pagan, and, in his heart of hearts and in this work, still accepts the fundamental orientation of the old religion and believes in fate's superiority to Christ. It can also be seen

Then, I have heard it told, Mary, the other woman, came, deeply distressed. Many of the Jewish people were walking after her. In her sorrow she told God's Son what was troubling her, what pain was in her heart. She groaned as she lamented the loss of Lazarus, that beloved man, she moaned and wept until the emotions of God's Son were moved and hot tears welled up as He cried.[192] Then He spoke to the women and told them to lead Him to where Lazarus was buried in the ground. There was a stone on top of the grave, a hard rock cover.[193]

The holy Christ ordered the stone removed so that He could see the body and look at the corpse. Then Martha, despite the presence of the crowd, could not avoid speaking her mind to the Mighty One. "My good Lord," she said, "if they take the stone off and remove it, I fear that a smell will come from there, an unsweet odor. I can tell you this in all truth and with no doubt because he has now been buried in the earth in that grave for four days and nights!" In answer

---

that the phrase 'by decree of holy fate' is in the niche in the epic that is almost always occupied by the phrase 'by the power of God' *thurh godes craft* or 'by His own power' *thurh is selbes craft*. 'By decree of holy fate' could also be interpreted as an unintentional slip back into the older Germanic religious language. The fact that it is inconsistent with the author's more common phrase 'by the power of God' would, therefore, not be anything significant.

I feel it is significant and not accidental. The author has intentionally inserted the word 'holy' from his Christian vocabulary and combined it with 'fate' to take the place of the expression 'the power of God.' It is his ultimate, if uneasy, synthesis: the 'fate' of the Saxons and the 'power of God, the Holy Spirit' (incarnate in Christ in the *Heliand*!) are one and the same. In Germanic terms: when one sees Christ, one is seeing fate. 'Fate' can thus be called, as here, 'holy fate,' and eventually be identified with the will of [the Christian] God. This marriage of concepts has a reciprocal effect. It tends to make 'fate' more 'holy,' and it also tends to make 'the will of God' fatal, more of an impersonal, inevitable force in the *Heliand*. See *The Saxon Savior*, pp. 33-53.

[192] In the biblical account, the crowd is amazed that Jesus is crying and say 'see how much He loved him' (Jn. 11) rather than Jesus crying out of emotional sympathy with Mary. The *Heliand* author must have felt that weeping for another man would have been considered inappropriate by the Saxon warriors.

[193] This is a Germanic grave, therefore, a burial in the earth. In the biblical account, Lazarus, like Christ, is not buried but placed in a cave-like tomb, with a vertical stone to close the entrance.

the Ruler said to the women, "Listen, did I not truly tell you before," He said, "if you believe, it will not be long before you will recognize the Chieftain's power here, the mighty strength of God?"

Then many people stepped forward and lifted up the hard stone. The holy Christ looked upward with His eyes and gave thanks to Him who made this world. "Victorious Chieftain,"[194] He said, "You are attentive to My words, I know that You are so always, but I am speaking to You in the presence of this great number of Jewish people so that they will truthfully know that you sent me into the world to teach them."

Then He called to Lazarus in a very strong voice, and told him to stand up and walk from his grave. The spirit was on its way, returning to the body! Lazarus's limbs began to stir, there was movement under the cloths, but he was still wound about, held tight by the corpse sheets. The ruling Christ told them to help him. Men went forward and unwound the cloth. Radiant, up rose Lazarus into this light! His life was granted to him so that he could continue to have his fated number of years in peace.

Mary and Martha were both rejoicing, and no man can truly tell another[195] how happy the two sisters felt in their hearts! Many of the Jewish people were amazed when they saw Lazarus walking safe and sound out of the grave—him whom sickness had taken, whom they had buried deep under the earth, lifeless. Now he could continue his life, hale and well, at home.

Thus the King of Heaven, the mighty divine Power, can protect everyone's life-spirit and help everyone against the hatred of the enemies—everyone to whom He grants His gracious favor.

---

[194] *sigidrohtin.* This single-word honorific, 'victory-chieftain' was no doubt a highly respected title won in battle.

[195] *ni mag that man odrumu / giseggian te sode.* This appears to be a known formula from the epic tradition as it is found also in the beginning of *Beowulf* as the flaming funeral ship sails away carrying its cargo to who knows what destination. See also song 24 of the *Heliand*.

Song 50

The clan-gathering of the Jewish warriors
decides to kill Christ.

The feelings of many men turned in favor of Christ, attitudes of mind changed, once they saw His holy works for themselves—such wondrous things never happened before in the world. Then again, there were also many people, people of very strong hostile feelings, who did not want to recognize knowledgeably the power of God; on the contrary, they fought against His great strength with their words. The Ruler's teachings were so loathsome to them that they sought out other people in Jerusalem (that was the foremost clan assembly site of the Jews, their chief place), a great crowd of cruelly determined men. They informed these people of Christ's works. They said that with their own eyes they had seen the earl alive, the one who had been in the ground, laid to rest in the earth for four days and nights—dead and buried—until Christ awakened him by His own words and actions so that the earl could see this world.

That was very repugnant to these arrogant men, Jewish people. They ordered their men to assemble the people there, arranged in their battle groups, the enormous gathering of their clan. They held a secret council about mighty Christ.[196] "That we simply tolerate this," they said, "is not the only counsel—too many of this clan will believe His teachings. Then people will come at us with armies of cavalry and our overlords will be warriors from Rome.[197] After

---

[196] The meeting of the high priest and the Pharisees has been transformed into the open-air Germanic *thing*, the annual gathering of the clan for decisions of law and councils of war.

[197] An amazing sentence—there is, of course, no mention at all of cavalry at this point, or any point, in the four gospels. Charlemagne had so developed the cavalry, that the Franks possessed the best mounted forces (later to be called knights) in the Northern world. Neither the Saxons nor the Vikings fared well against organized cavalry formations, especially once their lines became ragged. The author's deft and brief insertion of the fear of cavalry, brings the speaker's words into emotional accord with the military feelings of the Saxons, and into the political fear common to both peoples, Saxon and Jewish, of being ruled by warriors 'from Rome.'

that, we will either live dispossessed of our kingdom or we will suffer the loss of our lives, heroes, and our heads!"

Then a highly placed man spoke over the crowd of warriors. He was the bishop[198] of the people inside the hill-fort there, Caiaphas was his name. The Jewish people had picked him that year to take care of God's house, to guard the shrine. "I think it is astounding, renowned Jewish people," he said, "(you know all about so many things) that you really do not know that it is better counsel for anyone ever born, to terminate the aging of one man, to let him die a bloody death by your actions and lose his life-spirit for the sake of the clans, than to let all these warrior people be lost!"

That was not his will, however, which he was so truly expressing openly in front of the people for the benefit of mankind, proclaimed in front of the crowd, but rather it came to him from the power of God, because of his holy official position. He was in charge of God's house there in Jerusalem, he was the guardian of the shrine. It was because of this that he, the bishop of the people, said so truthfully how the Son of God was to free all the earth-people with His one life-spirit, with His life. That was a benefit for all people of earth, since the ruling Christ willed to bring in heathen people as well.

At that, those arrogant men, the Jewish warriors, found themselves in agreement and said to their battle groups, those renowned people, that they should not let their feelings be in any doubt. Whoever should find Him among the people, should immediately capture Him and bring Him out to the assembly of the

---

[198] The author uses the word *biscop* for high priest. The word is not Germanic but the Greek of the early church, *episkopos* 'overseer', and is the word used in the literal translation of the gospels into Old High German. In the author's day, of course, *biscop* meant bishop, as it does today. The question occurs, why did he not seek out a Germanic equivalent for high priest? After all, he uses four different Germanic "pagan" words for the temple and never uses the loan word *tempal*, which is the word used by the literal *Tatian*.

I think the question is answered in the reading. It strikes one much more forcefully even today to hear that 'bishops' are plotting the death of Christ rather than that some 'high wizards' are doing it. The clever use of a loan word here turns the *Heliand* right back on its Christian hearers. Germanic priests are not to be allowed, even by possible misunderstanding, to take the blame for killing Christ.

clans. They said that they could no longer tolerate that one mislead all the people.

Christ the Ruler knew the minds and attitudes of human beings very well, however, their cruel, hate-filled minds, since nothing in the middle world can be hidden from Him. From this point on He did not want to walk openly in the crowd among the earls of the Jews. God's Son waited for the radiant time which was ahead of Him, when He would suffer for these people, bear punishment for these warriors. He knew full well the day that had been fixed.

Our Chieftain decided to leave. The all-ruling Christ, holy Chieftain, then lived in Ephraim with His warriors at the high hill-fort until, following His will, he went back to Bethany amidst the mighty din of his good men. The Jews talked about that in every conversation—the huge numbers they saw following Him. "This is no good," they said, "for the security of our kingdom. Though we have spoken justly, our cause is not thriving at all. He wants to turn this people to His will. All the world is following Him because of His teachings, and therefore we will not be able to do anything harmful to Him—in front of the population."

Song 51

The Chieftain of human clans teaches
at the shrine.

God's Child then went into Bethany six nights before the Jewish people were to gather in Jerusalem on the holy days in order to observe the holy times, the Jews' Pascha.[199] God's Son, the Mighty,

---

[199] The *Heliand* here retains the original word, *pascha* [Lat. from Gk. from Hebr. *pesach* 'passover'], as is found throughout the Latin gospels. This was also done in song 1 with the word for gospel, *evangelium*. Some *Heliand* interpreters feel that contemporary hearers of the *Heliand* would have understood *pascha* in this passage as the 'Jews' Easter', on the grounds that Christian usage (as in *paschal candle*, etc.) would have been the only usage familiar to them. Others feel the word would have been understood as the 'Jews' Passover'. Educated monks would, no doubt, have understood it properly with both of these levels of meaning.

waited among the crowd. A great number of men, many people were present because of His words. Two women were around Him in that place, Mary and Martha; in thoughtfulness and generosity they served Him devotedly. The Chieftain of Clans gave them a long-lasting reward: He released them from every loathsome evil, made them safe from sin, and Himself commanded that they should be able to make their journey in peace, despite the enemies' hatred, with His good permission. They had performed their services as He had wished.

Then Christ the Ruler, the Chieftain of human beings, set forth with the people to go into Jerusalem, where the hateful Jewish leadership was during the holy time, guarding the shrine. There were many warriors there of very powerful clans who did not want to hear Christ's words, nor did they have any love in their feelings toward God's Child. Quite the opposite, they were so angry at Him, these haughty people, this violently hostile human clan, that, within them, they thought maliciously of Him and had His murder in mind. They understood Christ's teachings distortedly and wanted to punish the mighty One for His words, but there were so many people around—so many earls of the nobility were around Him all day long, the little people had surrounded Him with their persons because of His sweet word—so that the opponents among the Jewish folk did not dare to take Him; instead, they avoided Him because of the crowd.[200]

Then mighty Christ stood within the shrine. He spoke many a word of benefit to the sons of men. There were people around Him all day long until the light, the sun, went to its rest. Then many of mankind made their way home.

There was a great mountain nearby, outside the hill-fort. It was broad and high, green and beautiful. The Jewish people called it Olivet by name. Christ the Rescuer went up the mountain then with

---

Interestingly, the author makes no attempt in the passage to add an explanation or substitute the Germanic equivalent for the Pascha feast by naming it after the Germanic goddess of springtime and the direction 'East', *Ostar*, as was done in *Tatian*.

[200] In this passage the author produces an image of harmony in which both the upper class and the ordinary people unconsciously combine to protect Christ. In previous passages, the author has sided alternately with the upper class (for not coming to religion in order to find hand-outs) and with the "little people" (for being more generous-hearted and open to Christ).

His followers, and the night surrounded Him[201] so that none of the Jews really knew He had been there, when, as light came from the East, He stood at the shrine, the Chieftain of People. There He stood, receiving groups of people and telling them so much in words of truth that there is not a single person in this world, here in the middle realm, so clever—not one of the sons of men—who could ever get to the end of those teachings which the Ruler spoke at the altar in the shrine. He always told them with His words that they should get themselves ready for the Kingdom of God, every human being should, so that on that Great Day they will be honored by their Chieftain.

He told them what sins they had committed and always commanded that they be eliminated. He told them to have feelings of love for God's light and to leave all wickedness, all perverse arrogance, behind; to accept humility, to take it into their hearts. He said that the kingdom of heaven, the greatest of goods, would then be theirs. Many men were turned to His will after they heard the holy Word of God, heaven's King. They acknowledged His great strength, the coming of the Chieftain, the help of the Lord, and that the heavenly kingdom, the Rescuer, and God's mercy had approached the sons of men.

Some of the Jewish people were extremely angry—they were cruel-minded, vicious-spirited . . .[202] they did not want to believe His words, but instead waged war mightily against the power of Christ. Because of this wretched conflict, the people were not able to arrive at a firm grasp of faith in Him. They were never granted the benefit of being able to possess the kingdom of heaven.

God's Son then chose to walk away; the Ruler left the shrine, His followers with Him, and the Chieftain's Child climbed up the mountain. He sat there with His warrior-companions and told them many words of truth. They began talking about the shrine. The men

---

[201] Nature is also depicted as being in harmony with human goodness in this passage, as night imitates the protective behavior of the good earls and the "little people," and as the author extends the image of "surrounding" with synonymous verbs.

[202] One-half of a line is missing here from both the London and the Munich manuscripts.

spoke about God's house and said that there was no better sanctuary[203] on earth made by earls' hands, no better holy place[204] constructed with great effort by human labor. The powerful One spoke, the high King of Heaven—the others listened, "I can tell you," He said, "that the time will come when not one of its stones will be standing on top of another, it will fall to the ground and the fire will take it, the hungry flames, no matter how magnificent and well constructed it may be now. That is the fate of everything in this world—the green of the meadow fades away."[205]

Then His followers went up to Him and asked Him very quietly, "How long will this world in its happiness still stand before the end comes, the last day that the light will shine through the clouds in the sky; and when can we hope for You to come back to the middle world to judge mankind, those dead and those alive, my good Lord? We are very curious to know, ruling Christ, when that will happen."

Song 52

The coming of doomsday.

Christ the All-Ruler in His goodness gave the men this answer: "The good Chieftain has so concealed that," He said, "so deeply has that been hidden by the heaven-kingdom's Father, the Ruler of this world, that not a single one of the sons of men can ever know when the great time will happen in this world. Truly, not even God's angels who are always in His presence and who go before Him know, and so they cannot say truthfully in their words when it will happen, when He, the mighty Chieftain, will come to visit man. The holy Father in

---

[203] *alah.*

[204] *rakud.*

[205] This sentence is the *Heliand's* addition to the biblical account (Mt. 24:2). Christ is shown here both as soothsayer and in the Germanic tradition, giving fate and fatality its due. The last phrase *teglidid groni uuang* 'the green meadow disappears' may be a contemporary saying which the author chose to add.

heaven is the only one who knows. It is hidden from everyone else, living and dead, when His coming will happen.

"I can tell you, however, the amazing signs that will occur here before He comes to this world on the great day. They will happen to the moon's light and the same thing to the sun's—they will both turn black and will be surrounded by darkness. The stars, the bright tongues of flame in the heavens, will fall, and the earth will shake, the whole wide world will tremble! There will be many such signs. The great sea will rage, the ocean tide will terrify the inhabitants of earth with its waves. Then clans will wither away because of the great stress, people will shrivel up out of fear—and in no place will there be peace. In hatred, many wars will start all over this world, one clan will lead its army against another. There will be battles among kings with huge armies on the move. Many will meet a painful death—their clear war-fate[206]—(it is a horrible thing that people ever start such murder),[207] then there will be an enormous dying of human beings which will come over the whole world, greater than any that ever occurred in this middle world because of plague. People lie sick, they fall down and die, their days ended, their life time complete. An immeasurably great, deeply cruel hunger comes over the sons of heroes, the greatest of famines—and that is not the slightest of the agonies that will come to pass in this world before the day of doom.

"When you see these things happening in this world you can know for sure that the famous Last Day is approaching the people of the human race, and so is the power of God, the stirring of the might of heaven, and the holy coming of the Chieftain in His glory. Listen, you can recognize these things by using these trees as an image. When their buds swell and they go into flower and their leaves

---

[206] *open urlagi.* War and fate are identified in this powerful expression.

[207] This parenthetical expression of the author's sentiment about warfare is very useful in the interpretation of the *Heliand's* use of Saxon military concepts. The author clearly admires soldierly virtue and especially *gisidi* 'warrior-companion' loyalty; but he is not in favor of commencing actual warfare, least of all large-scale warfare. His blaming of 'those who start' war, may be both an anti-Carolingian comment, as well as an implicit acceptance of the need for military defense. He does not condone warlike behavior.

appear and their foliage opens up, the sons of people know that soon thereafter summer arrives—warm and pleasant with beautiful weather. So you will also know, by the signs I told you here, when the Last Day is drawing near for human beings. I tell you truthfully, this people, these clans, cannot pass away before My word is fulfilled and has come true.[208] The final turn[209] of the heavens and the earth will yet come, and My holy word will continue to stand fast and it will all be fulfilled and carried out[210] in this light just as I have said before these people.

"Stay truly awake! The great doomsday is certainly coming to you—and your Chieftain's might, the force of severe strength—and the famous time, the end-turn of this world! Therefore you should be on guard so that it does not catch you by surprise sleeping on your bed, full of wicked deeds and crimes. Mudspell[211] comes in the darkness of the night just as a thief comes—keeping his actions concealed. This is how that day will come to human beings, the last day of the light, with the people not knowing of it beforehand, just as the flood did long ago in Noah's times, when it destroyed mankind except for him and his family whom God, holy Chieftain, rescued from the

---

[208] The author has managed to finesse the problem of 'this generation will not pass away before all this has come to pass' by understanding 'generation' in a Germanic way as 'clan, type of people'. Thus the possible Saxon question based on the observation that 'that generation has passed away, and the predicted Day of Judgment has not happened' has been avoided. The *Heliand* understands Jesus' comment as meaning: the Jewish people cannot pass away before the Last Judgment.

[209] *giuuand* 'end, turning'. This is a curious word for 'end' since it is rooted in the concept of turning. It is not clear whether for the Saxons the word would carry overtones from the motion of the heavens or from the spinning of woolen thread —where it might refer to the last turn of the thread of the three fates. If either of these two possibilites is correct (and there may well be others), then the Measurer, time, or the fates, are lurking in the background.

[210] *gilestid* 'accomplished, carried out, done'. There is more than a hint in the addition of this verb that the words of Christ about the end of the world are not just prophesy, but are "performative." What He has said about the end will not just be "fulfilled," it will be "carried out," since the words of God in the *Heliand* are indeed expression, but they are cause as well; they are magic.

[211] *mutspelli* lit. possibly 'anger tale, the wrath spell'. The end of the world in Germanic religion, a story whose horrible words about the ends of the gods and men and this world, were expected to become "performative."

embrace of the water. This is also the way in which the hot fire came from heaven and surrounded the high hill-forts of Sodomland with black flames, cruel and hungry, so that not one man remained alive except for Lot alone. The Chieftain's angels led him out of there with his two daughters up onto a mountain. Everything else, the country and its people, were destroyed by the flames of the burning fire. The fire had come as suddenly as the flood had done before—so also will the last day come.

"For this reason, every single person should think about this beforehand! Every human being needs to do this, therefore let your feelings be concerned![212]

Song 53

Doomsday.

"Whenever it does happen that Christ the Ruler, the famous Son of Man, comes with the strength of God, with the force of the most powerful of kings, and with all the holy angels who are up there in heaven accompanying Him, to be seated in His own strength, at that moment all the sons of heroes, all the people of different clans, all people living, anyone ever raised by humans in this light, will be summoned together to Him. There He, the great Chieftain, will judge the people, all of mankind, according to their actions. He will at that time separate out the wrongdoers, the warped human beings on the heart side [left], and He will put the fortunate on the stronger [right] side.[213] He will then address the good and speak to them

---

[212] This verse is a direct address to the audience, marking it, and the following song of the Last Judgment, as significant.

[213] The word for left side *uuinistar* actually means 'the loving' or 'friendly side', presumably because the heart is perceived of as being to the left side of the chest. The word for the right side *suider* means 'stronger' and I presume that this is because the right hand was the sword and weapon hand. In any close fighting unit, shields would all have to be on the same side, on the left arm. At the time of the *Heliand* these words would probably have lost most of their original meaning and simply designated the direction right or left.

directly, 'Come,' He will say, 'you standing there are the chosen, and receive this powerful kingdom which has been prepared and constructed for the sons of men for after the end of this world. It has been consecrated for you by the Father of the sons of men. You may enjoy its benefits and rule its broad realm, since you often did My will, you followed Me gladly, and you were kind and generous to Me with your gifts when I was hard pressed by thirst and hunger, when I was captured by freezing cold. When I was in irons, chained up in prison, help from your hands often came to Me there, you were kind and generous-minded, your visits honored Me.'[214]

"Then those people will respond to Him. 'My good Lord,' they will say, 'When were you captured like that, hard pressed by such needs, as you are now saying and recounting in front of these people, Mighty One? When did a single person see You hard pressed by such needs? You have authority over all peoples, and over all the jewels they have ever acquired in this world.'

"Then God the Ruler will answer them, 'Whatsoever you did,' He will say, 'in your Chieftain's name, whatsoever you gave away for God's honor to the people who are the least—many of whom are now standing here, those who because of humility were poor people carrying out my will[215]—whatsoever you gave them of your wealth to add to my honor was received by your Chieftain Himself! Your help came to the Heaven-King![216] Because of this, the holy Chieftain wishes to reward your faith: He gives you life forever.'

---

[214] In this thoughtful passage the just are conceived of as those who, regardless of actual social rank, possess a good warrior-chieftain's attitude and virtues: *mildie*, kindness and generosity to those 'embattled' by life's hardships, and rendering support *helpa* to thanes "captured" by cold.

[215] This careful line can designate those who are poor because of submission (humility) to the will of God (they were so fated), or possibly Christian ascetics with a vow of poverty. It seems deliberately to exclude the same type of poor the author has previously seen as disreputable. See song 15 and note 86.

[216] As in folklore, the poor thane needing assistance turns out to have been the chieftain himself "in disguise." The author has touchingly reimagined Mt. 25:31-46 in a more folkloric manner and has reinterpreted Christian kindness as a Germanic Chieftain's *helpa*.

"The Ruler will then turn to the ones on the left, the wrongdoers, and the Chieftain will tell them that they will have to pay for their deeds, their wicked behavior. 'You will now have to leave Me,' He says, 'and you accursed must go to the eternal fire which was made ready for God's opponents, the enemy horde, because of your wicked behavior. You did not help Me when I was being tortured terribly by hunger and thirst, or when I had no clothes and went about in a state of misery. I had great need—but I never received any help— when I was put in irons, chained and locked up, or when the sickbed held Me captive with serious illness. You never thought it was important to visit Me when I was sick. It was of no worth at all to you to think of Me. Because of this you will now suffer from darkness in Hel.'

"Then these people will speak to Him in reply. 'But ruling God,'[217] they say, 'why do you wish to speak like this against these people, talking against so many? When did you ever need human beings or their goods? Why, all the wealth they have in this world You gave them!' Then God the Ruler answers, 'When you looked down on the poorest of the sons of men, the lowest of human warrior-heroes in your feelings, and let them be loathsome to you in your mind, refusing them your respect,[218] you were doing the same to your Chieftain, you were refusing Him your wealth. Because of this, God the Ruler, your Father, does not wish to receive you. You

---

[217] In the previous section God is often referred to as lord and chieftain, and the just refer to God as their lord, implying to the feudal audience that they feel loyalty ties to Him. In this section, the author has the unjust deal with God far more formally and distantly, by addressing Him with a more elevated title, leading the audience to feel that they have no loyalty tie to God. Finally, when God reproves the unjust for not helping Him, He uses the word that reminds them of their obligations and calls Himself Chieftain.

[218] This is a more psychological version of the stinginess of the unjust than in the biblical account (Mt. 25). The crime of the unjust in the *Heliand* is that of psychological stinginess, the refusal to be generous in giving respect and honor to the poorer thanes. The author betrays a surprisingly realistic concern about the hypocrisy of looking down on lower members of the same warrior class, while perhaps tossing some coins to the serfs in the village to satisfy the Christian obligation to help the poor.

shall go instead to the fire, to the deep death, where you shall serve the devils, the vicious enemies, since you were doing so before.'

"After those words He divides the people in two, the good and the bad. The damned, the warped human beings go off in a state of grief to hot Hel to receive their punishment: unending evil. The high King of Heaven then leads the pure[219] people up from there to the long-lasting light, where there is life forever, God's kingdom, made ready for the people who are good."

Song 54 PASSIO[220]

The Passion begins;
Judas betrays his own Chieftain to southern people;
Christ washes the feet of His earls and thanes.

And so, I have heard it told, the powerful Chieftain told the warriors there in His words about the final turn of this world and how it will continue on for as long as the sons of men are to inhabit it, and how at the end it will disintegrate and disappear. He also told His followers there in true words, "You all know," He said, "that two nights from now the time will have come, the Jews' Pascha, the time when they are to serve God at the shrine. There is no turning away[221] of this: there the Son of Man, the mighty One, will be sold to the massed people, fastened to the cross, and will suffer horrible tortures."

---

[219] *hluttaron* 'clear, pure'. The word carries the connotation of transparent, no admixture, and is used most often in the *Heliand* of water.

[220] The Latin word *Passio* 'The Passion' is found here in the Munich manuscript (M), in the London manuscript (C) *Passio Domini* 'The Passion of the Lord.'

[221] *geuuand* 'turning, turning point, end'. This is the same word used in the previous sentence for the 'final turn,' of the whole world. The connotation of inevitability links both pronouncements about ends, the world's and Jesus', reinforced not by the use of an analogous word, but the same word.

Many slithery-hearted thanes had assembled, southern people,[222] the manpower of the Jews, at the place where they were supposed to serve their God. All the law-speakers[223] had come, troops of them, they counted as the wisest among the crowd of men, a powerful clan. Caiaphas was there, the bishop of the people. They were conferring about God's Son, about how they could kill Him, an innocent man. They said that they should not touch Him [when He is] among the crowd on the holy day, "we do not want this huge crowd of warrior-heroes to get into an uproar, since this army is willing to stand and fight for Him. We will have to lay a trap very quietly for His life-spirit so that the crowd of Jews does not start a riot on the holy days."

Then Judas, a follower of Christ, one of the twelve, came up to where the Jewish nobles were seated in assembly. He said that he could give them good advice. "What will you trade me," he said, "what payment in jewels, if I give you the man without a battle and without a riot?" The minds of the people were filled with delight. "If you will do it," they said, "and if you keep your word, then you have the right to ask these nobles for the amount of good jewels you want." The assemblymen then promised him thirty pieces of silver altogether—which was, in his own judgment,[224] what he wanted; and Judas told the men assembled in bold words that he would give them

---

[222] See song 45. The prejudice against the Mediterranean peoples appears here as the author uses the same vocabulary for them as he used for Herod.

[223] *eosago* 'law-sayer'. Since Saxon law was not written, but was an oral tradition, the task of the lawyer was not so much to study the law but to know it—by memory, and to be the repository of his people's laws. This is very much different from the tradition of the scribes and Torah-lawyers of the New Testament, who constantly resort to the hallowed phrase 'it is written' in their arguments with Jesus. The Germanic law-sayers were indispensable in their culture for a lord to arrive at a just verdict in a difficult case, especially since law differed from clan to clan, and everyone had the right to be judged according to his own tribal law. It is thus all the more interesting that Jesus Himself is referred to by his opponent in song 46 as being an *eosago*.

[224] *an is selbes dom*. The phrase means both 'by his own determination' and 'in his own judgment, doom'—a sinister ambiguity. The author sees the thirty pieces of silver as Judas' own judgment—in both senses.

his Chieftain[225] for that. Judas then turned away from these people, His mind set on evil. He was calculating with such disloyalty how soon the time would come to him when he would be able to betray Christ to the hostile forces of the enemy.

At that time God's Child of Peace, Christ the true Ruler, knew that He would have to give up these dwelling places and set off on the journey to God's kingdom, to His Father's ancestral homestead. Not a single one of the sons of men ever saw greater love than the love He had for His men, His good followers. He arranged a banquet for them, seated them politely and spoke many words of wisdom to them. The day slipped on to the west, the sun went to its rest. It was then the Ruler requested with His words that water be brought to His hands, and the holy Christ arose at the feast and there washed His followers' feet with His hands, wiped them afterwards with His cloth, and dried them with loving care.

Then Simon Peter spoke with his Chieftain. "I do not think it is something proper, my good Lord," he said, "for You to wash my feet with Your holy hands." Then his Lord replied to him, the Ruler, with His words. "If you are not willing to accept that I wash your feet out of love, as I am doing for these other men here out of loving care, then you will never have a share with Me of the heaven-kingdom." At that, Peter changed his mind. "Have authority, my good Lord," he said, "for Yourself, over my feet, and over my hands and over my head too, Commander! Wash them with Your holy hands—for this reason: I would like to remain in Your favor and to have whatever part of the heaven-kingdom You are willing to give me, Chieftain, in Your goodness!"

Christ's followers, His earls and thanes, suffered His serving of them in patience, whatever their Commander, the mighty One, did

---

[225] To make Judas's act more appalling to the Saxons, the author does not use any of the more distant words for a ruling lord such as *herro* or *fro*, but the word for one's own family head and chieftain, *drohtin*.

out of love. And He intended to do a much greater thing to be of service to the human race.[226]

Song 55

The last mead-hall feast
with the warrior-companions.

God's Child of Peace went and sat down among the warrior-companions and gave them much long-lasting counsel. The light was coming back, morning was coming to mankind. Mighty Christ spoke to His followers and asked them where they were going to hold His feast-meal on the holy day, where He would observe the holy time with His warrior-companions. He then told His men to go to Jerusalem. "When you walk into the hill-fort," He said, "there will be a great deal of noise and commotion from the large throng. There you will see a man carrying a vat full of clear water in his hands. You are to follow him to whatever dwelling you see him go. Then say to the lord who owns the house that I am sending you there to prepare My feast. He will then show you a magnificent house, a high hall, which is everywhere hung with beautiful decorations.[227] There you are to prepare My banquet for Me. That is the place where I will definitely come with My warrior-companions."

---

[226] The point of the washing of the feet has been changed from a moral one to a contemplative one. In Scripture (Jn. 13) Christ says when He is finished with the washing, 'If I, who am your Lord and Master, have washed your feet, you should wash one another's feet.' The *Heliand* author avoids what, if literally understood, must surely have been unacceptable both as metaphor and behavior. The *Heliand* nicely finesses the 'impropriety' of a lord washing nobles' feet by having Peter bring this thought to expression. Peter objects in the *Heliand* not so much to having himself washed (as in Jn.), but to the action itself as improper, before he submits. More important for the author is the contemplative observation made in the thoughtful conclusion that the lowly service involved in the washing of human feet was nothing in comparison to the service He was about to render, at much greater price, to the human race.

[227] This probably means tapestries on the walls.

Soon thereafter, Christ's followers were on the road to Jerusalem. They found everything He had said in His directions to be true, nothing was in any way different. Then they prepared the feast. God's Son, the holy Chieftain, came to the house so that they could carry out the custom of their country and follow God's command, in accordance with the law of the Jews and their ancient customs from days long ago.

In the evening, Christ the All-Ruler went and took His seat in the hall. He told the twelve warrior-companions who were the most loyal[228] to Him in their feelings, in word and in deed, among the men to come to Him there. The holy Chieftain Himself knew their attitudes of mind. During the meal He spoke to them. "I am very glad," He said, "to be able to sit together with you and enjoy the feast, to share the Pascha of the Jews with you who are so dear to me."

"Now I will tell you that it is your Chieftain's will that I no longer enjoy food with men, with human beings, in this world until the kingdom of heaven is implemented. For Me, the pain and terrible torture which I am to suffer for this world and this people is now at hand." As He was speaking about this to the thanes, the holy Chieftain's mind became downcast, His mood darkened, and He spoke again to the warrior-companions, the good One said to His followers, "Listen, I promised you God's kingdom, the light of heaven," He said, "and you devotedly promised Me your thaneship. Now, you are not willing to carry it out, you are not being true to your word. I am telling you here and now in all truth that one of you twelve intends to sneak away from his promised loyalty and to sell me to the Jewish clan, to trade Me for silver. He wants to get buried treasure for himself, precious jewels, and for that, to hand Me over,

---

[228] *gitriuuiston* 'loyalest'. The ones who are not just loyal because it is their obligation to a Chieftain, but the ones who have the actual feeling of loyalty, are so called. As in the description of the unjust at the Last Judgment (see note 218) the *Heliand* insists on internal attitudes, 'feelings,' being what determines who is a 'good thane' of Christ.

his Chieftain and Lord!"[229]   That will be to his harm and
punishment, however. When he sees [his] fate[230], and catches a
glimpse of where this dreary task ends up, then he will know full well,
that it would have been a more pleasant thing for him, much better
by far, never to have been born alive in this light rather than to
receive the reward for his evil task and malicious advice."

At that, each of the earls began to look at one another, casting
worried glances. Their thoughts were in turmoil, their hearts in grief,
as they heard their Lord saying such lamentable words. The men
were worried. To which one of the twelve would He say that he was
the guilty harm-doer, the one who had set the price at the assembly?

Nor was it easy for any of the thanes to admit such evil
intentions—each man denied it—they all became frightened, no one
dared ask, until that worthy man, Simon Peter, who did not dare to
ask himself, made a sign to John the good. In those days John was
the favorite thane of God's Son, the one He loved the most. He was
allowed to rest on the lap of mighty Christ, and he was lying with his
head leaning on His chest. There he learned so many holy mysteries,
so many deep thoughts. He spoke to his Chieftain then and began
to ask Him, "who could it be, my Lord," he said, "who wants to sell
You, most powerful of kings, to Your enemies? We are very anxious
to know." Christ the Healer had His answer ready. "Look at the one
into whose hands I give some of My food in front of these men.
That man has evil intentions and a bitter mind, he will put Me in the
power of enemy murderers who will take My life-spirit and put an
end to My days."

After that He took some of the food in front of the men and put
it into the hands of Judas, that mean criminal, and spoke directly to
him in front of His warrior-companions and told him to leave His

---

[229] Judas' crime is seen in the *Heliand* as a violation of the warrior code of *gisidi*-loyalty. Judas is not seen as guilty of 'desertion under fire' or of 'treason to the cause' but of breaking the intimate feudal bonds of loyalty between a Chieftain and the thanes who were his personal warrior-companions.

[230] *thea uurdi* 'the fates'. When Judas, in other words, becomes aware of the fateful path he has taken, and sees the inevitable end to which this course of action leads, then . . . The phrase literally means, 'when he sees the fates' and perhaps this may have been a common, if frightening, expression.

people immediately. "Do what you are thinking," He said, "do what you are going to do—you cannot keep your intentions concealed any longer. Fate is at hand, the time has now come close."[231]

As soon as the disloyal traitor[232] took the food and put it in his mouth to eat it, the power of God left him. Cruel things started going into his body, horrible little creatures, Satan wrapped himself tightly around his heart,[233] since God's help had abandoned Judas in this world. This is the woeful situation of people who, under heaven, change lords.[234]

Song 56

The words of Christ give great powers
to the bread and wine.

Judas then went outside, he was set on treachery, the thane harbored cruel thoughts against his Commander. It was deep, dark night.

---

[231] *Thiu uurd is at handun,/ thea tidi sind nu ginahid* '[the] fate is at hand, the times have now come close'. This is a radical Germanic alteration of the parallel passage in Scripture (Jn. 13:31) 'Now the Son of Man is glorified, and God is glorified in Him.' Though some interpret this tragic line as referring to Judas's fate, I think that this is not the case and the line should be interpreted as an observation made by Christ about His own fate. This is the moment that sets His irrevocable fate in motion and He is depicted as knowing it. The words of this line are used more than once in the course of the Passion story, and they create a somber and tragic Germanic-religious undertone.

[232] *treulogo* lit. 'loyalty-liar'. The original is obviously much stronger than 'traitor,' since it implies that one has lied, or made a lie out of, one's bond of personal loyalty to the head of the clan.

[233] In the manner of a reptile. As in the confrontation between Christ and Satan in the scene of the Temptations of Christ (song 13), there are always hints that Satan moves like the snake. See song 13, note 58.

[234] This is obviously a strong warning to the Saxons, by characterizing vacillation between religions as a betrayal of one's loyalty to the Chieftain. Once that feudal bond is broken by a thane, the *Heliand* warns, he has no right to expect the Chieftain's reciprocal duty of help and support against enemies.

The Chieftain's Son remained at the feast, and there, for His followers, the holy King of Heaven, the Ruler, made both wine and bread holy. He broke it with His hands, gave it to His followers and thanked God, expressing His gratitude to the One who created everything—the world and its happiness—and He spoke many a word. "Believe Me clearly," He said, "that this is My body and also My blood. I here give both of them to you to eat and drink. This is what I will give and pour out on earth. With My body I will free you to come to God's kingdom, to eternal life in heaven's light. Always remember to continue to do what I am doing at this supper, tell the story of it to many men. This body and blood is a thing which possesses power: with it you will give honor to your Chieftain. It is a holy image: keep it in order to remember Me, so that the sons of men will do it after you and preserve it in this world, and thus everyone all over this middle world will know what I am doing out of love to give honor to the Lord.[235]

"Always remember how I commanded you here to hold firmly to your brotherhood. Have an attitude of devotedness in your mind and lovingness in your feelings toward one another, so that the sons of men, the people of earth, will all understand that you are obviously my disciples.

"I also want to let you know that a powerful enemy will tempt your minds, the one whose hatred is as cruel as a sword, Satan himself. He will approach boldly in order to deceive your souls.

---

[235] The Eucharist is treated by the *Heliand* poet as a "performative thing," an object which, like magic performative words, can accomplish the task it expresses. The hallowed Bread and Wine possess three "powers." First, it is the means of salvation, freeing people for heaven, since it is the body that will be given and the blood that will be spilled in the Crucifixion. The second is that the Bread and Wine are a *mahtig thing*, a power-filled (magic) thing, a holy image of Christ, a picture that enables (causes) Him to be remembered as often as "this thing" is done and the story of the Last Supper and Crucifixion is told. Third, it is a means of overcoming the limitations of time and fate. By remembering Him when people after the apostles in succeeding generations repeat His magic actions at the supper and see the Bread and Wine images, their fates and times (and His) will be overcome 'by His love'.

This scene is the author's poetic reversal of the magic of Cana in which Christ's words and actions in turning water into wine were intentionally hidden from all so that they could not be remembered or repeated from generation to generation.

Always keep the thoughts of your heart firmly set on God. When you pray I will stand at your side, so that the evil injurer can not cause doubts to arise in your feelings—I will help you against the enemy. He also came once to entrap Me, though He did not get his way at all with his lust for My body.

"Now, I do not want to hide from you any longer the troubles which will very soon be yours. You will desert Me, my warrior-companions, and your thaneship, before this dark night leaves people and the light of morning comes back to mankind." The mood of the men darkened quickly and their minds became worried, their hearts were grieved. Their Lord's words made them very concerned.

Simon Peter then spoke words of confidence, the thane said graciously to his Commander and Lord, "Even if this entire group of warrior-heroes," he said, "Your warrior-companions, should desert You, I am always willing to suffer any hardships together with You! I am always ready, if God lets me, to help You, to stand at your side without wavering. Even if these people lock You up deep in the dungeon, I have little doubt that I will stay with You in chains, lying with You whom I love so much. If they then want to take away Your life with the blade's hatred, my good Lord, I will give my life-spirit for You in the play of weapons; and I will not give any ground as long as my mind lasts and my arm has its strength!"[236]

His Lord then replied to him. "So," He said, "you are convinced that you have unswerving loyalty and bold courage. You have a thane's mind, you have good will, but I can tell you what will actually happen. You will become so weak-hearted—although you do not think so right now—that you will deny your Commander three times tonight before cockcrow. You will say that I am not your Lord, and that you renounce My protection."[237] The man said back to Him,

---

[236] Peter has made the speech of a loyal Saxon thane to his Chieftain. The audience would be able all the more to identify with him. Similar speeches before battle can be found in *Beowulf* (2631-62) and in the short *Battle of Maldon*. See *The Saxon Savior*, pp. 99-103.

[237] *mundburd* 'protection, guardianship'. The author has brought home the seriousness of Peter's denial in very Germanic terms. *Mund* is the relationship itself between chieftain and thane as well as the protection involved, and was held to be sacred from very ancient times. See Appendix 2.

"If it were ever to happen in the world," he said, "that I would have to die with You, facing death together, the day would still never come, beloved Chieftain, that I would be ready to deny You in front of these Jews." All the followers said the same thing, that they would be ready to suffer with Him at the assembly.

Song 57

Christ's deep fear before battle;
His last salute in the garden.

Then the Ruler Himself, the lordly King of Heaven, told them in His words that they should not let their minds doubt. He told them not to let deep thoughts . . .[238] "Do not let your hearts cloud up because of your Chieftain's words, do not be too frightened. I am going to see our Father Himself, and I will send you the Holy Spirit from the kingdom of heaven. He will console you and help you, and remind you of the many instructions I gave you in My words. He will put wisdom in your hearts, the happy teachings, so that you can continue the achievements in words and works which I asked of you in this world."

The powerful One then stood up in the shrine,[239] Christ the Rescuer, and went out by night with His thanes. Troubled and

---

[238] There is a lacuna here in the manuscript. Scholars have suggested that the missing word might be *dragan* 'to bear, carry, drag'. If so, the line might be finished 'weigh you down'.

[239] The author has made a touching slip here. He described the Last Supper as being held in a well-decorated Saxon mead-hall, to which the apostles were led, as in Scripture, by a man carrying water. The owner was not named. Now, however, that the bread and wine of the Eucharist have been shared there between Christ and His followers, the poet seems to forget that he identified the site as a hall and now calls it a Germanic *racod* or *rakud* 'shrine, temple', lit. 'god's house'. In the author's mind the place has become a *rakud*. Perhaps by this "slip," the mystically inclined author of the *Heliand* is suggesting to his hearers that we really do know both where this curious house is, reached through water, and the identity of its unnamed owner.

deeply saddened, Christ's followers walked with grief in their hearts. He brought them to the high Olivet mountain, the one He usually went up with His followers. (Judas was well aware of this, that deadly-minded man, because he was often on the mountain with them.) There God's Son spoke to His followers. "You are now so afraid," He said, "now that you know about My death. You are grieving and groaning, and the Jews are joyful, the merry crowd is in a good mood—the world is happy. This will all take a turn, however, and very quickly. They will then be troubled in their minds and mournful in their feelings, and you will be happy ever after for days without number—no end will ever come, no turn of fortune will ever come, to your good life! Therefore you need not feel bad about the task [I must do] nor feel regret about My departure, since from it will come help to the sons of men."

Then He told His followers to wait there, up on the mountain. He said that He wanted to climb up higher on the slope to pray, and told three thanes to go with Him, James and John and good Peter—daring warriors. They went gladly, together with their Commander. Up on the mountain God's Son asked them to bow themselves in prayer and to speak to God, asking Him sincerely to hold in check the strength of the tempters, the will of the evil ones, so that the opponent, the vicious injurer, could not bring doubt to their feelings. The powerful Son of the Chieftain bowed, the most Powerful of kings, and knelt down on the earth. He spoke to the good Father of all peoples, He said words of lamentation and grief. His mind was clouded and afraid; in His humanness His feelings were upset, His flesh was frightened. His tears fell,[240] His precious sweat dripped down just as blood comes welling out of wounds.[241]

---

[240] Tears have been added by the *Heliand* author. It is interesting that not only has none of Christ's fear of losing His life 'in battle' been suppressed, but the scene of the Agony in the Garden has been intensified by the author. Presumably, he felt the extreme realism of this part of the gospel story would be well understood by men who had already been on real battlefields.

[241] The bloody sweat of the Agony is used by the author to draw an implicit comparison to battle wounds. Christ's "battle" to save mankind has begun, he is already "wounded" and bleeding.

The spirit and the body were at war in God's Child. One was ready to be on its way—the spirit—to God's kingdom; the other stood there in distress—Christ's body—it did not want to give up this light, it was afraid of death. After He had addressed the mighty One, He continuously kept calling out more and more with His words to the Chieftain, to the high Heaven-Father, to the holy God, the Ruler. "If mankind cannot be rescued," He said, "unless I give up My body, which I love, to terrible torture for the sake of the sons of people—if You want it to be this way—then I want to drink it. I take this chalice in my hand and drink it to your honor, my Lord Chieftain, powerful Protector![242] Do not consider what might be good for My flesh, I will carry out Your will. You have authority over all things!"

He went back to the place on the mountain where He had left His followers waiting. God's Son found them in troubled sleep. Their minds were filled with sorrow that they would have to part with their Chieftain. (Every man should feel such sorrow when he has to leave a beloved lord and give up one so good!)[243] The Ruler spoke to His followers, He woke them up and greeted them with words. "Why do you want to sleep like this?" He said. "Can you not stay awake with Me for a time? Fate is at hand, so that everything will go just as God the Father in His might has determined it."[244] There is no doubt in My mind, My spirit is prepared to do God's will, ready to travel. My flesh is worried, my body is holding Me back, it is very loathe to suffer pain. Despite this, I will still do what My Father wants done. You keep your minds steadfast!"

He then went back once again to pray, the great Chieftain; and there He spoke many a good word. God's holy angel came from

---

[242] With the sparest of means the *Heliand* poet has transformed the Hebrew gesture of drinking as a symbol of acceptance into a Germanic one by inserting a thane's salute to the Chieftain before drinking the cup. The *Heliand* has Jesus add: *drinku ina thi te diurdu* 'I drink it to Your honor!' This is, I think, one of the finest touches in the epic. See *The Saxon Savior*, p. 104.

[243] This observation by the author seems to be a general comment, a defense of the virtue of loyalty. Judas represents those of the opposite attitude in the *Heliand*, those who "change lords" too easily.

[244] *Thiu uurd is at handun, / that it so gigangen scal, so it god fader / gimarcode mahtig.* Fate here is clearly the executive force of God, carrying out the Divine will.

heaven, strengthened His mind, and gave Him courage to face the chains.[245] He kept on praying continually, addressing His Father, the Ruler with His words. "If it cannot be otherwise, great Chieftain," He said, "except that I suffer terrible pain for these human beings, then I will adapt Myself to Your will."

He then left the place to go to His warrior-companions. He found them sleeping. He spoke to them quickly, and then went back a third time to pray. The Chieftain's Son said the same things which He had said before to the King of people, the all-ruling Father. Christ the Rescuer reminded the mighty One very earnestly of the good of mankind. Then He went back to His followers again[246] and soon spoke to them. "Sleep and rest," He said, "now the one who sold Me, who took money for Me, even though I am innocent of any sin, will soon be coming here in force." Christ's warrior-companions were awake after those words and they saw warriors coming up the mountain making a great din, angry armed men.

Song 58

Christ the Chieftain is captured;
Peter, the mighty swordsman, defends Him boldly.

Judas, the hate-filled man, was showing them the way; the enemy clan, the Jews, were marching behind. They were carrying fires with them, bringing lighted lamps and burning torches from the hill-fort, as they moved up onto the mountain for battle. Judas knew the place well to which he was to lead the people. As they were approaching the spot, Judas took the lead, ahead of the army, and told them a sign so that the earls would not capture some other man. "I will go

---

[245] The chains are the bonds of a captured prisoner of war.

[246] By rearranging the sequence of events in the Agony in the Garden in this effective manner, with the acceptance and angel coming early in the incident, and rapid-fire movement later, the poet has created an emotionally realistic scene of a distraught, almost panicked person who is running back and forth between imploring God and going to His friends.

up to Him first," he said, "kiss Him and talk to Him. That person will be Christ Himself, whom you are to capture by the might of the clan, tie Him up, up on the mountain, and bring Him back to the people at the fort. He has forfeited His life by His words."

The warriors marched forward, the grim Jewish army, until they had come to Christ. There He stood with His followers, the famous Chieftain. He was awaiting the workings of fate, the glorious time.[247] Judas, the man without loyalty, went up to Him, bowed his head to God's Child, and spoke to his Lord. He kissed the mighty One, keeping his word, and indicated Christ to the warriors just as he had said earlier in his words. The Chieftain of Peoples, the Ruler of this world, bore all that with patience, spoke to Judas in His words and asked him frankly, "Why are you coming to Me like this with an army? Why are you leading these people to Me and selling Me to this loathsome Jewish clan, and with your kiss identifying Me to this crowd?"

Then He went to speak to the other men, the warriors, and asked them in His words why they had come looking for Him at night bringing their warrior-companions with them, "as if you want to cause trouble for someone." The crowd spoke back to Him and said that they had been told that the Healer was up here on the hill, the one who creates mobs among the Jewish people and calls Himself God's Son. "We have come here looking for Him, we are anxious to find Him. He is from Galileeland, from Fort Nazareth." As the rescuing Christ told them in soothsaying that He was the one, the Jewish people became frightened; they were so terrified that they instantly fell backwards and everyone of them was on the ground. The army of warriors pulled back in retreat—they could not stand up to the Word, the voice, of God. But there were some real fighting men among them who ran back up the hill, strengthened their resolve, controlled their inner feelings, and went raging forward in hatred until they had Christ the Rescuer surrounded with their men.

---

[247] *bed metodogiscapu, / torhtero tideo* 'he awaited the Measurer's doings, the very radiant times'.

Christ's followers, wise men deeply distressed by this hostile action, held their position in front.[248] They spoke to their Chieftain. "My Lord Chieftain," they said, "if it should now be Your will that we be impaled here on their spear-points, wounded by their weapons, then nothing would be as good to us as to die here, pale from mortal wounds, for our Chieftain."[249]

Then Simon Peter, the mighty, the noble swordsman flew into a rage; his mind was in such turmoil that he could not speak a single word.[250] His heart became intensely bitter because they wanted to tie up his Lord there. So he strode over angrily, that very daring thane, to stand in front of his Commander, right in front of his Lord. No doubting in his mind, no fearful hesitation in his chest, he drew his blade and struck straight ahead at the first man of the enemy with all the strength in his hands, so that Malchus was cut and wounded on the right side by the sword! His ear was chopped off, he was so badly wounded in the head that his cheek and ear burst open with a mortal wound! Blood gushed out, pouring from the wound! The cheek of the enemy's first man had been cut open. The men stood back—they were afraid of the slash of the sword.[251]

Then the Son of God spoke to Simon Peter and told him to put his sharp sword back into its sheath. "If I wanted to put up a fight against the attack of this band of warriors, I would make the great

---

[248] As opposed to the gospel account, the *Heliand* poet has the warrior-companions/apostles, behave as in the epics, forming a defensive perimeter around their Chieftain and offering to stand their ground with Him to the death. Contrast with Jn. 18.

[249] From this song onward the Passion is viewed as a battle, a last stand of a brave chieftain with his thanes. See *The Saxon Savior*, p. 95 ff.

[250] This probably would have reminded the audience of the famous Nordic berserkers, the most famous representatives of the *furor teutonicus* in warfare. Peter, however, is not a simple berserker, he flies into a rage out of loyalty. He cannot permit his Chieftain to be chained up. He does not rage blindly into the lines of the enemy, but moves up to stand in a defensive position in front of his Commander. This entire episode with Peter is the best known section of the *Heliand*.

[251] In the original there is a wordplay that is very hard to translate. People stand back because of fear of the *billes biti* 'the bill's bite'. A sword can be referred to poetically as a bird's bill because of the similarity of shape—and because both sword and bill can bite!

and mighty God, the holy Father in the kingdom of heaven, aware of it so that He would send me so many angels wise in warfare that no human beings could stand up to the force of their weapons. No human army, however huge, could ever stand fast against them nor afterwards still be in possession of their life-spirits. But, the ruling God, the all-mighty Father, has determined it differently: we are to bear whatever bitter things this people does to us. We are not to become enraged or wrathful against their violence, since whoever is eager and willing to practice the weapon's hatred, cruel spear-fighting, is often killed himself by the edge of the sword and dies dripping with his own blood. We cannot by our deeds avert anything."[252]

He then went up to the wounded man and skillfully put the parts of his body back together, his headwounds, so that the sword-slash was quickly healed.

God's Son spoke to the hostile warriors. "It seems very amazing to Me," He said, "that if you wanted to do some harm to Me, why did you not capture Me when I was among your people in the shrine and was soothsaying with My words? There was sunshine then, the precious light of day! You did not want to do any harm to Me then in all that light—and now you bring out your people at night in darkness just as one does when it is a thief one wants to catch, a criminal who has forfeited his life-spirit." The Jewish warriors then grabbed at God's Son, a cruel clan, a hate-filled mob. The angry army of men massed around Him—they did not see their

---

[252] Scripture gives only one reason for not resorting to the sword, "those who live by the sword will perish by the sword" in Mt. 26:52. The *Heliand* has Christ add this second more Germanic reason based on the irresistibility of fate. *uui mid usun dadiun ni sculun / uuiht auuerdian.*

crime[253]—they fastened His hands together with iron handcuffs and His arms with chains.

There was no need for Him to suffer such terrible pain, such horrible hardship and suffering, but He did it for the sake of this warrior clan, because He wanted to save the sons of people, to haul them up from Hel to heaven—to wide-flung happiness! That is why He did not say a thing about what they wanted to do to Him in their spiteful hate.

Song 59

Peter denies he is a warrior-companion of Christ.

Then the angry Jewish people became haughty, their leaders were very proud of themselves for having been able to put the holy Christ in body irons and bring Him back in chains. The enemy then set off to return from the mountain to the hill-fort. The Son of God, his hands bound, walked among the warriors down to the valley feeling sad and upset. His close warrior-companions had run away on Him, just as He had Himself told them earlier. It was not because of any cowardice, though, that they abandoned the beloved Son of God, but because a long time ago it had been said—the words of the soothsayers—that it would happen in this way. Therefore, they could not have avoided it.

---

[253] This observation is an insertion by the author. It does occur in Scripture, of course, but only at the Crucifixion ("Father, forgive them, for they know not what they do") and not at this point in the gospel account. The poet may be anxious that the listeners not take the "Jewish warriors'" behavior as an affront which they might have to avenge.

There may also be another level here. Similar excusing words were used of Herod's soldiers when they were carrying out the massacre of the holy innocents. In that incident it seemed to imply a memory of Frankish soldiers' behavior toward the Saxons. The same memory may be being evoked in these verses, especially since Christ is taken prisoner with the iron manacles and chains that many of the audience may once have worn when they were converted to Christ and the Empire. See *The Saxon Savior,* p. 108.

Peter and John were walking behind the crowd; the two men were following at a distance. They were very anxious to know what the cruel Jews wanted to do to God's Child, their Chieftain. Then they came to the valley between the mountain and the hill-fort, the place where their bishop lived, the guardian of their shrine. There, proud earls led Him through the fence. A great fire was blazing in the courtyard with a crowd around it; it had been made for the warriors of the army. The Jewish people went up to it to warm themselves, they let God's Son stay waiting in His chains. There was tremendous noise and commotion, the shouting of braggarts.

John was known to the leadership and was therefore able to crowd into the courtyard with the people. Peter, the best of all thanes, stood outside. The guard at the gate would not let him follow his Lord until John asked a friend, one of the Jews, to let Peter come on into the courtyard. At that point, a clever, nasty woman walked up to Peter—she was a maid-servant of one of the Jewish commanders. This unattractive maiden spoke to the thane. "Why, you might be one of the followers, from Galilee, of the One standing over there with His arms in chains." Peter immediately became frightened; his courage went soft. He said that he did not at all understand the woman's words nor was he ever a thane of that Commander. He avoided Christ in front of the crowd and said that he did not recognize the man. "What you are saying is not familiar to me," he said. God's strength, toughness, had gone out of his heart.

Changing places, he moved among the soldiers until he came to the fire, and went to warm himself. There another woman began to say frightful words about him. "Here all of you can see your enemy," she said, "this man is clearly one of Christ's followers, one of His own warrior-companions!" After that, men of the enemy began moving closer in a hostile manner, questioning him intensely about which army he belonged to. "You do not belong to these fort-people," they said, "we can see from your behavior, both in your words and in your ways of acting, that you are not one of these people. You are from Galilee."

He did not want to admit it in the slightest, and so he stood there contesting it, and swore a strong oath that he was not a member of that warrior-company.[254] He had no control over his words. It was supposed to happen that way. It had been thus determined by the One who is the Protector of Mankind in this world.[255]

Then a man approached the group of soldiers and came up to Peter. He was a relative of the man whom Peter had cut with the sharp edge of his sword, and he said that he had seen Peter up on the mountain "in the tree-garden where we put irons on your Lord's hands, and put Him in chains." Out of fear Peter denied his beloved Lord; he said that he would forfeit his life if any earthly human being there could truthfully say that he was one of that man's warrior-companions and was a follower of His path.[256]

At that moment a cock crowed for the first time. The holy Christ, the Best man ever born, standing there in chains, looked over His shoulder at Simon Peter. The Son of the Chieftain looked at the earl.

Peter immediately felt pain within him, there was hurt in his heart, confusion in his mind. He was deeply concerned about what he had just said. He remembered the words which Christ the Ruler had Himself said to him before, that in the dark of the night, before cockcrow, he would deny his Lord three times. This memory swelled up within him, a bitter feeling in his breast, and he walked out of the

---

[254] *that he thes gesides ni uuari.* The denial is very strong in the original, since Peter is denying that he is a part of his Chieftain's personal *gesidi*, whose prime responsibility is unwavering loyalty in battle situations. The author must have felt that Peter's behavior, good and bad, is so humanly intelligible in warrior society that it cannot fail to gain a sympathetic response from the audience, and so he suppresses none of this scene.

[255] As in the earlier part of the *Heliand* fate was made responsible for unfortunate occurrences, such as the death of the widow of Naim's son, in the Passion, fate or the will of God (or the predictive words of the prophets) are made responsible for unfortunate behavior by the apostles.

[256] The beautiful irony in Peter's statement is, of course, that he said "any earthly person." There is someone else standing nearby.

place in a rage,[257] the man went off from the crowd because of his deep concern and feelings of sorrow. He was crying over his own words, his own failure. He was so worried that hot and bloody tears came pouring up from his heart.[258] He thought he could never again make up in the slightest for his deceitful deeds or return to his Lord and be in His favor.

There is no hero so old that he has ever seen any man's son more deeply regret his own words with tears and lamentation. "Well, mighty God," he said, "I have so ruined myself that there is now no need for me to give thanks for my time in the world. If now, Commander, when I reach old age I am to do without Your favor and the kingdom of heaven, then I see no reason to be in any way grateful, beloved Chieftain, that I ever came into this light. I am now unworthy, my Lord Ruler, of walking among Your followers, I am too sinful to be with Your warrior-companions. I will avoid them in my feelings, now that I have said such criminal things." Thus the best of men lamented in deep misery and regret that he had denied his beloved Lord.[259]

People should not be amazed, warriors need not wonder, why God would have wanted such a loveable man and powerful thane to have such an evil thing happen to him as to deny his beloved

---

[257] By using the same word *gibolgan* 'enraged' here that the poet used to describe Peter's striding to Christ's defense on the mountain, the sad fact of Peter's vacillation is highlighted with tragic symmetry, and an appealing spiritual connection is made to the Saxons' situation of vacillation.

[258] Despite Peter's denial of Christ, the author suggests a profound bond of personal similarity between Christ and his "fallen" thane. Just as Christ felt his fear of death so intensely that His sweat became a sweat of blood, the author imagines Peter's grief as being so intense and from the heart that Peter's tears become tears of blood.

[259] The author's concern for Peter is made all the more clear by contrasting this greatly expanded scene with the very brief, though poignant, mention it is given in Scripture (Lk. 22:34): "And Peter went out and wept bitterly."

Shame is considered in the *Heliand*, as in the High Middle Ages, to be a sign of mature knightly virtue, demonstrating the presence in the warrior of deeply held feelings of loyalty. (Cf. The young Parzifal's blatant need to learn to feel shame after committing an unknightly crime.) Because of this Germanic tradition the author is able to keep all of Peter's behavior in his gospel-story.

Chieftain so shamefully because of a servant-girl's words. It was done for the sake of those people, for the sake of the sons of men. The holy Chieftain intended to make Peter the first man in the leadership of His household, and wanted Peter to realize how much strength there is in the human spirit without the power of God. He let Peter commit sin so that afterwards he would better appreciate people, how all human beings love to be forgiven when they have done something wrong. People love to be freed from their loathsome sins and crimes—just as God, the King of Heaven, forgave Peter the wrong he had done.[260]

Song 60

Christ is brought before the assembly as a prisoner

Therefore a man's boasting is not very reliable (it is merely the bragging of a young field-hand), if God's help has left him because of his sins; once that happens, it is not long before the thoughts of a man's heart turn cowardly—no matter what solemn threats he may have uttered before, boasting of his battles, his fighting skill and his strength. This became very clear to that great and excellent thane when his Commander's holy help left him. No one, therefore, should brag about himself too strongly, since a man's will and confidence often disappear if the ruling God, the high King of Heaven, does not strengthen his heart.[261]

Meanwhile, the Best person ever born was waiting, suffering the iron bonds for the sake of mankind. Many of the Jewish people surrounded Him, taunting Him loudly and ridiculing Him, while He

---

[260] The *Heliand* gives a special explanation for God's letting Peter sin—so that he will be a forgiving ruler. Luke's gospel does not need to give an explanation, since it does not present Peter's denials as fated by the will of God.

[261] This paragraph seems curiously out of place. Its admonition to the Saxon warrior on the ultimate source of courage in battle is appropriate enough, but it seems to be the ending of the previous song rather than the beginning of this one. Song 60 could well begin with the following paragraph.

stood there in chains and bore with patience whatever evil things this clan's people did to Him.

Then the light came back, morning came to mankind. Many of the Jewish forces assembled, they had the malicious minds of wolves. Many of the law-interpreters gathered there in the morning, angry and adamant, people of ill-will set on treachery. These fighting men walked together in battle-groups to the secret council. They began to consult with one another on how they could lead the mighty Christ by means of liars' perjury into saying something sinful with His own words, so that they could then subject Him to terrible torture and sentence Him to death.

That day they were unable to find testimony damning enough to justify punishing Him or condemning Him to death, depriving Him of His life because of it. Then, toward the end, two liars came forward and walked up to the battle-group of men. They began to tell the law-interpreters that they had heard Christ Himself saying that He was able to knock down God's shrine, the highest of all houses and, with the powerful skill of His hands and with His own strength, build it up on the third day—something no other man could do.

Christ kept silent and endured it. Never could people ever say so many lies about Him that He would avenge it on them with evil words.

Then there arose among the warriors a deadly-minded man, the bishop of those people, the leader of the clan, and he asked Christ, solemnly adjuring Him in his own name, to testify under oath. He spoke to Christ in God's name and requested Him earnestly to tell them if He were the Son of the living God "who created this light, Christ the eternal king. We are not able to recognize this at all, not from Your words and not from Your deeds." The true Son of God replied to him, "You are saying it now, in front of these Jews, you are soothsaying that I am the very one![262] These people do not believe this of Me and therefore do not wish to let Me go—they are not worthy of My words. But now I will say to you anyway in all truth

---

[262] *that ik it selƀo bium.* lit. 'that I myself am it.'

that you will yet see Me, the great Son of Man, sitting on the right side of God, in the great power of the all-ruling Father, returning from there through the clouds of the sky, and passing judgment on all the clans of warrior-heroes in accordance with what their deeds deserve!"

The bishop then became enraged, his mind was bitter, he went into a furor over what Christ said and slit his clothing, he cut it open in front of his chest. "Now all of you need not wait any longer," he said, "for testimony from witnesses, now that such words have come from Him, such blasphemy from His own mouth! Many men have now heard it here, many fighting men within this holy shrine heard Him say how powerful He is—He said He is God! What sentence of doom do you Jews wish to pass on Him for this? Is He now deserving of death because of such words?"

Song 61

Christ stands in chains before Pilate of Pontusland; Judas, the deserter, hangs himself.

All the warriors of the Jewish army said that He deserved the punishment of His life-spirit being taken. (Yet it was not because of anything that He did that the Jewish people in Jerusalem condemned Him, the sinless Son of the Chieftain, to death.) The Jews were boasting of their feats: of what was the greatest harm they could do to God's Son as He was held in iron bonds. They surrounded Him with warriors and hit Him on the cheeks with their hands—that was all done to ridicule Him—the enemy horde heaped words of mockery and scorn upon Him. God's Child stood His ground among the enemy. His arms were chained, He suffered in patience whatever bitter things the people did to Him. He never flew into a rage over the attacks of these warriors.

Then wrathful men took Him, God's Son, still in irons, and led Him to where the clan had its assembly house.[263] There were many thanes there, surrounding their military governor. He was their lord's delegate from Fort Rome and held the lord's authority over this kingdom. He had come from Caesar, the emperor, and was sent to the Jewish clans to rule the realm—he gave them advice and support. Pilate was his name, he was from Pontusland, born to that clan. He had assembled powerful forces at the assembly house, batallions of men. It was there that truthless men, Jewish people, handed over God's Son to the enemy.[264] They said that He deserved to forfeit His life-spirit, that He should be executed by the sharp attack of the weapon's edge.

The crowd of Jews did not want to throng into the assembly house, the people stood outside and spoke from there with those who were inside. They did not wish to associate with the many foreigners so that they would not hear a thing that day of any unjust words or rash judgment, they said that they wanted to keep their holy time,

---

[263] *thinghus* '[Germanic] assembly house'. The Roman praetorium is referred to by the Germanic term for the sacred legal assembly place of the clan. Since the imperial delegate of Caesar is obviously in charge, despite the fact that the scene (in the *Heliand*) is in the local people's assembly place, the author has shifted the site of Christ's hearing before Pilate to the politically uncomfortable Saxon *thinghus* assembly with an imperial legate present. In the New Testament the local assembly place for the Jews, the Sanhedrin, is never conflated with Pilate's praetorium.

We may also have here more reason for the author's changing of the reason for the Jews' not wishing to enter the praetorium. If, in the *Heliand,* the praetorium becomes a (Jewish) *thinghus*, Jews could not defile themselves by entering their own sacred assembly place. Therefore it becomes necessary for the author to give as a reason the possibility of hearing unholy language from the foreigners on the holy day that keeps the Jews out.

[264] The Jews' turning Jesus over to the Roman authorities is seen in the Bible as a legal necessity (forced upon the Sanhedrin by the occupying power) for the execution of the death penalty. In the *Heliand* it is seen as that and something far worse: the betrayal of a man by turning him over to the enemy. Thus the similarity in the *Heliand's* treatment of Judas and the Jews in the Passion.

their Pascha, clean.[265] Pilate received the Ruler's Son, the One who had committed no sin, from the treacherous injurers.

Judas's mind began to be troubled as he saw his Chieftain being handed over to death. After that, he began to regret his deed as he kept thinking that he had sold his innocent Lord. He then took the silver in his hands, the thirty coins that had been paid to him for his Commander, and went to the Jews and told them the cruel and sinful thing he had done, and gladly offered to return the silver. "I earned it so atrociously with the blood of my Chieftain," he said, "that I know it will do me no good."

The Jewish clansmen did not want to accept it and they told him that from now on it was his business to worry about a sin like that, what he had done to his Lord. "You take care of it yourself," they said. "Why are you coming to see us about this? Do not blame it on these people!" Judas then walked away from there and went, deeply troubled, to God's shrine, and threw the silver inside, into the sanctuary. He did not dare to own it any longer. Very frightened, he walked along—just as the ferocious sons of the enemy fiends told him to do. They had taken such cruel hold of the man's mind—God was enraged at him—that he made himself a noose. The deserter bowed down, putting his head into the deadly rope to strangle and hang himself, and chose his punishment: the hard oppression of Hel, hot and dark, the deep valley of death—because he had been unfaithful to his Chieftain.[266]

---

[265] Scripture mentions the refusal of the Jews to enter the Roman praetorium in order to remain undefiled for Passover (Jn. 18:28) but does not bring out the irony that the same people who had such fine religious sensitivities are quite at home turning an innocent man over to the enemy. The *Heliand* poet goes even further in his irony by making explicit what the source of defilement might be: a defilement of the ears by hearing the foreigners say something unjust or make some rash judgment—the very activity in which the Jewish authorities are at the same moment engaged.

[266] There is no mention of fate. The warning to the Saxons about being a "deserter" is thereby made all the more a matter of personal responsibility.

Song 62

Pilate, Caesar's thane, speaks with God's Son.

God's Son waited at the assembly house, enduring the pain of the iron bindings, until the people came to agreement among themselves about the torture they wished to inflict upon His life-spirit. The delegate of Caesar from Fort Rome arose from the benches and angrily went to speak with the Jewish leadership who were standing in the courtyard in their battle-groups. They did not want to come into the house on the day of Pascha.

Pilate began to question the Jewish people boldly about what the man had done to deserve the death penalty. "Why are you so angry with Him, why are your minds so hostile to Him?" They said that He had done a great deal of harm, of evil, to them. "These people would never have given Him over to you if they were not sure beforehand that He was a criminal, guilty by His words. He has misled many of this people with His teachings, and has confused them by putting doubt in their minds about whether we should pay taxes to Caesar's imperial court. We can tell you that about Him, giving truthful witness. He also says strong words: He says that He is the Christ, the king of this realm—He is that enormously impudent!"

Caesar's imperial delegate said in return, "If He does outrageous things so openly in front of so many, then take Him back to your own people and pass judgment on Him in accordance with what the law of your ancestors commands and determine if He should pay with His life-spirit, if He is worthy of death." Then they said that none of them were allowed to execute anyone by hand on the holy day or to kill anyone with weapons during the holy time.[267]

At that, Caesar's thane, the delegate from Fort Rome who was over this clan, turned angrily away from the warriors. He commanded the Son of God to approach him, and questioned Him intensely and straightforwardly about whether He was the clan king

---

[267] Recent excavations in Denmark's bogs and at Sutton Hoo in East Anglia, both indicate that strangulation may have been used for religious (burial) and legal executions in the North.

of these people. The Chieftain's Son had His answer ready. "Is what you are saying coming from yourself," He said, "or did other earls here say it to you speaking about My kingdom?" Caesar's delegate replied with pride and anger as He conversed there in the sacred building[268] with the ruling Christ. "I do not come from this country of Jewish people," he said, "I am not a fellow clansman of Yours, nor any relative of these men. The crowd put this affair into my hands, Your fellow clansmen, Jewish people, handed You over to me in irons. What harm have You done that You have to suffer the bitter pain of iron shackles from Your own kinsmen?"

Christ, the Best of healers, answered him directly as He stood there in chains in the sacred building. "I too do not come from this country," He said, "nor from this world's time. Were it otherwise, My followers would be courageously resisting the attackers, battling the enemy clan, so that no one could hand Me over in chains to the hate-filled Jewish people to suffer terrible torture. The reason I was born in this world was to give witness, to give knowledge to you about true things by My coming. People who come from truth are able to recognize that easily. They can understand My words and believe My teachings."

Caesar's delegate could not find anything reprehensible about God's Son, not a single deceitful word for which He would owe His life. He then went back again and spoke angrily with the crowd of Jews. They paid close attention as he said in front of the people that he was unable to find any blasphemous language in the prisoner such that He would be deserving of losing His life-spirit, worthy of death.

The Jewish people stood there, stupefied, accusing God's Son with their words. They said that He first started insurrection in Galileeland, "and from there he traveled through Judea to here, creating doubt in peoples' minds and feelings. For this He deserves to die; He deserves to be punished by the edge of the sword if ever there was someone who was worthy of death because of His deeds."

---

[268] *rakude* 'shrine, temple, god's property'. The place of assembly, the *thinghus*, is treated as a sacred area in the *Heliand*.

Song 63

Warriors bring Christ in irons to King Herod; arrogant earls ridicule God's Child of Peace.

So the Jewish people accused Him with words because of the hate in their minds. Then the military governor in his slyness heard them say from which clan Christ, the Best of men, came. The good One came from the famous clan, from Galileeland.[269] That was a great group of nobly born men! Herod powerfully ruled the kingdom there which was given to him by the emperor for him to enforce justice among the people, preserve the peace, and to hand down judgments. Herod was also that same day in Jerusalem with his men; he was with his warriors at the shrine. That was the custom then, to observe the holy time there, the Pascha of the Jews.

Pilate then commanded his warrior-heroes to take the prisoner, as He was, in His chains;[270] and he ordered his earls to put the captive, God's Son, in Herod's hands, since Christ was from the clan-territory and people under Herod's authority. The fighting men carried out their lord's word. They led the holy Christ, the Best Son ever born to the light of men, to the head man of the people, in chains. Christ walked with His arms and legs in iron shackles until they reached the place where King Herod was seated on his bench. A crowd of warriors surrounded him, proud fighting men. They were very anxious there to see Christ Himself. They thought He might show them some great and mighty sign just like the many He did in His godlike power for the Jewish people.

---

[269] People and land are identified in the *Heliand*. The idea of "nation" as connoting a political entity composed of different ethnic groups (modern nation states like the U. S. A.) is not present. "Nation" in the *Heliand* is a familial entity based on birth into a specific clan territory—as nation (based on *natus* 'birth') originally meant.

[270] The reader will have noticed the constant reference to Jesus as being a prisoner in chains. This seems to be a poetic effort to stimulate sympathy for Christ among the Saxon hearers, and, even more, empathy. Many of the Saxon hearers of this epic must have been themselves or by proxy of their relatives, precisely in this situation from the ruling Christian authorities. The New Testament, of course, knows no such emphasis on chains and body irons in Christ's Passion.

With great curiosity the king asked Him questions in many words. He kept trying to get to the bottom of Christ's attitude and feelings—what He wanted to set up for the benefit of the human race. The mighty Christ stood there, enduring and keeping silent. He did not want to give an answer to Herod the king, nor to his earls, not a single word.

Then the angry Jewish people stood there harassing and accusing God's Son until the point when the king's attitude and that of all the king's retainers became hostile to Him. In their hearts they despised Him. They did not recognize the might of God, the Lord of Heaven. Their minds were in darkness, they were blinded by evil. Patiently the Chieftain's Son endured all their violence, words and deeds, every spiteful thing they wanted to do to Him. To mock Him, they ordered that His limbs be wrapped in white clothing so that He would become a joke to the young people there.[271] The Jews, arrogant earls, were delighted when they saw Him being held up to ridicule.

King Herod sent Christ back from there to the other clan people, ordering a strong man to lead Him.[272] They spoke disrespectfully to Christ, using outrageous words, as He walked along in chains, loaded down with ridicule.[273] But His mind was not in doubt, He bore it all with patient humility. He had no intention of paying them

---

[271] In Scripture, Herod has a white robe placed on Christ's shoulders, presumably to ridicule any claim of kingship on Christ's part (Lk. 23:11). In the *Heliand* the humor may be more sinister. By describing the white clothing as being wrapped around Jesus' limbs, the prisoner is psychologically threatened by being given the form of a future corpse!

[272] The contemporaneous *Utrecht Psalter* has an illustration depicting this. The prisoner is led by a single guard holding a long chain which is shackled to the metal fastening between the captive's handcuffs.

[273] In the New Testament account it is only mentioned twice that Christ is bound. In the *Heliand* it is repeated again and again in a spellbinding contemplative refrain. It is impossible for the audience or the reader to think of the Passion in the *Heliand* without imagining Christ standing there in chains or being led around in irons. No Saxon who had been marched off by the Christian Franks in the same manner to baptism or death could fail to be moved by the touching similarity, the mystical vision of the poet who saw his captive Saxons as Christ.

back for their evil words, mockery and insults.[274] They brought Him back inside the house, up to the palace where Pilate was at the assembly place.[275] The thanes gave over the Best of persons into the hands of murderers, just as He Himself, guilty of no sin, chose. He wanted to rescue the sons of men from suffering and death. The Jews full of hate, stood in front of the guest hall. Sons of the fiend[276] had so incited the crowd that they did not hold themselves back in the slightest from the cruelest of deeds.

Caesar's thane, the hardened military governor, then went over to speak to the crowd. "Look," he said, "you sent this captive to me in this hall, and you yourselves handed Him over, maintaining that He has ruined many people, misleading them with His teachings. I am unable, however, to find anything from these people, the Jewish folk, that He should pay for with His life in front of this crowd. That became clear today. Herod could not—and he knows your law, the traditional laws of your people!—Herod could not see cause to put the man's life in jeopardy, to have Him die today, because of some sins or other, and leave His life behind. Now, before these people here, I will threaten Him with legal process in severe language, I will correct His attitude, and I will let Him continue to enjoy living among mankind."

The Jewish clan yelled out together in very loud voices and demanded ardently that Christ's life-spirit be killed with pain, that He be thrown onto a cross and tortured terribly. "With His words He has earned the death penalty! He says that He is the Chieftain, that He is really God's Son! He will pay for that atrocious language as is

---

[274] These two sentences could be taken merely as a description of Christ's attitude, but in the context of this song, and with the unusual inclusion (in Christ's case) of the remark that 'His mind was not in doubt,' it seems clear that the author is exhorting the Saxons to patient and undoubting behavior under oppression.

[275] *palencia* is the word used for 'palace'. This is late Latin, contemporaneous with the author. He avoids the biblical, more classical word *praetorium*, perhaps on the grounds that it conjured up no visual image for the hearers. He then identifies the *palencia* with the Germanic *thingstedi* 'assembly place'. Two sentences later Pilate will refer to the same place as a *gastseli* 'guest-hall', thus arriving at the visually more familiar mead-hall.

[276] *gramo[no] barn* 'sons of the hostile one[s]; devils'.

written in our law: such blasphemous utterances are paid for with one's life!"

Song 64

The Jewish warriors threaten Pilate with the ill-will of the emperor at Fort Rome.

The ruler of the people felt a strong twinge of fear as he heard them saying that they had actually heard the man speaking, telling people in public that He was God's Son. The military governor then turned and went back in the house, into the assembly hall, and spoke in daring words to God's Son, asking Him what kind of man He was. "What kind of human being are You?" he said. "Why do You conceal Your feelings from me? Why do You hide Your deepest thoughts? Do You not know that Your fate, Your life, is totally dependent on what I decide? The Jewish warriors handed You over to me, giving me the power either to have You impaled on spear-point, to kill You on a cross, or to let You live—whichever of the two I myself and my people think is the better course of action."[277] God's Child of Peace said in return, "Do you not know that in all truth you could not have power over Me if Holy God Himself had not given it to you? However, the ones who handed Me over to you out of hatred, and sold Me out as I was held in chains—they have greater sins."

The hostile-minded governor, the thane of the emperor, would gladly have let Him go after that, since he did have authority over the man in the sight of the people. The Jewish clansmen, however, attacked this desire of his with their every word. "You are not a friend of Caesar, someone of whom he is fond, if you let Christ leave here safe and sound. That might one day come to cause trouble and pain for you, since whoever speaks the words He does, whoever

---

[277] Impalement on a spear (Germanic) and crucifixion (Roman) are made into the poetic equivalent of each other and thus constitute one of the two choices which Pilate has.

raises himself so high that he says that he would like to have the title of kingship—without the emperor giving it to him!—is bringing disorder into Caesar's world empire by disdaining the emperor's word and by ignoring the emperor in his attitude. Therefore, you should punish such audacity, such impudent words—if you are concerned about your lord and your lord's friendship, you will take this man's life."

The military governor understood that the Jewish leadership was threatening him with his commander. He went back then to the assembly place and took his seat. A huge crowd of warriors was gathered there. He ordered Christ the Ruler brought before the people. The Jews were demandingly asking how soon they could see the holy Child hanging, dying in pain on a cross. They said that there was no other king among their own aristocracy except for the noble emperor Caesar from the Roman hill-fort. "He reigns here over us, therefore you should not let this One go! He has said so many wicked things to us that He has destroyed Himself by His deeds. He has to suffer death, punishment, and extreme torture!"

The Jewish people said many different sinful things about mighty Christ. He stood there, keeping silent in patient humility. He did not answer their hostile words, He wanted to free the whole world with His life—that is why He let the evil clan subject Him to whatever terrible torture they desired. He did not want to let all the Jewish people know openly that He was God Himself. For, if they really knew how much power He had over this middle world, their feelings would turn cowardly within their breasts and they would never dare to lay their hands on the Son of God, and then the kingdom of heaven, the brightest of worlds, would never be unlocked to the sons of men. Because of this, He hid it in His heart and did not let the human clan know what they were doing.[278] Fate was coming closer

---

[278] The apologetic reasoning in this section is not in the evangelist's account of the Passion, and represents an attempt to justify Christ's apparent total passivity in the "face of the enemy." The argument that no one would have carried out the Crucifixion once they realized who He was, and thus that human salvation would not have occurred in the manner that had been foreordained, is a way to explain the passiveness both as an act of unselfishness and as submission to one's fate/the will of

then, the great power of God, and midday,[279] when they were to bring His life-spirit to its death agony.

At that same time there was also in the hill-fort a famous criminal—also lying in chains, for he had committed many murders and killed many people in the kingdom. He was a man so notorious at stealing that no one was his equal. He was also a prisoner there because of his sins, Barabbas was his name. He was well known to many people from hill-fort to hill-fort because of his wicked crimes. There was a custom in the country of the Jews that, every year on the holy day they could request that a prisoner be set free for the love of God, and that the head of the fort, the people's governor, would then grant a prisoner his life. The military governor thus began to ask the Jewish leadership and people as they stood before him which one of the two they would decide in favor of, "which of the two prisoners standing here facing the people?" The leaders of the Jews had incited all the poor people[280] to ask for the life of the one who devastated the country—the thief who plied his vicious trade so often in the darkness of night!—and for Christ to be killed on a cross.

It became well known everywhere which way the clanspeople decided in their verdict. They then had to do it: hang the holy Son. Later on, it would become cause for worry to the military governor that he had seen through the case, that he knew that the leadership was persecuting the rescuing Christ out of jealous hatred, and yet he had listened to them and carried out their will. For this he received

---

God.

[279] *Thiu uurd nahida thuo, / mari maht godes endi middi dag.* Fate is now clearly identified with the will of God, which, like fate of old has inexorably prespecified everything that comes to pass, including even the very time, noon on Good Friday, when the Crucifixion is destined to begin. The mention of the time, midday, brings the ancient association of the fates and time together, with their task of measuring the length of existence of any mortal being. The mention of midday thus adds a very somber and pagan tone, reminding the Germanic listener of one of the old words for the divine being: *Metod* 'the Measurer.' See *The Saxon Savior,* pp. 53-54.

[280] The implication being that the more well-to-do, thanes, are not as easily manipulated as the poor. The gospels do not make any comment on the economic or social standing of the people in the crowd as the *Heliand* does, no doubt in order to appeal to its specific addressees.

punishment, repayment in this light, and for a long time afterwards. He was woeful later, when he gave up this world, later on.[281]

Song 65

Caesar's thane puts the Best of all men into the hands of the Jews.

The enemy, the worst of the wicked, Satan himself, became aware of all this when Judas's soul arrived down at the bottom of cruel Hel. At that moment Satan knew for certain that the One who was standing there in chains was the Ruler, Christ, the Son of the Chieftain. Satan then knew for sure that Christ wanted to set the whole world free from the oppression of Hel by His hanging, freeing everyone to go to God's light. That gave Satan a feeling of great pain and was profoundly disturbing to his mind. He immediately wanted to come to Christ's aid to help prevent the sons of men from taking Christ's life or killing Him on a cross! He wanted Him to remain alive, so that human beings would not become safe and secure from their sins and the inferno.

Satan then set off for the place where the military governor's family lived in the hill-fort. The sinister enemy began showing mysterious signs very clearly to the governor's wife so that she would use her words to help Christ, Chieftain of the human race, to remain alive (He was then already predestined to die).[282] Satan knew truly

---

[281] The word used here so many times is *sidor* 'later, afterwards, later on'. The Christian idea of eventual punishment for culpable acts and the Germanic idea of the inescapability of one's fate at the specified time in the future, are powerfully combined by using the word *sidor* from the epic tradition.

[282] In a clever if somewhat intimidating reversal, the *Heliand* poet draws a necessary conclusion. If fate and the will of God are one, anyone who opposes fate (what happens in this world and when), opposes the will of God. Christ is fated by the will of God to be crucified at noon on Good Friday. While those who are instruments of this predetermination, Pilate and the Jewish leaders, for example, are not excused from condemnation for having cooperated in bringing it about, the only one who opposes the inevitable is Satan. Satan will not win, of course, but the author

that Christ would take away his power and he would no longer hold his great sway over the broad middle-world. The woman was very worried, she was frightened by the visions that were coming to her in broad daylight. They were the doings of the deceiver, who was invisible, hidden by a magic helmet.[283] She sent a request to her lord in her words, commanding that he be told truthfully what was coming to her in visions because of the holy man. She asked her lord to help the man and to save the man's life. "I have seen so many strange things here on account of Him that I know that the sins of any earl who dares to kill that man's life-spirit will be horribly increased."

The messenger then went on his way until he found the place where the military governor was seated in the midst of the throng, next to the stone street (a road made by joining rocks together). There he went up to his lord and told him his wife's words. The governor became very upset, inside he was churning, the thoughts of his mind turned despondent. Both things were painful to him: that they should kill an innocent man; and that he did not dare to dismiss the case in the presence of these people because of what they had said. Then, in his heart, his mind gradually inclined toward the Jewish leadership, toward acting according to their will. He did not defend himself in the slightest from the serious sin he was there doing to himself.[284]

---

does have an explanation for the dream of Pilate's wife, the source of which is unexplained in the gospels. Even Satan makes all too human efforts to fend off what is inexorably coming to pass.

[283] Satan is using a *helidhelm* 'concealing helmet' to remain invisible. This magic helmet may have been a commonplace of Germanic folklore since we have more evidence of its "use" in other Germanic stories such as the *Nibelungenlied*, where Siegfried uses it somewhat disreputably in a bedroom adventure.

[284] In the *Heliand* sin seems most often to be conceived of as something evil done to oneself, a self-inflicted wound, because of its ultimate effect not on the person who is the object of the sin, but on the person who commits the sin. Because sin is a self-hurting action, it is not surprising that the poet sees the act of sinning not so much as something done out of one's own will (who would want to hurt oneself?), but rather a takeover of one's body and mind and behavior by the will of "the enemies." See for example the *Heliand's* rendition of "lead us not into temptation," in the Lord's Prayer, song 19. In this scene Pilate is depicted in the same manner, losing his will

Then, as he sat there before the people, he ordered them to bring him clear spring water in a basin for his hands. Caesar's thane, the strict military governor, washed himself in front of the clan and spoke to the leadership, saying that he cleared himself then and there of these sins and evil deeds. "I do not want to be in any way responsible," he said, "for this holy man. You carry all this out yourselves—every word and action you are doing here to punish Him." Then all the leaders of the Jews, the huge crowd, all shouted out together, saying that they would take responsibility for the terrible things done to the man. "Let His gore pour over us, His blood and His death-curse,[285] and let it pour over our children, and over our descendants hereafter! If we are doing anything sinful, we will take full responsibility," they said, "even for the killing itself!"

The Best of all men was then, in front of the Jews, put in the hands of those who hated Him. As the heinous enemy took Him, He was held tightly by the pressure of iron bonds; and a great crowd of cruel people surrounded Him. The great Chieftain endured patiently whatever the clanspeople did to Him. They ordered Him to be whipped prior to killing His life-spirit and ending His days. They spat in His eyes to ridicule Him, warriors slapped His cheeks with their hands and they took His clothes from Him. Those vicious criminals stole His red cloak and did even more things to Him to show contempt. They ordered a terrible headband to be made by twisting hard thorn-branches together and then placed it on Christ the Ruler Himself. The warrior-companions then went up to Him, addressed Him in the royal manner, and fell on their knees, bowing their heads to Him. It was all done out of mockery, but the Chieftain of Peoples bore it all with strength because of His love for human beings.

---

to that of others.

[285] *baneđi* 'death-curse, murder-cry, death-lament, death-cry'. As is clear from the preceding, the translation is not entirely certain. Part of the difficulty stems from the word itself, which seems to be a Celtic loan-word. *Ban* is clearly 'death' or 'murder', *edi* is a solemn utterance such as a curse, lament, or complaint. From its use in its context here the word could mean either the victim's death-cry, and/or the death-curse that falls upon those who murdered him.

Then they ordered warrior-heroes to use the edges of their battle-axes to make a mighty cross out of a hardwood tree with their hands. They told Christ, the holy Son of God, to bring it by Himself, they commanded our Chieftain to carry it to the place where He was to die, covered with blood, though He had done nothing wrong.

The Jews walked along, willing warriors, leading the ruling Christ to death. A loud, terrible sound could be heard there. There were women walking behind them, crying and lamenting; groaning men from Galilee who came with them following the long roads. Their Lord's death was a great sorrow to them.

Then He spoke. The Best of sons looked back and told them not to weep. "Do not let My going away trouble you," He said, "instead you should be crying and lamenting with bitter tears over your evil deeds. The time will come when Jewish mothers and wives who never had a child in their time will be the happy ones. At that time you will pay horribly for your injustice. At that time you will dearly want high mountains to cover you and bury you in the depths. Death would be by far preferable for you in this country than to endure the torture and pain that will be coming here—to the people of this clan."

Song 66

The Chieftain is hanged on the criminal tree.

There on the sandy gravel they erected the gallows, up on a field the Jewish people set it up—a tree on a mountain—and there they tortured God's Son on a cross.[286] They eagerly pounded cold iron, sharp-pointed new nails—horrible fastenings—through His hands and

---

[286] Throughout this song the cross is continually interpreted, usually in a phrase immediately following its mention, by its Northern equivalent: a tree or gallows. Even the cross itself when mentioned is often shaded with descriptions that insist on its treelikeness. The Crucifixion is thus brought home to people accustomed to seeing prisoners of war, criminals, and even oxen, hanging from trees sacred to Woden as a religious sacrifice. See Appendix 1.

His feet with hard hammerstrokes. His blood ran down onto the earth, oozing from our Chieftain, but He did not want to take vengeance on the Jews for the terrible deed. Instead He asked mighty God the Father not to be angry with the people of the human race,[287] "because they do not know what they are doing," He said.

The warriors, men of daring, divided the clothing of Christ, the robes of the Chieftain. About one item the fighting-men could not come to an agreement until they cast lots in their group to see which one of them would have the holy coat, the most beautiful garment ever worn.

The herdsman of the people, the military governor, ordered that they should write on the cross, above the head of Christ, that this was the king of the Jews, Jesus from Fort Nazareth, nailed here because of jealousy and hate on a new gallows, the wooden tree. The people asked him to change the words to: this is the One who liked to say of Himself that He had authority over these warrior-companies, that He was king of the Jews. Caesar's delegate, the hard military-governor, said in reply, "It has been written for you thus over His head, so wisely cut into the wood, that I cannot now change it!"[288]

The Jewish people put two condemned criminals on crosses for punishment on both sides of Christ to have them suffer great pain on the criminal-tree[289] as reward for the evil things they had done. The people spoke words of mockery to holy Christ and shouted

---

[287] In this and other passages it is clear that the Jews in the Passion are a stand-in for the whole human race. The *Heliand* poet's negativity with regard to the behavior of the Jews in Christ's Passion is also negative with regard to human behavior under these circumstances and not just the behavior of one clan. This is shown by phrases referring to the Jews being paralleled (as here) by phrases in which "human beings" is given as the equivalent for "the Jews."

[288] Pilate's reason given in scripture (Jn. 19:22) is simpler: "What I have written, I have written." In the *Heliand* a second more wry Northern note is added by changing the verb for to write from *scriƀan* 'to write with ink on paper' to *uuritan* 'to carve runes in wood'. Thus Pilate in the *Heliand* is able to find it not just personally undesirable to change the inscription, but also rather difficult, since he had arranged that the runic inscription be wisely carved into the wood over Christ's head.

[289] *uuaragtreuue*. This expression is normally taken as a kenning for the gallows. There may be a possibility, however, that it is not a kenning, but may refer to a tree designated for criminal executions by hanging.

scornful words. They looked at the Best of all human beings suffering on the cross—"If You are king over everything," they said, "the Son of the Chieftain, as You Yourself have said, rescue Yourself from this torment! Free Yourself from this hate, walk away from it hale and well! These people, these sons of heroes, will believe You then!"

Someone who was standing there in front of the gallows, a very arrogant Jew, said blasphemously to Him, "This world would be in a lot of trouble," he said, "if You were in authority over it! You said that You could knock down the entire high house of the heavenly King, the greatest construction there is in stone, in one day, and have it standing again three days afterwards—a claim no other person of this people has ever dared to make. Look how You are now fastened, suffering great pain, and You are not able to do anything to improve Your terrible situation."

Then one of the thieves also nailed there joined in with hostile words, just as he heard the clanspeople saying—he was not a thane of good will or feelings. "If You are the king," he said, "Christ, God's Son, then get down from the cross, slip out of the rope,[290] and help and heal all of us here together. If You are the King of Heaven, the Ruler of the world, let it show in Your deeds; show Your greatness in front of this crowd!" Then the other man who was also hanging where he was fastened and suffering horrible pain, said to him, "Why do you want to say something mocking like that to Him? Here you are: held to the gallows, broken on the tree. Both of us are suffering badly because of our sins, it is our own actions that have brought us to this punishment. He stands here innocent of any crime, free of any sins—He never did anything malicious. It is only because of this clan's hatred that He is willing to suffer pain in this world."

"I do want to believe," he said, "and I would like to ask the Land's Protector, God's Son, that You think of me, and help me, Best of counselors, when You come to Your kingdom—be gracious

---

[290] The author has the thief speak both Roman and Germanic: come down from the nails holding you to the cross; slip out of the rope from which You are hanging from the tree.

to me then."[291] Christ the Rescuer replied to him immediately in His words. "I say to you truthfully," He said, "that before today is over, you and I will together in Heaven's kingdom see the light of God in Paradise—even though you may now be in such pain."

Mary, Christ's mother, was standing there under the tree. She was pale, she saw her Son suffering, enduring horrible torture. There were also women with her who had come because of their love for the mighty One—John, Christ's follower, was also standing there very sad beneath his Lord, his mind in grief—they were all sorrowful because of the death. Then the mighty Chieftain, Christ, spoke to His mother, "I will now commend you to My follower who is standing here present. Go along with his warrior-company and treat him like a son." He then spoke to John and told him to take good care of her and to love her with the generous kindness one should have for his mother, this woman with no wickedness. In his clear-minded way, John then took her under his protection just as his Lord had commanded him.

Song 67

The Chieftain of mankind dies by the criminal-tree rope;
His spirit escapes.

At midday a great sign was wondrously shown over the whole world when they lifted God's Son up onto the gallows, up onto the cross—it became known everywhere: the sun went dark, its brilliant, beautiful light was unable to shine. It was wrapped in shadow, dark and gloomy, and in a deep sinister fog.[292] Of all overcast days it was the dreariest and darkest ever in this wide world for as long as Christ the Ruler was suffering on the cross, until none[293] that day. At that

---

[291] When the good thief decides to believe, he immediately begins speaking to Christ in the forms and epithets appropriate for a Germanic lord.

[292] As in the scene of Christ walking on the water, fog is added to keep the incident near the North Sea!

[293] *nuon* 'none, the ninth hour [of the Roman day]' 3:00 PM.

time the fog lifted and the darkness dissipated, the sun's light began to grow brighter in the sky.

Then the Strongest of kings called up to God as He stood there fastened by the arms, "Father all-mighty," He said, "why have You abandoned Me like this, beloved Chieftain, holy King of Heaven? Why is Your help and Your support so far away? I am here among the enemy being tortured terribly!"[294] The Jews laughed at Him in mockery. They heard the holy Christ, the Chieftain facing death, asking for a drink, saying that He was thirsty. The clanspeople did not let up, those hateful adversaries, they wanted very much to bring Him something to drink, something bitter! Those outrageous people had made an unpleasant sour mixture of vinegar and bile. A man stood ready, a person guilty of many crimes whom they picked out and enticed with their speech into doing it. He took a sponge soaked with this most loathsome wine, fixed it onto a long shaft—he tied it onto a pole—and then held it up to God's Son, putting it to the mighty One's mouth.

Christ recognized their murky deed, He realized that they were being deceitful. He did not want to taste any more bitterness. Instead, God's Child called out loudly to the heavenly Father. "I entrust My spirit into Your hands, into God's will,"[295] He said, "My spirit is now ready to go, ready to travel." The Chieftain of Mankind then bowed His head, the holy breath escaped from the body.[296]

---

[294] Christ's plea to His Father is strengthened in the *Heliand* by being movingly recast as a captured Companion and Thane's appeal to His Chieftain, reminding Him of His obligation as a Chieftain to render help and support to a faithful Thane now in peril from the enemy.

[295] By the slight expansion of the text to include God's will, the Christ of the *Heliand* is ready to trust both God the Father and fate (God's will). The addition of "ready to travel" makes the transcendence of death almost an everyday concept.

[296] A beautiful suggestion is only slightly concealed in the final verb: the Prisoner has *escaped*.

As the Protector of the Land died on the rope,[297] amazing signs were worked immediately so that the Ruler's death, His last day, would be recognized by the many speechless beings.[298] Earth trembled, the high mountains shook, hard rocks and boulders in the fields cracked apart. The colorful curtain so wonderfully woven which had for many a day been hanging without harm inside the shrine (people, heroes' sons, were never allowed to look at the holy things hidden behind the curtain) was torn in two down the middle—Jewish people could then see the treasure-hoard![299] Graves of dead men opened up; and, by the Chieftain's power, they got up out of the earth alive in their bodies, and were caught sight of there, to the amazement of human beings. What a powerful thing that was, that Christ's death should be felt and acknowledged by so many beings which had never before spoken a word to human beings in this world!

Jewish people saw these awesome things, but their slithery attitude had become so hardened in their hearts, that there was no sign shown to them—be it ever so holy—that could ever make them trust any better in Christ's power or in His universal kingship over this world. Some who were there to guard the bodies did say in their words that it was truly the Ruler's Son, God's Own, who was dying on the gallows, the Best Son ever born. Many women were crying

---

[297] Jesus' dying on the cross is, in Germanic terms, a hanging. The listeners heard clear echoes of the hanging of Woden in the cosmic tree when he tried to learn the answer to the riddle of death, and discovered the mysterious runes. See *The Saxon Savior*, pp. 76-7.

[298] This lovely romanticist explanation is not in the New Testament. Scripture merely states that the natural reactions—earthquake, rock fractures, etc. occurred at Christ's death. In the *Heliand*, these natural movements are acknowledged as being expressive language, "words" of the creatures that cannot talk, so that they too can acknowledge in their own language what has happened. There is no wonder that the *Heliand* poet finds this small incident important enough to merit a mini-frame structure (the frame is closed several lines down) on its own, it is so similar to his own language task.

[299] The veil of the temple concealed the holy of holies, the room which once contained the ark of the covenant. The *Heliand* interprets this concealed sacred possession of the Jewish people as a hidden Germanic treasure in the tradition of the last scenes of *Beowulf,* and the treasure of the Nibelungs hidden in the Rhine.

and beating their breasts. The horrible torture hurt their hearts, their Lord's death put them into deep sorrow.

It was a Jewish custom not to let prisoners remain hanging on the holy day once their lives had glided away and their souls had sunk. Cruel-minded, hateful men approached the place where the two thieves stood nailed, both of them suffering in pain alongside Christ. They were still alive until cruel Jewish people broke[300] their legs, so that they then took leave of life and departed for the other light. There was no need for them to force the death of Christ the Chieftain by any further outrage. They found Him already gone, His soul had been sent on the true road to the long-lasting light. His body's limbs were growing cold, His life-spirit was far from the flesh.[301]

One of the enemy came closer, hate in his mind, carrying a well-nailed spear tightly in his hands. With incredible force he thrust it, cutting a wound in Christ's side with the spearhead, opening up His body. The people saw that both blood and water were pouring out from there, welling out of the wound. All of this was just the way He wanted it and had predetermined beforehand for the benefit of mankind, the sons of men. Now it had all come to pass.[302]

---

[300] In the gospel accounts, Pilate sent Roman soldiers to do this. The *Heliand* author has only Jewish soldiers carry out the crucifixion, possibly for the reason of simplifying the antagonists, "the enemy," in his epic and because he often uses the Jewish people as the stand-in for the human race.

[301] Christ has escaped from his captors; and when they came to inflict more torture upon Him, they were confronted by the fact that He was "gone."

[302] At this point in the *Heliand*, the author has Christ take the God/fate relationship a last step toward synthesis. Christ is now not confronted by an "approaching fate/will of God" as in the Passion, He is here seen as having been the one who had arranged all His destiny beforehand, He Himself had predetermined all that subsequently befell Him. He is God's will/fate incarnate. In Germanic cosmology there may be no more ultimate way of stating Christ's divine status.

Song 68

The body is removed from the gallows tree
and buried in the earth;
Christ's spirit returns at night to the corpse;
Christ rises.

When the bright sun, together with the heavenly stars, had sunk nearer to its rest on that gloomy day, our Chieftain's thane set off on his way. An intelligent man, he had been a follower of Christ for a long time, although not many people really knew of it, since he concealed it with his words from the Jewish people. Joseph was his name, secretly our Chieftain's follower. He did not want to follow wicked people of the clan into doing anything sacrilegious, and so he waited among the Jewish people in holiness for the kingdom of the heavens.

At that moment he was on his way to speak with the military governor, to deal with emperor Caesar's thane. Joseph urged the man earnestly to release Christ's body from the cross on which it now was, dead, freeing the good man from the gallows, and to lay it in a grave, commit it to the earth. The military governor had no desire to refuse what Joseph wanted, and so he granted him the authority to carry it out. From there, Joseph set off for the gallows, walking to the place where he knew that God's Son, the corpse of his Lord, was hanging. He removed it from the new gallows pole and pulled the nails out of it. He took the beloved body in his arms, just as one should with one's lord, wrapped it in linen, and carried it devoutly—as the Chieftain deserved—to the place where they had hewn out the inside of a rock with their hands, a place where no hero's son, no one, had ever been buried. There they committed God's Son, the holiest of corpses into the folds of the earth in the way customary in their country, and closed the most godlike of all graves with a stone.[303] The poor women who had seen all of this man's terrible death sat there crying and distraught. Then the weeping women decided to go away from there—they noted carefully the way back to the grave—they had seen enough of sorrow and overpowering sadness. The poor distraught women were all called Mary. Evening came then, and the night fog.

The next morning many of the hateful Jewish people were assembled . . .[304] they were holding a secret meeting. "You are well aware how this whole kingdom was divided and the people were confused because of this one man. Now He lies buried, overcome with wounds, in a deep grave. He always said that He was to get up from death on the third day. This clan's people believe much too much in His words. Order the grave now to be put under guard and watched, so that His followers do not steal Him from the rock and then say that the powerful One has arisen from His rest. The clan's fighting men will be even more provoked if they start to spread that story around here."

Warriors were picked from the Jewish battle-group for the guard. They set off with their weapons and went to the grave where they were to guard the corpse of God's Son. The holy day of the Jews had now passed. The warriors sat on top of the grave on their watch during the dark starlit night. They waited under their shields[305] until bright day came to mankind all over the middle world, bringing light to people.

---

[303] The *Heliand's* depiction of the burial of Christ is a very carefully made synthesis of the Mediterranean and Germanic traditions. Though Christ is brought to a tomb hewn out of a rock as in the Bible, he is buried in the ground, in the floor of the tomb, in a Germanic earthen grave. The stone that sealed the entrance way to the tomb in the scriptural account is placed directly over the grave in the *Heliand*. Carolingian law forbade this type of mound grave for Saxons (and insisted that the dead be brought to the church's cemeteries), but in the *Heliand* Christ Himself is buried in the ground with a stone slab above in the old Germanic pagan style, enabling his Resurrection to be visualized as a resurrection from the soil, a Saxon Resurrection.

[304] There is a lacuna here in the manuscripts (*M* and *C*).

[305] *bidun undar iro bordon* lit. '[they] bided under their boards'. Though this could mean 'they waited under arms', it seems more likely to indicate that they were using their shields as a kind of cover against the elements.

It was not long then until: there was the spirit coming, by God's power, the holy breath, going under the hard stone to the corpse![306] Light was at that moment opened up, for the good of the sons of men; the many bolts on the doors of Hel were unlocked; the road from this world up to heaven was built![307] Brilliantly radiating, God's Peace-Child rose up! He went about, wherever He pleased, in such a way that the guards, tough soldiers, were not at all aware of when He got up from death and arose from His rest.

The Jewish warriors, the fighting men with their shields, were sitting outside, around the grave.[308] The brilliant sunlight continued to glide upward. The women were on their way, walking to the grave, women of good family, the Marys most lovely. They had traded many jewels, silver and gold to buy salves, and given much wealth to get roots,[309] the best they could obtain, so that they could pour salve on the corpse of their beloved Lord, the Chieftain's Son, and into the wounds carved into Him. The women were very concerned in their minds and some were speaking about who could roll the huge stone off to one side of the grave. They had seen the men lay it over the corpse when they had buried the body in the rock.

---

[306] This is the *Heliand's* expansion, the biblical texts make no attempt to provide a poetic description of the moment of Resurrection itself. Thus in the Germanic religious imagination a dead person's shade, his moving spirit, his breath/life may well have been pictured in this wandering way.

[307] Of the three immediate results of the Resurrection here mentioned, the first two have been heard before in the poem; it is the third that provides a new climax. "The road to heaven has been built." This may have been suggested to the poet because of the presence of such an important road in Germanic mythology. (There is no such image in the New Testament Resurrection accounts.) The *bifrost* 'the *Milky Way*' was thought to provide such access to heaven (and to earth) for the gods to travel and, more importantly here, for the souls of the dead with the help of the Valkyries. Germanic Christianity, too, would have to have such a road to the light, and the author finds its entrance here at Christ's grave.

[308] This is not a contradiction of the previous passage in which they were described as sitting on top of the grave. This is simply the usual style of the author of interweaving the Northern and Southern conceptions of a single event. In this case he gave the Germanic version first; now he gives the Mediterranean.

[309] As in the preceding, the olive-oil salves are from the biblical account, the roots (and the herbal medicinal concoctions made from them) are the Germanic equivalent.

When the noble ladies had come into the garden so that they could look at the grave itself, an angel of the All-Ruler came down out of the skies above, moving along on its coat of feathers[310] like a roaring wind so that all the ground was set to shaking; the earth reverberated; and the resolve of the earls, the Jewish guards, weakened; and they fell down out of fear. They did not think that they would have their life-spirits—simply be alive—much longer!

Song 69

The angel of the All-Ruler tells the women that the Chieftain is on His way to Galileeland.

The guards were lying there, the warrior-companions were as if half dead. Suddenly the great stone lifted up, uncovering the grave, as God's angel pushed it aside. The Chieftain's great messenger then sat down on the grave. In his movements and in his face, for anyone who attempted to look directly at him, he was as radiant and blissfully beaming as a brilliant light! His clothes were like a cold winter's snow.[311] The women saw him sitting there on top of the stone which had been removed, and terror came over them because of the nearness of such radiance. All of the noble ladies were shocked and became very frightened. They did not dare to take a step farther toward the grave, until God's angel, the Ruler's messenger, spoke to them in words and said that he was very aware of their errand, their works, their good will and intentions, and told the women not to be afraid of him. "I know that you are looking for

---

[310] *federhamo* 'feather shirt'. It seems like the author is either alluding to some mythic, Germanic, magic feather garment that is now lost to us, or he is deliberately making the feathers of angels' wings (conceived according to the imagery of Mediterranean or Byzantine art) intelligible to his audience by making them into a sort of magic coat that enables its wearer to fly!

[311] *uuintarcaldon sneuue* 'winter-cold snow' or perhaps 'new-fallen snow'. The adjective is the author's quietly effective expansion of the text. Scripture (Mt. 28:3) simply has "snow."

your Chieftain, Christ the Rescuer, from hill-fort Nazareth, whom the Jewish people tortured, crucified and, though innocent, laid here in the grave. He is not here now, He has gotten up for you. This place, this grave in the sand, is empty. You may come up much closer to it now. I know that you long to look inside this rock. The places are still clearly visible where His body was lying."

The pale women felt strong feelings of relief taking hold in their hearts—radiantly beautiful women.[312] What the angel of the All-Ruler said to them about their Lord was a most welcome message for them to hear. He told them to go back again from the grave, and journey to Christ's followers and to tell His warrior-companions in soothsaying words that their Chieftain had gotten up from death. He told them especially to tell Simon Peter[313] the wonderful and welcome message in words, and to let him know: the Chieftain is coming! He is already in Galileeland Himself, "where His followers, His warrior-companions, will see Him again, just as He promised them in His own true words." Just as the women were intending to leave, two other angels in completely white, brilliantly shining clothing stood there in front of them. The angels spoke to them in holy words. The women's minds were stupefied, they were in sheer terror! They could not look at God's angels because of the radiance, the brilliance was far too strong for them to gaze at.

The Ruler's messengers spoke to them immediately and asked the women why they came looking where the dead are for Christ, the Chieftain's Son, who was a living person and full of life-spirit. "You will never find Him here in this rock-grave now; He has already risen up in His body. You should believe this, and remember the words which He often said to you so truthfully when He was one of your companions in Galileeland—how He, the holy Chieftain, was to be

---

[312] Though the women are outwardly pale with worry, their very worry and their relief, which in this case is belief, renders them spiritually as radiant as the angel.

The reader may also have noticed that the *Heliand* author is generally not above seeing to it that the men in his story who believe in Christ are intelligent and the women who do so are beautiful.

[313] Peter is also singled out in Mark's gospel (16:7) "tell his disciples and Peter" by the use of his name. The poet underlines the point in this line, since Peter is for him the archetypal Saxon warrior.

given over and sold into the hands of sinful, hate-filled men, that they would torture, crucify, and kill Him, and that for the good of the people He would get up, alive, on the third day, by the Chieftain's power. Now He has done all this, it has been accomplished among human beings. Hurry now, go forth quickly and let His followers know!

Song 70

The grave-guards are bribed with jewels;
Peter, John, and Mary Magdalene come to the grave.

"He has travelled on ahead of you and has gone away to Galileeland, where His followers, His warrior-companions, will see Him again." It was an immediate pleasure for the women to hear such words being spoken, proclaiming the strength of God—even though they were still shaken and still felt afraid. They set off from there, walking away from the grave, and told Christ's followers of the strange visions they had seen when they had been grieving and were waiting for some relief or consolation.

Then the Jewish guards who had been sitting over the grave all night long guarding the body, keeping watch over the corpse, arrived at the hill-fort. They told the Jewish leaders what terror, what strange visions had come to them at the grave. In their words they told them everything that had happened by the Chieftain's power, and they did not mentally hold anything back. The Jewish people offered them many jewels, gold and silver, paying them great buried treasure, to get them not to say anything again about it, nor to tell the story to the crowd. "Just say that you felt tired, and, weary of mind, you fell asleep, and that His warrior-companions then came back and stole Him from the rock. Always be forceful about this, keep saying it with confidence! If this becomes known to the military governor, we will help you against him and see to it that not the slightest harm, nothing bad, is ever done to you." The guards accepted the great amount of precious jewels from the people, and began to do all this. They made it known to people throughout the land—but they were not following their own will when they decided to spread such lies about the holy Chieftain.[314]

The minds and emotions of Christ's followers became hale and well once again as they listened to the good women telling the story of God's might! Their mood turned joyful then—John and Peter ran to the grave as fast as they could. John the good got there first, and he stood over the grave until, right afterward, Simon Peter, the earl famous for his strength, arrived and went in to the grave.[315] He saw the corpse clothing of God's Son lying there, the linen cloth with which the body of his Lord had been gently wrapped before. Lying in a separate place was the piece of material that had been around the head of holy Christ, the powerful Chieftain, while He was at rest.

Then John too went inside the grave to see the strange thing. At that moment his belief opened up and he knew that his Chieftain would come back up out of the earth to this light, arisen from death! John and Peter then left; the followers of Christ, the warrior-companions, were gathering together.

At another moment, one of the women was standing there crying sorrowfully over the grave in her grief—it was Mary Magdalene. The thoughts of her heart, her feelings, were in turmoil because of sorrow. She had no idea where she should look for her Lord or where she could get His help. She could not control her lamentation, she could not stop crying. She did not know where to turn, her thoughts and emotions were in a state of confusion.[316] Then she

---

[314] As in previous instances, evil for good people is seen as ignoring one's own (good) will, and allowing oneself to become a mere instrument of the (bad) will of others. See the Lord's Prayer, song 19.

[315] In Scripture no reason is given for Peter's failure to run as fast as John to the tomb (Jn. 20:4). The *Heliand* poet finds a way both to admit the fact and provide a flattering excuse for his hero, Peter is too strong to run that fast. He also makes it clear that the time difference was minimal!

[316] The author here greatly expands Scripture to give a surprisingly explicit psychological picture of Mary Magdalene. John's gospel merely has a single line: "But Mary was standing outside weeping at the tomb . . . " (20:11). The *Heliand's* extended emphasis is focused on her internal turmoil: almost uncontrollable sorrow, a deep sense of loss and helplessness, the confusion of thoughts and feelings.

In an era in which warfare was the accepted path for the warrior class, this cannot have been a rare state of mind, but rather one to which anyone who had lost

saw the mighty Christ standing there, although she could not recognize Him as someone familiar until He wanted to let her know and told her that it was Himself.

He asked why she was crying so hard, so bitterly, with such hot tears. She said that it was about her Lord, that she did not know where He had gotten to. "If you can show me, my lord, if I may be so bold as to ask you, if you removed Him from this boulder, tell me in your words where He is. It would be the greatest of all joys for me to see Him!" She did not know that it was the Chieftain's Son who had spoken the kind words to her. She thought that it was the gardener, a lord's farm-guard. The holy Chieftain, the Greatest of Rescuers, then spoke to her and said her name. Quickly she came closer to Him, that woman of such good will, and recognized Him, her Ruler. She could not contain herself! In her love she wanted to grasp Him in her hands, the woman wanted to hold the Chieftain of Peoples, except that the Peace-Child of God fended her off with His words. He said that she was not to touch Him at all with her hands. "I have not yet gone up," He said, "to the heavenly Father. But now you hurry off quickly, and let the earls know, my brothers, that I am about to go and see the All-Ruler, our Father—both yours and Mine, the true God!"

Song 71

Christ the Ruler joins the warrior-company of earls on the road to Emmaus Castle.

The woman was ecstatic that she could make known such a wonderful thing—to say that He was healthy and well. She was ready immediately to perform this task and brought the men, the earls, the welcome message that she had seen the ruling Christ healthy and

---

a loved one could relate. Perhaps the author was thinking of some of the distress he had seen among the Saxon (and Frankish) women, and their sense of irreparable loss. Perhaps further he is suggesting to them that their loss may not be eternally irreparable.

well, and she told them how He had Himself sent her to them with brilliant signs. However, they still did not want to trust the woman's words, that she brought such a welcome message directly from God's Son. Instead, the warrior-heroes sat there in a desolate mood, grieving.

Once again the holy Christ, the Chieftain, showed Himself clearly after He arose from death, to the joy of the women, when He met them on the road. He spoke to them familiarly and they bowed down before Him to His knees and fell at His feet. He told them that there should be no attitude of fear in their hearts, "but instead go and tell My brothers these words: that they should follow after Me and go to Galileeland. There I will meet them again."

Then there were two of the followers who were also on their way from Jerusalem the same day, early in the morning—earls on business. They wanted to reach the castle[317] at Emmaus. They began a long conversation among themselves about their Lord as these heroes traveled down the road. Then the holy One came walking toward them, God's Son. They were not able readily to recognize the strong One. He did not yet want to let them know who He was, but He joined their warrior-company and asked what the matter was which they were discussing. "Why are you walking along so sadly," He said, "are you both in mourning, your spirits filled with sorrow?" The earls immediately spoke to Him in reply and gave this answer, "How can You ask this question," they said, "are You from Jerusalem, are You of the Jewish people . . ."[318]

. . .

. . . the Holy Spirit from the meadows of heaven with the great power of God. Then He led His followers out, away from there, until He

---

[317] *castel*, from military Latin *castellum* 'small fortified army camp'. This is the only time that this Romance word appears in the *Heliand*. It is obviously very close to its English equivalent *castle*, and may perhaps have been used for a stone fortification.

[318] The London manuscript, *C*, ends here, and the Munich manuscript, *M*, has several pages missing.

brought them to Bethany. There He lifted up His hands and hallowed all of them and consecrated them with His words. He then set off from there, upward, and went to the high heavenly kingdom and His holy throne. He is seated there on the right side of God, the all-mighty Father, and from there the ruling Christ observes everything that happens in the whole world.[319]

On that same site, the good warrior-companions fell to prayer and then they went back to the hill-fort at Jerusalem—the followers of Christ went rejoicing! Their minds were happy as they stood in the shrine. The Ruler's strength . . .[320]

---

[319] In Scripture Christ is seated at the right hand of the Father, but there is no comment on His gazing down on the world. In Germanic mythology it is an ultimate characteristic of Woden that, after his suffering on the tree, he always looks down on this world from his throne and is aware of all that happens. Christ in the *Heliand* has surpassed Woden. Not only has He overcome fate's power over people, He has also overcome His own fated death by His own strength, "the power of the Chieftain." He is therefore worthy of taking Woden's place and of being seated upon the throne, and thus of assuming the old god's final function of observing all that happens in this world.

[320] Munich manuscript, *M*, stops here.

Appendix 1

Germanic Religious Customs
in Adam of Bremen's
History of the Archbishops of Hamburg-Bremen

Adam came to Bremen in approximately the year 1066 and died about twenty years later. His *History* contains some observations on the popular practice of Germanic religion from earlier authors and as it was still known in his time, especially in Sweden where the temple at Uppsala still stood. The excerpts that follow are from Francis J. Tschan's translation of the *History of the Archbishops of Hamburg-Bremen* (New York: Columbia University Press, 1959), pp. 10-11, 207-208.

> For they worshiped those who, by nature, were not gods. Among them they especially venerated Mercury [Woden?], whom they were wont on certain days to propitiate, even with human sacrifices. They deemed it incompatible with the greatness and dignity of heavenly beings either to confine their gods in temples or to mold them in any likeness of the human form. They consecrated groves and coppices and called by the names of the gods that mysterious something which alone they contemplated with reverence. . . . they even regarded with reverence leafy trees and springs. They worshiped, too, a stock of wood, of no small size, set up in the open. In native language, it was called *Irminsul*, which in Latin means 'universal column,' as it it sustained everything. These excerpts about the advent, the customs, and the superstitions of the Saxons (which superstitions the Slavs and Swedes still appear to observe in their pagan rites) we have taken from the writings of Einhard.

That folk [the Swedes] has a very famous temple called Uppsala, (scholion: Near this temple stands a very large tree with wide-spreading branches, always green winter and summer. What kind it is nobody knows. There is also a spring at which the pagans are accustomed to make their sacrifices, and into it to plunge a live man. And if he is not found, the people's wish will be granted.) situated not far from the city of Sigtuna and Bjorko. (scholion: A golden chain goes around the temple. It hangs over the gable of the building and sends its glitter far off to those who approach, because the shrine stands on level ground with mountains all about it like a theatre.) In this temple, entirely decked out in gold, the people worship the statues of three gods in such wise that the mightiest of them, Thor, occupies a throne in the middle of the chamber; Wotan and Frikko have places on either side . . . The people also worship heroes made gods, whom they endow with immortality because of their remarkable exploits. . . .

For all their gods there are appointed priests to offer sacrifices for the people. If plague and famine threaten, a libation is poured to the idol Thor; if war, to Wotan; if marriages are to be celebrated, to Frikko. It is customary also to solemnize in Uppsala, at nine-year intervals, a general feast of all the provinces of Sweden. From attendance at this festival no one is exempted. Kings and people all and singly send their gifts to Uppsala and, what is more distressing than any kind of punishment, those who have already adopted Christianity redeem themselves through these ceremonies. The sacrifice is of this nature: of every living thing that is male, they offer nine heads, (scholion: Feasts and sacrifices of this kind are solemnized for nine days. On each day they offer a man along with other living beings in such a number that in the course of nine days they will have made offerings of seventy-two creatures. This sacrifice takes place about the time of the vernal equinox.) with the blood of which it is customary to placate gods of this sort. The bodies they hang in the sacred grove that adjoins the temple. Now this grove is so sacred in the eyes of the heathen that each and every tree in it is believed divine because of the death or putrefaction of the victims. Even dogs and horses hang there with men. A Christian seventy-two years old told me that he had seen their bodies suspended promiscuously. Furthermore, the incantations customarily chanted in the ritual of a sacrifice of this kind are manifold and unseemly; therefore it is better to keep silence about them.

Appendix 2

Germanic Social Ties and Personal Loyalty

In the Roman administrative system, administrators could be changed regularly without fear of disobedience on the part of lower-level personnel, since the loyalty of the inferior was not to the person who was in charge, but to that person's office. In Germanic society loyalty was to the person. In Germanic gospel translations, *disciples* 'students, learners' are called *jungaron* 'followers', which literally means 'young men'. In Germanic warrior-society, the coloration of this important concept thus shifts from 'young men of studiousness' to 'young men of loyalty'. The same is true for *gesith* 'warrior-companion'. The following background excerpts are from *The Cambridge Illustrated History of the Middle Ages*, Vol. 1, ed. Robert Fossier, transl. Janet Sondheimer (Cambridge: Cambridge University Press, 1989), pp. 83-84.

Men Bound by Ties of Service and Fidelity

Since everything was geared to victory, it is not unusual to find the Celts and Germans making use of slaves as soldiers, a practice the Romans shunned on principle. It was customary according to the law of the Bretons for a master to have a slave carry his weapons. Among the Franks, the Celtic word *gwass*, Latinized as *vassus*, designates a slave charged with a particular duty, which might entail the bearing of arms. *Vassus* produced the diminutive *vassalus*, which gave rise to 'vassal.' The 'lads' who clustered in battle around a 'veteran' (in Latin *senior*, meaning 'older', which later gave rise to *seigneur*) eventually came to form a kind of bodyguard in which the comradeship of arms was strong enough to break down juridical barriers. The warmth of fellow-feeling experienced in these moments of crisis could naturally lead from friendship to freedom. Under the Romans, as we saw, it was the law which defined, indeed created, social relationships; among the Germans, on the contrary, changing social relationships produced modifications in the law. . . .

Freedom, innate or acquired, in fact typified the majority of retinues surrounding kings, chieftains and other great personages. The Visigothic and Ostrogothic kings had their *saiones*, all-purpose retainers whose job was to see that orders were executed. Essentially they were members of the king's following, with the capacity to give the weak the protection they themselves received from their royal master. . . . In a separate category were the *gasindi* (literally 'serving men') usually slaves or freedmen, who performed sundry duties about the palace and owed fidelity to their prince. Bodyguards of similar type and with a similar name, *gesiths*, are found among the Anglo-Saxons. Those of lowly condition received food and clothing from their master, as his name indicates (*hlaford* 'giver of bread', whence 'lord'), while others received a grant of land, in temporary or permanent ownership. All owed military service to their protector. Turning lastly to the Franks, we find the same phenomenon. As well as his *scara* or permanent corps of warriors, the king had his *antrustiones*, who were in a way his bodyguards. They went through a special ceremony in which they commended themselves to him, kneeling with their hands placed between his. They swore their fidelity and '*truste*' (the Old High German '*treue*' means the same). Placed from now on under the protection, or '*mainbour*,' of the master who maintained him, the *antrustion* defended his master by force of arms. Anyone daring to kill an *antrustion* was liable to the enormous *wergild* ['blood-money'] of 600 solidi. This gives an idea of the importance of the *antrustions* and of the bonds between man and man, in this instance between superior and inferior.

Another practice found everywhere among the Celts and Germans is that of adoptive paternity, whereby teenage boys were taken into another household to be trained as warriors and servitors, and at a later date even as officials. Known to the Anglo-Saxons as '*fosterage*,' this system created real physical bonds, with adolescents undergoing rapid initiation into the adult world. Faithful in life and death to their foster-father, these 'nurslings,' as they were often described among the Franks and Visigoths, were a force to be reckoned with, especially when their more than ordinary solidarity was underpinned by oaths of commendation. Friends, followers, young men: such were the characteristics of these gangs of fighters, who were soon to be found in the service not only of kings, but also of clan chieftains and heads of extended families.

Appendix 3

Magic in the *Heliand*

Magic may not be what one would expect to find in a faithful poetic version of the Christian gospel, and thus perhaps scholars have not attempted to study the *Heliand* for the possible presence of Northern magical concepts. The *Heliand* does, however, I believe, reveal various distinct traces of Germanic magic. These traces can be identified quite clearly in one case, namely in the devil's use of a "magic helmet" to conceal himself from Pilate's wife. In other cases there is somewhat greater difficulty in identifying magic practices because of the author's careful use of ambiguous language and his preference for an indirect and suggestive method in conjuring up the aura of magic. In several incidents, however, it is my thesis that he forces the reader to surmise the presence of magic by surrounding the event with dramatic secrecy, or he refers to "powers" in the description of the event or object. This magic interpretation of a scene occurs in the expanded description of the "powers" possessed by the consecrated bread and wine in the Last Supper scene, in the curious secrecy that is made to surround Christ's transformation of water into wine at Cana, in the introduction of the *Pater Noster* as a secret runic mystery, and in the depiction of the creation of the world—and the writing of the gospel—as instances of word magic ordained by God.

Both De Vries's classic study, *Altgermanische Religionsgeschichte*,[1] and Flowers's more recent linguistic study, *Runes and Magic*,[2] do

---

[1] Jan de Vries, *Altgermanische Religionsgeschichte*, 2 Bände (Berlin: de Gruyter, 1956).

not deal directly with the *Heliand*, but they provide very useful descriptions of both magic formulae and magic objects and images in Germanic religion, and they provide helpful literary and linguistic descriptions of the nature and practice of those beliefs. Their work provides additional markers that make it possible to undertake a textual search for Germanic magical elements in the *Heliand*. Flowers's very helpful adoption in the Germanic realm of the linguistic term "performative speech" (words that possess the power to carry out what they say, such as spells, runes, curses) suggests also the extension of the same concept to the realm of "performative things." This category would include objects that, by their own power, produce effects—usually by causing what they depict or signify to happen—without any need for divine assistance. The major examples would be magic helmets, swords, spearpoints, and stones, and especially "performative images," carved or natural images that can cause what they depict to happen to the viewer. (The gaping mouth of a snake's head carved on the prow of a ship was viewed as having the power to harm the native spirits of the land it approached and had to be removed before making landfall;[3] the head of a decapitated horse on a pole carved with runes and pointed toward an enemy's farmstead was sure to cause him ill fortune [*Egil's Saga*, Ch. 72].)

If we begin with the most obvious example of something magical in the *Heliand*, it would be the *helidhelm*. In various forms, including the *Tarnkappe* of later medieval literature, this 'hiding-helmet' possessed the power to render its wearer invisible. One can well imagine how the pressed warrior of a close hand-to-hand battle might wish with all his heart that such a magic helmet existed. The following passage in the *Heliand* is the earliest mention of such a helmet in Germanic literature.

---

[2] Stephen E. Flowers, *Runes and Magic, Magical Formulaic Elements in the Older Runic Tradition* (New York: Peter Lang, 1986).

[3] The example is taken from De Vries's citation of Icelandic law prohibiting a ship from approaching Iceland without first removing the dragon head from the prow. See De Vries, op. cit., pp. 260 and 318.

. . . That uuif uuard thuo an forahton,
suido an sorogon, thuo iru thiu gisiuni quamun
thuru thes dernien dad an dages liohte,
an helidhelme bihelid. (5449-52)

'. . . The woman [Pilate's wife] was very worried, she was
frightened by the visions that were coming to her in broad
daylight. They were the doings of the deceiver [Satan], who was
invisible, hidden by a magic helmet.'

No doubt the author could have retained the dream device used
in the New Testament for this scene (he had no difficulty using the
dream sequence for the warning of the Magi to return to their
country by another route), but he seems to have wanted to use this
harmless device from Germanic mythology to make the devil seem
more at home, as it were, in Germanic Christianity! Another fairly
obvious and charming example of a magic description of a miracle is
the *Heliand*'s version of the multiplication of the loaves and fishes
(Matthew 14: 13-21). As the thanes/disciples go among the huge
crowd with their paltry five loaves they, like sorcerer's apprentices,
are described as becoming aware that the bread *undar iro handun
uuohs* 'that the bread between their hands was growing' (2859).
Matthew's gospel, on the other hand, is prudently silent on this point!

A more difficult passage, and one of much greater importance,
is the description of the institution of the Eucharist at the Last
Supper. Here the *Heliand* differs considerably from the gospel
versions of the institution by the addition of explanatory material to
the story. The most significant addition is the line in which the
author has Christ say (after He has told his twelve apostolic thanes
that the bread is truly His body and that the wine is His blood): *thit
is mahtig thing.* This line is a difficult challenge to anyone attempting
to translate it. It can be rendered literally: 'this is [a] strong thing'.
The literal translation is true to one of the two common meanings of
mahtig 'strong'. The literal translation, however fails to capture the
other meaning of *mahtig* 'magic, powerful (in a magical sense)'. It is
difficult at first sight to decide which of these two explanations of the
Eucharist the poet is attempting to convey to his audience: Is the

Eucharist 'something strong' or is it something that 'possesses [magic] powers'? What exactly is the type of 'strength' being referred to, and why add this remark to the biblical account?

I think three approaches can help answer the question. First, Flowers, in his discussion of power concepts in Germanic magic, confirms the use of *mah-tiz* in the sense of 'having magic power'[4] as well as its use in the physical sense. To his discussion I would like to add the observation that the line itself, *thit is mahtig thing*, is striking in its omission of the indefinite article. Literally the line—from the standpoint of Modern German usage of the indefinite article with personal nouns—may imply that having power is all that the object is about, that having power is of the essence of the object. Unfortunately, one cannot be absolutely certain about the meaning of the omission of the indefinite article in Old Saxon. Thus the translator's woes with *thit is mahtig thing*; but the translator's woe may perhaps be the interpreter's weal. By pointing to the bread and wine, and saying "that is [a] power-thing," the Christ of the *Heliand* locates, in my opinion, the Eucharistic elements among the familiar Germanic world of intrinsically powerful magic objects, such as the 'hiding-helmet', things that possess in themselves the secret power to accomplish what they depict.

Fortunately for the theologian, the *Heliand* poet then lists perfectly orthodox theological functions of the Eucharistic bread and wine and delightfully has Christ describe those functions as if he were revealing to his twelve thanes secret magic "powers" possessed by the Eucharistic power-objects, and urging them to use them.

> gilobiot gi thes liohto, quad he, that thit is min lichamo
> endi min blod so same: gibu ik iu her bediu samad
> etan endi drinkan . . .
> . . . thit is mahtig thing,
> mid thius sculun gi iuuuomu drohtine diurida frummien,
> habbiad thit min te gihugdiun, helag bilidi,
> that it eldibarn aftar lestien,

---

[4] op. cit., p. 127.

uuaron an thesaru uueroldi that that uuitin alle,
man obar thesan middilgard, that it is thurh mina minnea
    giduan
herron te huldi. (4638-51)

"'Believe me clearly," He said, "that this is My body and also My
blood. I here give both of them to you to eat and to drink. . . .
This body and blood is a thing which possesses power: with it
you will give honor to your Chieftain. It is a holy image: keep
it in order to remember Me, so that the sons of men will do it
after you and preserve it in this world, and thus everyone all over
this middle world will know what I am doing out of love to give
honor to the Lord.'"

The whole scene therefore makes the Eucharist comprehensible
in terms of Germanic religion. Were the poet not to have described
the bread and wine as possessing magic power, it is very possible his
hearers would have treated the bread and wine of the sacrament as
merely being un-magical things, objects containing no real performa-
tive power and therefore incapable of producing of themselves the
desired theological effects they depict. In cross-culturally interpreting
the Eucharist in this manner, the *Heliand* poet in the early ninth
century may be one of the first to have participated in the shift of
sacramental emphasis from the earlier Semitic and biblical focus on
God himself (as the personal prime cause of the performative effect
of any sacrament or miracle), to the instrumental, or secondary,
causes beloved of Northern Europeans: the water used in baptism,
the oil used in ordination and confirmation and anointing the sick,
and, of course, the bread and wine, together with their accompanying
verbal formulae and gestures (perceived and presented as performa-
tive spells). It is at this time, the eighth and ninth centuries, that the
enormously popular veneration of holy "things" possessing powers,

usually the power to heal, begins: holy water, holy oils, holy relics.[5] The *Heliand* may be an instructive instance of the need, among the Saxons at least, for the concept of magic in order to come to a serious understanding of the "powers" Christians possessed. "Magic thing" was the *Heliand* poet's way to express the supernatural effectiveness of the Eucharist's bread and wine—-as a performative image (though infinitely more positive than the carved snake head on the prow or Egil's horse head). This seems appropriate and powerful in the Germanic world, whose religious mythology and vocabulary had such respect for the "instruments" through which religious effects were produced, and had perhaps somewhat less respect for the limited power of their mortal gods. This Northern-European religious mindset is ancestral to the one that eventually insisted on non-divine explanations for natural phenomena by using instruments and formulae related to secondary causality rather than attributing the occurrences of nature primarily to the will of the First Cause. This being the case, perhaps the *Heliand* poet's cross-cultural translation of *magic power* for the miraculous and sacramental may have been more than optional; it may have been accurate and realistic. It seems then, that with reference to the bread and wine of the Eucharist, *thit is mahtig thing* in the *Heliand* should be construed to mean: 'this is a magic thing' or, more conservatively, 'this is a thing that possesses power'.

The wedding feast at Cana (song 24 of the *Heliand*; in the New Testament, John 2:1-12) is a case where the presence of magic is strongly suggested to the reader/hearer but done almost entirely by indirection. This is seen best by contrasting the biblical account with that in the *Heliand*. From John's gospel:

> When they ran out of wine, since the wine provided for the wedding was all finished, the mother of Jesus said to Him, "They

---

[5] A very interesting historical study of the reciprocal religious effect on Christianity of the conversion of the Germanic North can be found in the dissertation of James C. Russell, *The Germanization of Early Medieval Christianity* (Fordham University, 1990), especially pp. 205-07 and 332-45. A revised version of Russell's dissertation is forthcoming from Oxford University Press in 1992.

have no wine." Jesus said, "Woman, why turn to Me? My hour has not yet come." His mother said to the servants, "Do whatever He tells you." There were six stone water jars standing there, meant for the ablutions that are customary among the Jews: each could hold twenty or thirty gallons. Jesus said to the servants, "Fill the jars with water," and they filled them to the brim. "Draw some out now," He told them, "and take it to the steward." They did this; the steward tasted the water, and it had turned into wine. Having no idea where it came from—only the servants who had drawn the water knew—the steward called the bridegroom and said, "People generally serve the best wine first, and keep the cheaper sort till the guests have had plenty to drink; but you have kept the best wine till now."

Interestingly, Jesus does nothing—says nothing over the water, performs no ritual gesture—he simply instructs that water be poured in and then immediately drawn out. This contrasts significantly with the *Heliand* version:

> Uuerod bliðode
> uuarun thar an luston liudi atsamne
> gumon gladmodie. Gengun ambahtman,
> skenkeon mid scalun, drogun skiriane uuin
> mid orcun endi alofatun; uuas thar erlo drom
> fagar an flettea, tho thar folc undar im
> an them benkeon so bezt bliðsea afhobun,
> uuarun thar an uunneun. Tho im thes uuines brast,
> them liudiun thes liðes: is ni uuas farleðid uuiht
> huergin an themu huse, that for thene heri forð
> skenkeon drogin, ac thiu scapu uuarun
> liðes alarid. Tho ni uuas lang te thiu,
> that it san antfunda frio sconiosta
> Cristes moder: geng uuið iro kind sprecan,
> uuið iro sunu selbon, sagda im mid uuordun,
> that thea uuerdos tho mer uuines ne habdun
> them gestiun te gomun. Siu tho gerno bad,
> that is the helogo Crist helpa geriedi

themu uuerode te uuilleon. Tho habda eft is uuord garu
mahtig barn godes endi uuid is moder sprac:
'huat ist mi endi thi', quad he, 'umbi thesoro manno lid,
umbi theses uuerodes uuin? Te hui sprikis thu thes, uuif, so filu,
manos mi far thesoro menigi? Ne sint mina noh
tidi cumana.' Than thoh gitruoda siu uuel
an iro hugiskeftiun, helag thiorne,
that is aftar them uuordun uualdandes barn,
heleandoro bezt helpan uueldi.
Het tho thea ambahtman idiso sconiost,
skenkeon endi scapuuardos, thea thar scoldun thero scolu
    thionon
that sie thes ne uuord ne uuerc uuiht ne farletin,
thes sie the helogo Crist hetan uueldi
lestean far them liudiun. Larea stodun thar
stenfatu sehsi. Tho so stillo gebod
mahtig barn godes, so it thar manno filu
ne uuissa te uuarun, huo he it mid is uuordu gesprac;
he het thea skenkeon tho skireas uuatares
thiu fatu fullien, endi hi thar mid is fingrun tho,
segnade selƀo sinun handun,
uuarhte it te uuine endi het is an en uuegi hladen,
skeppien mid enoro scalon, endi tho te them skenkeon sprac,
het is thero gesteo, the at them gomun uuas
themu heroston an hand geƀan,
ful mid folmun, themu the thes folkes thar
geuueld aftar themu uuerde. (2005-48)

'The warriors were merry, the people were enjoying
themselves together, the men were feeling good. The servants
went around pouring from pitchers, they had clear wine in steins
and barrels. The conviviality of the earls in the drinking hall was
a beautiful sight, and the men on the benches had reached a very
high level of bliss, they were really happy! Then the wine ran
out on them; the people had no more apple wine. There was not
the smallest drop left in the house that the servants could still
bring to the crowd; the vats were empty, the liquor was gone.

Now it was not very long before the loveliest lady, Christ's mother, found out about it. She went and spoke with her Child, with her Son Himself, and told Him in words that the hosts did not have any more wine for the guests at the wedding. Then she asked the holy Christ earnestly to arrange some help for the people, for the sake of their happiness. The mighty Son of God had His answer ready and said to His mother, "What is it to Me and you," He said, "what happens to these peoples' liquor, to these warriors' wine? Why are you talking so much like this, woman, admonishing Me in front of all these people? My times have not yet come."

The holy virgin, however, trusted well in her mind that, even after these words, the Ruler's Son, the Best of healers, would help. Then the most beautiful of women told the servants, those pouring and those in charge of the wine barrels, all the ones who were serving the crowd, that they were not to let out a whit of the words or actions that the holy Christ would tell them to do for the people.

Six stone vats were standing there empty. God's mighty Child gave His orders very quietly so that a lot of people would not know for sure how He said it with His words. He told those who were pouring to fill the vats there with clear water, and then He blessed it with His fingers, with His own hands—He worked it into wine! Then He ordered it poured into a drinking vessel, drawn off with a pitcher, and then speaking to a servant, He told him to give it to the most important person at the wedding, to put it right into the hands of the one who had the most authority over these people after the host. . . .'

The changes are clear. The author makes the scene magical by his addition of the element of secrecy. Mary goes around to all the servants, both the ones who are serving the wine and the ones in charge of the wine barrels and tells all of them not to let out a bit of what they see Christ do or hear Him say. Christ is then described as giving His orders quietly; He does not want a lot of people knowing the words He uses to change the water into wine. Even Christian ritual is brought anachronistically into the scene as Christ is made to make the sign of the cross over the water and with His own hands work the water into wine.

The scene is implicitly a magical one, Christ is shown working in the manner of a wizard who knows which spells and gestures to use, and who is most anxious to restrict this secret knowledge as much as possible. By making Mary and Jesus both share this concern, the incident is made magical without ever using the word! Implicit in it is the Germanic belief in secret spells and in their intrinsic performative ability. The author seems to say that if many people were to learn the secret instructions given to the waiters or the secret words, the spell that Christ used to change water into wine, then, with or without his consent, there would not be a lake or stream in all of Germany whose drinking water would be safe from being transformed into the finest vintage by those who had overheard the spell!

The Lord's Prayer is also treated as just such a spell, magic words which can bring about what they say. The "Our Father" is thus not considered to be a group of wishful petitions, but rather as magically capable of performing the intent of the petitions: granting immediate access to God the Father, and giving protection from evil to the person reciting the spell. The *Heliand* does this by changing the introductory section which precedes the Lord's Prayer. The change can be seen by contrasting the introduction to the prayer in the biblical version (Luke 11:1-2) with that of the *Heliand* (song 19). In Luke the disciples say: "Lord, teach us to pray, just as John [the Baptist] taught his disciples." In the *Heliand* the parallel line is significantly different:

Herro the godo. . . us is thinoro huldi tharf
te giuuirkenne thinna uuilleon, endi oc thinoro uuordo so self,
alloro barno bezt, that thu us bedon leres,
iungoron thine, so Iohannes duot,
diurlic doperi, dago gehuuilicas
is uuerod mid uuordun, huuo sie uualdand sculun,
godan grotean. Do thina iungorun so self:
gerihti us that geruni. (1588-95)

'Our good Lord . . . we need Your gracious help in order to carry out Your will and we also need Your own words, Best of all born, to teach us, Your followers, how to pray—just as John, the good baptist, teaches his people with words every day, how they are to speak to the ruling God. Do this for Your own followers—teach us the secret runes.'

Teach us the secret runes, *gerihti us that geruni*, transforms the "Our Father" into a spell of great performative "power," and locates prayer among the Germanic religious categories along with charms and spells.[6] It clearly removes prayer, and especially the Lord's Prayer, from the category of pious, nothing-effecting wishes and petitions. The word *geruni* itself contains both the idea of secret and mystery, and the runes themselves, the letters of the Germanic alphabet, which were used both secularly and in magic ritual. The runic alphabet has been found incised on spear heads and weapons to give them greater effectiveness, and there are many accounts of their use both for blessing and curse. The runes were a powerful gift to mankind from Woden, and thus it is only fitting that Christ should give his followers strong magic runes as well.

The concept of the Lord's Prayer as being runic magic may seem farfetched, and the reader may wish to settle for simply understanding *geruni* as 'secret' or as 'mystery'. My argument against this is: there is a precedent—however unlikely that may seem—outside the *Heliand* for the identification of the very letters of the *Pater Noster* as magic runes. In *The Dialogues of Solomon and Saturn*, an Old English philosophical and poetic discussion of pagan and Judaeo-Christian wisdom, the fighting power of individual letters of the *Pater Noster* is described in brutally visual detail. The following excerpt is a description of what just the first five letters, *P, A, T, E,* and *R* (the most fierce of all!) can do to a troublesome spiritual or worldly enemy:

---

[6] For a further possible connection with the Woden tradition, see G. Ronald Murphy, S.J., *The Saxon Savior: The Germanic Transformation of the Gospel in the Ninth-Century Heliand* (New York: Oxford University Press, 1989), pp. 75-94.

Prologa prima   'the first prologue ['letter']
đam is ·ᛈ· P · nama   whose name is **P**
hafađ gudmecga   this warrior has
gyrde lange   a long rod
gyldene gade   with a golden goad,
and a đone g[rim]man feond   and the grim enemy fiend he
suuidmod suuipeđ   keeps beating with it ferocious-
                                             ly;

and him on suuade fylgeđ   following on his track comes
·ᚠ· A ·ofermaegene   **A**—with super-strength!—
and hine eac ofslyhđ   and also beats on him.
·ᛏ· T ·hine tesuuađ, and hine   **T** harasses him and stabs him
on đa tungan stickađ   in the tongue,
uuraested him đat uuoddor   twists his throat for him,
and him đa uuongan briceđ.   and smashes his cheeks.
·ᛗ· E ·hine yflađ,   **E** attacks him,
suua he a uuile   [E is] always ready
ealra feonda gehuuone   to stand fast
faesta gestandan;   against every enemy;
đonne hine on undanc, ·ᚱ· R ·   then, little to his pleasure, **R**
eorringa geseced;   will angrily come after him,
bocstafa brego   the prince of letters
bregdeđ sona   will soon whirl
feond be đam feaxe   the enemy by the hair
laeteđ flint brecan   and let flint break
scines sconcan...[7]   the phantasm's legs . . .'

In the manuscript the scribe has been careful to use both the
runic and the Latin letters for *PATER*. This amazing conflation of
Christian prayer and Germanic rune magic ends with an exhortation

---

[7] John M. Kemble, *The Dialogue of Salomon and Saturnus* (London: printed for
the Aelfric Society, 1848) p. 141. I have followed the Kemble text here for the Old
English, but his translation I have adapted to a more modern English.

to the reader "advocating the use of the Lord's Prayer as an effective war-spell in battle.⁸"

Fordon naenig man	'Therefore, no man should
scile oft ordances	ever without cause
utabredan	draw forth
uuaepnes ecgge,	the weapon's edge
deah de him se uulite cuueme	(even though its gleam pleases him),
ac symle he sceal singan	rather he should always sing
Pater Noster	the *Pater Noster*
and daet Palmtreo	and pray the Palm-tree
biddan mid blisse,	with joy,
daet him bu gife	so that it will give him both
feorh and folme	life and [a strong] arm
donne his feond cyme.⁹	when his enemy comes.

It might be helpful to know if the West Saxon *Solomon and Saturn* is contemporaneous with the *Heliand*, since this would all the more strengthen the reading of the *Heliand* verse in question, *gerihti us that geruni*, as 'teach us the secret runes'. The *Heliand* author merely indicates that the Lord's Prayer has runic power, and is in no way as explicit as the author of *Solomon and Saturn*, never in any way referring to specific letters of the prayer. Still, he does imply that it is secret and runic, and may perhaps have shared something of the kind of spirit that is found in *Solomon and Saturn*. Unfortunately scholarly speculation has been unable to tie down a specific date for the West Saxon work. Dates have been suggested as early

---

⁸ Ralph W. V. Elliott in *Runes, An Introduction* (New York: St Martin's Press, 1989) p. 89. Elliot is here alluding with approval to R. I. Page's concession that the *Pater Noster* in *Solomon and Saturn* is a genuine example of rune magic.

⁹ Kemble, p. 145. Once again I have adapted Kemble's translation, but retained his reading of the text. The meaning of *Palmtreo* 'palm-tree' is uncertain. It seems to be an alternate name here for the Lord's Prayer.

as 627 and as late as just before the year 1000.[10] Menner would place it in the ninth century, making the work roughly contemporaneous with the *Heliand*, or perhaps somewhat later. One line of the text may suggest an earlier date, however. In describing the horrible fate of the fiends at the hands of the "Our Father," the poem mentions a time when the devil will wish he were back in hell: *donne hine forkinnað / da cirican getwinnas* 'when he will be rejected / by the twin churches'.[11] I would suggest that this friendly awareness of the existence of *twin churches* in England might be the type of reaction of approval that a writer might have had at the time of, or just after, the Synod of Whitby, when the Irish and the Roman churches in England finally reconciled their differences (especially over the date of Easter). If this interpretation of *da cirican getwinas* as 'the twin churches' is correct, the magic *Pater Noster* of the *Solomon and Saturn* might be dated much closer to the time of the synod, 663-64, and might thus have been an influence on the later (and more moderate) poet of the "secret runes" of the *Heliand*'s "Our Father."

If we turn to the author's description of the creation of the world in the introductory song of the *Heliand*, we see that he describes creation as taking place through performative words, or rather through a performative word. This thought enables him to tie together the two types of magic words: the magic words of Germanic religion and the creative, i.e., performative and therefore magic, word of God. The poet describes the task of the evangelists: to write down:

all so hie it fan them anginne thuru is enes craht

---

[10] Cf. Robert J. Menner's exhaustive survey in *The Poetical Dialogues of Solomon and Saturn* (New York: The Modern Language Association of America, 1941) pp. 12-17.

[11] Menner quite rightly takes Kemble to task for attempting to emend this line to *da cyrican ge tunas* in order to translate it 'when him shall repudiate both churches and houses', but Menner then suggests that "two churches" refers to the letters N and O. This suggestion seems unlikely in view of the ferocious warrior conduct of the letters in the poem. Cf. Menner, op. cit., p. 113.

uualdand gisprak, thuo hie erist thesa uuerold giscuop
endi thuo all bifieng mid enu uuordo
himil endi erđa endi al that sea bihlidan egun
giuuarahtes endi giuuahsanes: that uuard thuo all mid uuordon
   godas
fasto bifangan. . . . (38-43)

'all the things which the Ruler spoke from the beginning, when
He, by His own power, first made the world and formed the
whole universe with one word. The heavens and the earth and
all that is contained within them, both inorganic and organic,
everything, was firmly held in place by Divine words.'

It seems then that the author had found magic aplenty in the
biblical world when he looked at it through Germano-Christian eyes,
but especially in the book of *Genesis*, where everything made in the
six days of creation, beginning with *Fiat lux!* 'Let there be light' on
the first day, is brought into being and held there by performative
words, by a divine spell. It is not too far a jump then to seeing the
written gospel itself as God's spell; and finally, even Christ as a
performative word, the magic Word, of God. It is, I am sure, not by
accident that everywhere in the *Heliand* Christ is described as being
mahtig, possessing powers, and as performing every miracle, like a
wizard, *thurh is selbes craft* 'by his own power'. This Germano-
Christian synthesis of magic words, God's words, and Christ who
knows the secret word-spells, is one that makes the whole of the
Bible a book of charming performative magic in the vision of the
Heliand. This synthesis is a realization that the unknown author does
not conceal; it is the first line of his poem:

Manega uuaron, the sia iro mod gespon,
. . . , that sia bigunnun uuord godes,
reckean that giruni, that thie riceo Crist
undar mancunnea mariđa gifrumida
mid uuordun endi mid uuercun. (1-5)

'There were many whose hearts told them that they should begin
to tell the secret runes, the word of God, the famous feats that
the powerful Christ accomplished in words and deeds among
human beings.'

Appendix 4

Symmetrical Structure in the *Heliand*

The reader of the *Heliand* has the feeling that the gospel story in the poem has been somehow rearranged, restructured, and gently eased into a more rounded-out narrative form.[1] The most recent comprehensive effort, however, to describe and identify this restructuring has met with failure and has not gained acceptance from scholars in the field. Johannes Rathofer's monumental attempt at delineating the structure of the epic in his *Der Heliand: theologischer Sinn als tektonische Form* 'The *Heliand*: Theological meaning as expressed in structural form'[2] has been firmly rejected, and his symbolic-mathematical method of interpreting the sequence of the *fitts* 'songs, episodes' using the London manuscript *C* has been seriously questioned. His effort to see in the *Heliand* a division into four books, four books that by their very existence create what Rathofer thought was an almost simultaneously visible *figura crucis*, has been rejected by Taeger on the convincing basis of lack of codicological evidence and the impossibility of making such a presumptive quadripartite division "visible" as a cross in the course of chanting the long epic.[3] Despite Rathofer's painstaking research, Taeger concludes that it has failed, but concedes one possible positive result: Rathofer may have identi-

---

[1] Among the readers of the *Heliand* I would like to thank and credit my student Mary Ballard for her many thoughtful insights and her assistance with this paper.

[2] It appeared as vol. 9 of *Niederdeutsche Studien* (Cologne: Böhlau Verlag, 1962).

[3] See his remarks in his introduction to *Heliand und Genesis*, hrsg. Otto Behaghel, 9. Auflage, bearb. von Burkhard Taeger (Tübingen: Niemeyer, 1984), xx-xxii.

fied the central focal song of the *Heliand*, the 38th, and may have thereby suggested that some structure of the other songs might exist around the 38th song. The Transfiguration would thus be the center point of the epic.[4]

The purpose of this paper is to examine that possibility and to suggest that sufficient evidence exists for a deliberate overall structure of the component songs of the *Heliand*. It is based on the initial assumption that the Transfiguration on the Mount is indeed the center of the epic. It is also based on the conclusion that, due to the formal unwieldiness of the gospel story itself, the poet could not order the entirety of the gospel's incidents into parallel episodes in his composition, but rather selected a number of them based on his spiritual insight into their appropriateness. This is perhaps what is implied in the Latin *Praefatio* where the poet's method is described as taking holy Scripture and . . . *juxta historiae veritatem quaeque excellentiora summatim decerpens* . . . 'in a summary way excerpting, from the point of view of the truth in the story, the things that are more outstanding.'[5] Though there is some difficulty with the *Praefatio* (it seems to refer to a work containing the whole of the Old and New Testament), its further elaboration of the poet's method seems a perfectly accurate reference to the *Heliand*: . . . *et interdum quaedam, ubi commodum duxit, mystico sensu depingens* . . . 'and, every once in a while, wherever it seems appropriate, depicting the mystical meaning [of the things that are more outstanding] . . .'[6]

For some years I have also felt that the *Heliand* had an *inclusio* or symmetrical type of structure centered on the 38th song, but I could not think how to locate and define the extended structure.

---

[4] "Der Versuch, die Zählung der Fittengliederung nicht nur als ursprünglich zu erweisen, sondern auch noch zahlensymbolisch auszudeuten, ist gescheitert; übriggeblieben ist höchstens die Möglichkeit, den 'Heliand' als eine Zentral-komposition, mit der Verklärung Christi auf dem Berg Tabor als in die Mitte des Werks gestellte, vorweggenommene Überwindung des Leidens." (p.xx)

[5] *Heliand und Genesis.* Herausgegeben von Otto Behaghel, 9. Auflage, bearbeitet von Burkhard Taeger (Tübingen: Max Niemeyer Verlag, 1984), p. 1. All Old Saxon citations are from this edition; the English and Latin translations are mine (see n. 9 below).

[6] *Ibid.*

Since the unknown author seems to have used an *inclusio* structure to retell and to elaborate certain of the smaller scenes in the *Heliand* (such as the 'Walking on the Water')[7] for his purposes, it would not seem unreasonable to expect that he had eased the whole of the gospel (insofar as the evangelists' story permitted such rearranging) into the same form. This would seem to be a formidable task since none of the four gospels—and *a fortiori* Tatian's harmony of the four gospels—is structured in this measured epic manner. Did the *Heliand* poet do it by design, or are its parallel songs few and accidental? The route I chose to take to answer this question was one of looking for more obviously visible imagery, clearly parallel content, centered on both sides of the 38th song, rather than a numerical analysis of the songs independent of their content.[8]

The striking thing about the Transfiguration scene particularly emphasized in the *Heliand* is its climactic brilliance with the breaking into "middlegard" of the *lioht odar* 'the light of the other world' and its occurrence on a mountain. The dazzling description suggests, by similar vocabulary and imagery, both the depiction of the light of the other world coming to the horse-guards ('shepherds' in the gospel story) at Bethlehem in the Christmas song (5) and the description of the dazzlingly bright angel who comes with thunder to sit on the open tomb of the Resurrection (69). There is no question in my mind that the *Heliand* poet is completely fascinated with light, and uses it to shine a brilliantly focused beam on the beginning, the middle, and the end of his version of the gospel. The problem is, of course, that this same device is to be found in the gospels themselves, and it is hard to isolate the structure of the *Heliand* from the point of view of its light imagery except to say that, like the gospels, it uses light at the three critical points, to emphasize the incursion of the Divine into the terrestrial world. In contrast, the impressive image of the mountain

---

[7] Cf. G. Ronald Murphy, S. J., *The Saxon Savior* (New York: Oxford University Press, 1989), pp. 68-73.

[8] In using this approach I realize I am following in the footsteps of Cedric Whitman and his classic analysis of the narrative structure of the *Iliad* in his *Homer and the Heroic Tradition* (Cambridge: Harvard University Press, 1958).

is more useful as a beginning point for looking for more detailed structure.

The mountaintop at the center of the *Heliand* suggests two other mountain scenes in the epic in which the author brings the gospel story to a striking climax in Germanic imagery: the epic "battle scene" on Mt. Olivet, in which Peter defends his Chieftain with the sword, and the brilliant recasting of Christ's teachings in Germanic terms in the Sermon on the Mount. The scene on Mt. Olivet is in song 58, exactly twenty songs away from the Transfiguration's song 38, and the Sermon on the Mount reaches the conclusion of its first part in song 18—also twenty songs away from song 38. I do not think this placement is accidental. These three mountain scenes with their glorification of Christ and his "thanes" are the most "visible" foundation of the symmetrical structure of the *Heliand*. One might have expected from Christian tradition that the mountain of the Crucifixion, Mount Calvary, would have been given the most important dramatic role. The *Heliand* poet may have wanted, in order to combat the vacillation of his Christian Saxons, to emphasize the sole incident when Christ-the-Chieftain's leading thane, Peter, fought for him (on Mt. Olivet) rather than when he deserted him (on Mt. Calvary).

One of the things that must have given the author difficulty in attempting any thoroughgoing restructuring of the gospel story as a central composition with parallel scenes is the extreme length of the Sermon on the Mount. Rather than cut any of it, however, the author seems instead to have decided to count the first portion of it (songs 15-18) as one song unit. I say this because the author placed a formulaic caesura at the end of the 18th song, a formula found almost word for word in songs 16, 17, and 18. This unique formulaic description of the men standing around Christ listening to his chieftain-like instructions binds these three songs to one another and to song 15 where the men are called up onto the mountain to hear their Chieftain's secret instructions:

> Stodun uuisa man,
> gumon umbi thana godes sunu gerno suuido
> uueros an uuilleon: uuas im thero uuordo niud,

thahtun end thagodun. . . (16, 1281b-1286a)

'Wise men were very eager and willing to stand around God's Son, intent on His words. They thought and kept silent...'[9]

Helidos stodun,
gumon umbi thana godes sunu gerno suido,
uueros an uuilleon: uuas im thero uuordo niud,
thahtun endi thagodun. . . (17, 1383b-1387b)

'The heroes [warriors] were very eager and willing to stand around God's Son, intent on His words. They thought and kept silent . . .'

Helidos stodun,
gumon umbi thana godes sunu gerno suido,
uueros an uuilleon: uuas im thero uuordo niud,
thahtun endi thagodun . . . (18, 1580b-1586a)
[identical with 17, 1383b-1387b]

The great length of the Sermon seems to have forced the author to consider these songs (15-18) as a single unit in balancing them against a single song (58) from the other side of the central song (38) of the epic.

If we next move ten songs away from the Sermon-on-the-Mount unit, from song 15 to 5, we arrive at the coming of Christ to Bethlehem, the Nativity. If on the other side of the composition we move ten songs away from the "battle" on Mt. Olivet, from song 58 to 68, we arrive at the Resurrection, also described, in parallel with the Nativity scene, as a "coming." Christ's spirit makes its way through the dark night to the corpse:

Sia obar themo grabe satun,
uueros an thero uuahtun uuannom nahton,

---

[9] English translations are from this volume.

bidun undar iro bordon, huan er thie berehto dag
oƀar middilgard mannon quami,
liudon te liohte. Thuo ni uuas lang te thiu,
that thar uuard thie gest cuman be godes crafte,
halag aðom undar thena hardon sten
an thena lichamon. (68, 5765-5772)

'The warriors sat on top of the grave, on watch during their
star-lit night. They waited under their shields until bright day
came to mankind all over the middle world, bringing light to
people.

It was not long then until: there was the spirit coming, by
God's power, the holy breath, going under the hard stone to the
corpse!'

The Birth and the Resurrection have been made equidistant from
the Transfiguration at the center, each being 30 songs from the
center (counting the first part of the Sermon on the Mount [15-18]
as one unit).

Furthermore, if one goes on from the Nativity, song 5, to the first
song of the *Heliand*, one has a distance of exactly five songs. By
parallel, from the Resurrection to the end of the *Heliand*—if this
analysis is correct—there would also have been five songs and thus
the last song of the poem would have been song *72. Since we have
almost all of the text except for *72 and part of 71, by this account
astonishingly little of the epic would be missing.

Confirmation of this general structure can be gained by
proceeding from the center outward, and usually in simple multiples
of five or ten. The death of John the Baptist occurs in song 33, five
songs before the Transfiguration, Jesus foretells His death in song 43,
five songs after the Transfiguration scene. Evidence that this
particular parallelism is deliberate can be found in the fact that song
43 is primarily devoted to the very important scene in the *Heliand* of
the curing of the blind man outside Jericho, one of the few incidents
into which the author intrudes with a lengthy interpretation and a
personal exhortation to the hearer/reader. Christ's foretelling of his
death does not fit into this incident at all, and yet the death

description has been inserted into the song (43) in a rough way that makes it seem like a passage out of place. Out of place or not, I believe the author felt he had to have it at the beginning of the song to effect a clear structural parallel to the beheading of John the Baptist in song 33.

Ten songs after the Transfiguration Jesus raises Lazarus from the grave at the request of Lazarus's sisters, ten songs prior to the Transfiguration Jesus raises up the cripple who has been lowered through the roof by his friends. These incidents may seem analogous only by reason of being a restoration to health and otherwise not excessively similar. The *Heliand* poet seems to have had the same feelings, since he has gone to some pains to make the incidents more spiritually similar. He does not do this as one might expect by trying to make the cripple's cure more similar to that of Lazarus, by describing it, let us say, as a beginning of "a new life." The author finds a parallelism in the fact that both Lazarus and the cripple were restored to health because of the persistent loyalty of friends and relatives. Here he is looking at both incidents through the eyes of Germanic warrior culture and sees *triuue* 'loyalty' as active in both. He thus changes the gospel story to show this virtue more clearly. Little is necessary in song 28. The poet simply refers to the men who are carrying the sick man and who lower him through the roof not as friends but as *erlos* 'warriors' who were this man's *gesidos* 'warrior-companions, vassals', who are thus performing a loyal service for their lord. A bit more is necessary in the scene of the raising of Lazarus, but the material is there. Christ comes from far away to help Lazarus. In the gospel story he comes because Lazarus's two sisters, Mary and Martha, summon him, giving as their reason "the one whom you love is sick." In the *Heliand*, Christ comes at the summons of the sisters, but because of his loyalty to them. They are the cause of his coming, not Lazarus. Thus in both songs, 28 and 48, a potential parallel is enhanced and brought to expression in the *Heliand*. At one and the same time incidents, the cripple and Lazarus, are culturally accommodated in their content and, by their parallel placement in the poem, they are accommodated to epic form.

If we go further from the central scene, fifteen songs prior to the Transfiguration on Mt. Tabor, we come to song 23. In this episode

Jesus concludes the Sermon on the Mount by warning about the Great Day, the Last Judgment; fifteen songs subsequent to Mt. Tabor, in song 53, the author has placed Jesus' description of Doomsday, the day of the last judgment.

It seems that the epic restructuring into parallel scenes on both sides of the center was not possible for every fifth scene in the gospel, since the matter itself would not everywhere lend itself to such parallelism. The Crucifixion, for example, in the *Heliand*, according to this schema, is placed parallel to the coming of the Magi, something that does not tally. I have concluded that the poet merely adjusted and jiggled his matter (especially in the first part, by omission of parables such as the Prodigal Son and the Good Samaritan) to make some epic parallelism possible. Usually, it seems he did it on every fifth song. There are, however, other examples as well. In song 4 the Angel appears to Mary to announce the Incarnation, in song 69 the angel appears to the women, *Mariun* 'the Marys', to announce the Resurrection. In one rather delightful example, songs 8 and 65, the Magi are warned in a dream not to go back to Herod, and Pilate's wife is warned in a daydream by the devil in a hiding-hood not to harm Christ. A more somber tone is struck by the parallelism of songs 22 and 54: in the first, Christ warns his followers of the dangers of money and tells them never to accept payment for their services, in the 54th, as I am sure one can guess, Judas is accepting the thirty pieces of silver from the Jewish leaders.

One of these parallel scenes is unusually touching. The desperate prayer of Jesus to his Father in the Agony in the Garden (song 57) to avert his coming crucifixion, is placed parallel to the gentle moment in song 19 when he teaches his thanes to pray the "Our Father." Such a placement in itself invites meditation and indicates how well the poet could "depict the mystical meaning." It is indeed moving to think that the Christ who is praying in agony to his Father to remove the evil that is about to befall him, once taught his followers to pray to the Father in these words:

Gef us dago gehuuilikes rad, drohtin the godo,
thina helaga helpa . . . Ne lat us farledean leða uuihti
so forð an iro uuilleon, so uui uuirdige sind,

Figure 1. The symmetrical arrangement of songs in the *Heliand*.

Song:	Content:
4	Angel announces the Incarnation to Mary.
5	Nativity: The coming to earthly light.
8	Dream: Warning the Magi to return by another way.
15-18	**Sermon on the Mount (Part 1).**
19	Jesus teaches the prayer "Our Father . . ."
22	"Accept no payment" teaching.
23	The Great Day (Last Judgment).
28	The cure of the bed-fast man.
33	Death of John the Baptist.
38	**Transfiguration on Mount Tabor.**
43	Death of Jesus foretold.
48	The raising of Lazarus.
53	Doomsday: The Last Judgment.
54	Judas accepts his payment, 30 pieces of silver.
57	Jesus prays in His agony in the garden to the Father.
58	**Peter's defense of his Lord on Mount Olivet.**
65	Dream: Warning Pilate's wife about Jesus.
68	The Resurrection: The coming back of the Lord.
69	Angel announces the Resurrection to the Marys.

ac help us uuidar allun ubilon dadiun. (19, 1610-1612)

'Give us support each day, good Chieftain, Your holy help . . .
Do not let evil little creatures lead us off to do their will, as we
deserve, but help us against all evil deeds.'

It seems that there is more than enough evidence for deliberate
symmetrical structuring of a significant number of the songs of the
Heliand. If this overall analysis is correct, there may be many
parallels that I have not seen, and the project invites help, further
study, and meditation. I have included in Figure 1 a diagram which
I hope will invite further discussion of the *Heliand*, a literary and
spiritual gem of the Germanic-speaking peoples.

Finally I would like to mention three possible motives for the
poetic restructuring of the gospel in the *Heliand.* One was to make
the gospel story seem to be, as far as possible, a heroic epic in form
as well as in content. The poet had turned the entire arrest scene,
the Passion and Death into an epic in content, why not have the
whole poem be structured for song in form as well? A poetic form
that alluded to the ancient and familiar Germanic musical past? The
second motive may well have had to do with his reinforcing the
notion of fatedness in the poem. There is a certain predictive and
confrontational relationship between Christ and fate in the first part
of the epic, and an acceptance of the inevitability of fate as divine will
on Christ's part at the end. If this is so, then the poet of the *Heliand*
was also careful to help his hearers/readers participate in the uneasy
relationship between Christ and fate, to realize that the pain of the
growing relationship of Germanic and Christian religious feelings was
birthpain. Parallel structure of beginning and end helps the poet by
expressing the fatedness of that 'bright-shining' relationship not only
through content, but also in form. The third motive is perhaps the
most obvious and the most important of all: setting scenes in parallel
invites meditation. The juxtaposition of two analogous scenes, as in
so much of medieval church art, invites the beholder to meditate on
the similarities, to seek and find a richer meaning in the harmony of
the two, *mystico sensu.*

Select Bibliography

Primary Sources

Heliand und Genesis. Herausgegeben von Otto Behaghel. 9. Auflage bearbeitet von Burkhard Taeger. Tübingen: Max Niemeyer Verlag, 1984.

Tatian, Lateinisch und Altdeutsch mit ausführlichem Glossar. Herausgegeben von Eduard Sievers, 2. neubearbeitete Ausgabe. Paderborn: Ferdinand Schöningh, 1966.

Secondary Sources

Adam of Bremen. *History of the Archbishops of Hamburg-Bremen.* Translated by Francis J. Tschan. New York: Colombia University Press, 1959.

Alexander, Michael. *The Earliest English Poems.* Berkeley and Los Angeles: University of California Press, 1970.

Anderson, Theodore M. "The Caedmon Fiction in the Heliand Preface." *PMLA* 89 (1974), 278-284.

Baetke, Walter. *Vom Geist und Erbe Thules.* Göttingen: Vandenhoeck, 1944. See especially "Die Aufnahme des Christentums durch die Germanen," 82-105.

Becker, Gertrand. *Geist und Seele im Altsächsischen und im Althochdeutschen; der Sinnbereich des Seelischen und die Wörter gest-geist und seola-sela in den Denkmälern bis zum 11. Jahrhundert.* Heidelberg: C. Winter Universitätsverlag, 1964.

Bede's Ecclesiastical History of the English People. Edited by Bertram Colgrove and R. A. B. Mynors. Oxford: The Clarendon Press, 1969.

Belkin, Johanna und Meier, Jürgen. *Bibliographie zu Otfrid von Weissenburg und zur altsächsischen Bibeldichtung (Heliand und Genesis)*. Berlin: E. Schmidt, 1975.

Beowulf. [Reproduced in facsimile from the unique manuscript British Museum MS. Cotton Vitellius A. XV, transliteration and notes by Julius Zupitza.] London and New York: Oxford University Press, 1959.

Berr, Samuel. *An Etymological Glossary to the Old Saxon Heliand*. Bern and Frankfurt: Herbert Lang, 1971.

Bischoff, Bernhard. "Die Schriftheimat der Münchener Heliand-Handschrift." *Beiträge zur Geschichte der deutschen Sprache und Literatur* 101. Tübingen: Max Niemeyer Verlag, 1979, 161-70.

Bonifatii Epistulae; Willibaldi Vita Bonifatii. Editionem Curavit Reinholdus Rau. Darmstadt: Wissenschaftliche Buchgesellschaft, 1968.

Bostock, J. Knight. *A Handbook on Old High German Literature* (2nd edition, revised by K. C. King and D. R. McLintock). Oxford: Clarendon Press, 1976.

Bretschneider, Anneliese. *Die Heliandheimat und ihre sprachgeschichtliche Entwicklung*. Marburg: Elwert, 1934.

The Cambridge Illustrated History of the Middle Ages. Edited by Robert Fossier, translated by Janet Sondheimer. Cambridge: Cambridge University Press, 1989.

Carolingian Chronicles: Royal Frankish Annals and Nithard's Histories. Translated by Bernhard Walter Scholz with Barbara Rogers. Ann Arbor: University of Michigan Press, 1972.

Davidson, H. R. Ellis. *Gods and Myths of Northern Europe*. Harmondsworth: Penguin Books, 1964.

De Boor, Helmut. *Die deutsche Literatur: von Karl dem Grossen bis zum Beginn der höfischen Dichtung, 770-1170*. 5. Auflage. München: C. H. Beck'sche Verlagsbuchhandlung, 1962.

DeWald, Earnest Theodore. *The Illustrations of the Utrecht Psalter.* Princeton: Princeton University Press, 1932

Dufour, Xavier Leon. "Jesus' Understanding of His Death." *Theology Digest* 24 (Fall, 1976) 293-300.

De Vries, Jan. *Altgermanische Religionsgeschichte*. Berlin: Walter de Gruyter, 1957.

Düwel, Klaus. *Runenkunde*. Stuttgart: Metzler, 1968.

Ebrard, Johann Heinrich August. *Die iroschottische Missionskirche des sechsten, siebenten, und achten Jahrhunderts und ihre Verbreitung und Bedeutung auf dem Festland*. Hildesheim und New York: Georg Olms Verlag, 1971. (Reprint of the 1873 Gütersloh edition.)

Eggers, Hans. "Altgermanische Seelenvorstellungen im Lichte des Heliands." *Jahrbuch des Vereins für niederdeutsche Sprachforschung* 80 (1957), 1-24. [Also in Eichhoff and Rauch *Der Heliand*.]

Eichhoff, Jürgen und Irmengard Rauch. *Der Heliand*. Darmstadt: Wissenschaftliche Buchgesellschaft, 1973.

Einhard, *The Life of Charlemagne*, translated from the *Monumenta Germaniae* by Samuel Epes Turner. Ann Arbor: University of Michigan Press, 1960.

Elliott, Ralph W. V. *Runes, An Introduction*. New York: St. Martin's Press, 1989.

Flint, Valerie I. J. *The Rise of Magic in Early Medieval Europe*. Princeton: Princeton University Press, 1991. [An excellent interpretation of the role of magic in Northern Christianity.]

Flowers, Stephen E. *Runes and Magic, Magical Formulaic Elements in the Older Runic Tradition*. New York/Berne/Frankfurt: Peter Lang, 1986.

_____. "Toward an Archaic Germanic Psychology." *Journal of Indo-European Studies* 11, Nos. 1 and 2 (1983), 117-38.

Foerste, William. "Otfrieds literarisches Verhältnis zum Heliand." *Niederdeutsches Jahrbuch* 71/73 (1950), 40-67.

Friesse, E. R. "The Beginnings of the Heliand." *Modern Language Review* 50 (1955), 55-57.

Genzmer, Felix. *Heliand und die Bruchstücke der Genesis*. Stuttgart: Reclam, 1982.

Göhler, Hulda. "Das Christusbild in Otfrids Evangelienbuch und im Heliand." *Zeitschrift für deutsche Philologie* 59, 1-52.

Green, Dennis Howard. *The Carolingian Lord: Semantic Studies on Four Old High German Words: balder, fro, truhtin, herro*. Cambridge: Cambridge University Press, 1965. [An admirable work of exceptional balance and thoroughness.]

Grosch, Elizabeth. "Das Gottes- und Menschenbild im Heliand." *Beiträge zur Geschichte der deutschen Sprache und Literatur* 72 (1950), 90-120.

Hagenlocher, Albrecht. *Schicksal im Heliand; Verwendung und Bedeutung der nominalen Bezeichnungen*. Köln/Wien: Bohlau, 1975.

_____. "Theologische Systematik und epische Gestaltung. Beobachtungen zur Darstellung der feindlichen Juden im *Heliand* und in Otfrids Evangelienbuch." *Beiträge zur Geschichte der deutschen Sprache und Literatur* (Tübingen) 96 (1974), 33-58.

Heffner, R. M. S. "Concerning the Heliand Verses 5-8." *Monatshefte* 56 (1964), 103-05.

Heuss, Walter. "Zur Quellenfrage im Heliand und im althochdeutschen Tatian." *Niederdeutsches Jahrbuch* 77 (1954), 1-6.

Hodgkins, Thomas. *Charles the Great.* Port Washington, New York: Kennikat Press, 1970.

Huber, Wolfgang. *Heliand und Matthäusexegese: Quellenstudien insbesondere zu Sedulius Scotus.* München: Hueber, 1969.

Kemble, John M. *The Dialogue of Salomon and Saturnus.* London: The Aelfric Society, 1848.

Kennedy, Charles W. *An Anthology of Old English Poetry.* New York: Oxford University Press, 1960.

Krogmann, Willy. "Crist III und *Heliand.*" *Festschrift für Ludwig Wolff zum 80. Geburtstag.* Herausgegeben von Werner Schröder. Neumünster: Wachholz, 1962, 111-19.

Landström, Bjorn. *The Ship, An Illustrated History.* Garden City, New York: Doubleday, 1967.

Leges Saxonum und Lex Turingorum (Fontes Iuris Germanici Antiqui in Usum Scholarum ex Monumentis Germaniae Historicis Seperatim Editi). Herausgegeben von Claudius Freiherrn von Schwerin. Hannover und Leipzig: Hahnsche Buchhandlung, 1918 [Contains the *Capitulatio de partibus Saxoniae*].

Lehmann, Winfred P. *The Alliteration of Old Saxon Poetry.* Oslo: Aschehoug, 1953.

The Letters of St. Boniface. Translated by Ephraim Emerton. New York: Columbia University Press, 1940.

Lindow, John. *Comitatus, Individual and Honor: Studies in North Germanic Institutional Vocabulary.* Berkeley: University of California Press, 1976.

Lintzel, Martin. *Der sächsische Stammesstaat und seine Eroberung durch die Franken.* Berlin: Verlag Dr. Emil Ebering, 1933.

Magnusson, Magnus. *Vikings!* New York: Elsevier-Dutton Publishing Co., 1980.

Masser, Achim. *Bibel und Legendenepik des deutschen Mittelalters.* Berlin: Erich Schmidt Verlag, 1976.

_____. "Pilatus im Heliand." *Niederdeutsches Jahrbuch* 96 (1973), 9-17.

Menner, Robert J., ed. *The Poetical Dialogues of Solomon and Saturn.* New York: The Modern Language Association of America, 1941.

Metzenthin, Ernst Christian Paul. *The Home of the Addressees of the Heliand.* Menasha, Wisc.: George Banta Publ. Co., 1922.

Mittner, Ladislaus. *Wurd: das Sakrale in der altgermanischen Epik.* Bern: Francke Verlag, 1955.

Murphy, G. Ronald. *The Saxon Savior: The Germanic Transformation of the Gospel in the Ninth-Century Heliand.* New York: Oxford University Press. 1989.

_____. "The *Heliand*, a Ninth-century Saxon Epic: The Opening Verses in Translation." *The Georgetown Journal of Languages and Linguistics* 1, No. 1 (1990), 129-43.

_____. "Magic in the Heliand." *Monatshefte* 93, No. 3 (1991).

_____. "Structure in the Heliand." *The German Quarterly* 65, No. 2 (1992).

Neumann, Friedrich. *Geschichte der altdeutschen Literatur* (800-1600). Berlin: Walter de Gruyter & Co., 1966.

Pertz, Georgius Henricus. *Scriptores Rerum Germanicarum, Ex Monumentis Germaniae Historicis.* Hannover: Hahn, 1865.

Peters, Elisabeth. *Quellen und Charakter der Paradiesesvorstellungen in der deutschen Dichtung vom 9. bis 12. Jahrhundert.* Breslau: M. & H. Markus, 1915.

Pickering, F. P. "Christlicher Erzählstoff bei Otfried und im Heliand." *Zeitschrift für deutsches Altertum und deutsche Literatur* 85 (1954-1955), 262-91.

_____. "Wieder 'Apokryphes im Heliand.'" *Zeitschrift für deutsches Altertum und deutsche Literatur,* 85 (1954-1955), 262-91.

The Poetical Dialogues of Solomon and Saturn. Edited by Robert J. Menner. New York: The Modern Language Association of America, 1941.

Preisker, Herbert. *Deutsches Christentum; die neutestamentlichen Evangelien im altdeutschen Heliand.* Langensalza; Berlin: Verlag Julius Beltz, 1934.

Priebsch, Robert. *The Heliand Manuscript, Cotton Caligula A. VII in the British Museum, A Study.* Oxford: The Clarendon Press, 1925.

Quispel, G. "Der Heliand und das Thomasevangelium." *Vigiliae Christianae: A Review of Early Christian Life and Language* XVI (1962), 121-53. Amsterdam: North-Holland Publishing Co., 121-53.

_____. "Some Remarks on the Gospel of Thomas." *New Testament Studies* 5 (1959), 262-90.

Rabani Mauri. *Commentariorum in Mattheum Libri Octo,* Lib. VIII, cap. xxvii, p. 1131 in J.-P. Migne, Patrologia Latina, vol. 107 (Paris: Migne, 1864).

Rathofer, Johannes. *Der Heliand: theologischer Sinn als tektonische Form; Vorbereitung und Grundlegung der Interpretation.* Köln: Bohlau, 1962.

_____. "Hraban und das Petrusbild der 37. Fitte im Heliand." *Festschrift für Jost Trier zum 70. Geburtstag.* Herausgegeben von William Foerste und Karl Heinz Borck. Köln/Graz: Bohlau, 1964.

236 / The Heliand

_____. "Zum Aufbau des Heliand." *Zeitschrift für deutsches Altertum und deutsche Literatur* 93 (1964), 239-72. [Also in Eichhoff und Rauch, *Der Heliand*.] Darmstadt: Wissenschaftliche Buchgesellschaft, 1973.

_____. "Zum Eingang. Ein textkritischer Versuch im Lichte der Quelle." *Niederdeutsches Wort* 9 (1969), 52-72.

Rauch, Irmengard. "Another Old English–Old Saxon Isogloss: (REM) Activity." *De Gustibus: A Festschrift für Alain Renoir.* Edited by J. M. Foley. New York: Garland (in press).

Reed, Carrol. "Gnomic Verse in the Old Saxon Heliand." *Philological Quarterly* 30 (1951), 403-10.

Robinson, George W. *The Life of St. Boniface by Willibald.* Cambridge, Mass.: Harvard University Press, 1916.

Robinson, Potter Rodney. *The Germania of Tacitus: A Critical Edition.* Middletown, Conn.: The American Philological Association, 1935.

Rompelman, Tom Albert. *Heliandprobleme.* Wilhelmshafen: Schriftenreihe der nordwestdeutschen Universitätsgesellschaft, 1957.

Rupp, Heinz. "The Adoption of Christian Ideas into German, with Reference to the Heliand and Otfrids 'Evangelienbuch'." *Parergon* 21 (1978), 33-41.

_____. "Der Heliand. Hauptanliegen seines Dichters." *Deutschunterricht* 8 (1956), Heft 1, 28-45. [Also in Eichhoff und Rauch *Der Heliand*.]

_____. "Leid und Sünde im Heliand und in Otfrids Evangelienbuch." *Beiträge zur Geschichte der deutschen Sprache und Literatur* (Halle) 78 (1956), 421-69 & 79 (1957) 336-79.

Russell, James C. *The Germanization of Early Medieval Christianity.* Dissertation, Fordham University 1990 (Ann Arbor: University Microfilms International, No. 9105787).

Russell, Jeffrey B. "St. Boniface and the Eccentrics." *Church History* 33 (1964), 235-47.

Schmidt, Kurt Dietrich. *Die Bekehrung der Germanen zum Christentum.* Göttingen: Vandenhoeck und Ruprecht, 1939.

Schröder, Werner. *Kleinere Schriften zur althochdeutschen Sprache und Literatur.* Bern/München: Francke Verlag, 1966.

Schwab Ute. "Zur zweiten Fitte des Heliands." *Mediaevalia Litteraria* (1971), 67-117.

Scott, Mariana. *The Heliand, Translated from the Old Saxon.* Chapel Hill: University of North Carolina Press, 1966.

Sehrt, Edward Henry. *Vollständiges Wörterbuch zum Heliand und zur altsächsischen Genesis.* 2. Auflage. Göttingen: Vandenhoeck und Ruprecht, 1966.